AGGREGATED
DISCONTENT

AGGREGATED DISCONTENT

Confessions of the Last Normal Woman

HARRON WALKER

Random House
New York

Random House
An imprint and division of Penguin Random House LLC
1745 Broadway, New York, NY 10019
randomhousebooks.com
penguinrandomhouse.com

Aggregated Discontent is a work of nonfiction.
Some names and identifying details have been changed.

LIBRARY OF CONGRESS CATALOGING-IN-PUBLICATION DATA
Names: Walker, Harron, author.
Title: Aggregated discontent / Harron Walker.
Description: First edition. | New York : Random House, 2025.
Identifiers: LCCN 2024047785 (print) | LCCN 2024047786 (ebook) |
ISBN 9780593450048 (hardcover) | ISBN 9780593450062 (ebook)
Subjects: LCSH: Walker, Harron. | Women journalists—United
States—Biography. | Transgender people—United States—Biography. |
Journalists—United States—Biography. | LCGFT: Essays. |
Autobiographies.
Classification: LCC PN4874.W265 A3 2025 (print) |
LCC PN4874.W265 (ebook) |
DDC 070.92 [B]—dc23/eng/20241216
LC record available at https://lccn.loc.gov/2024047785
LC ebook record available at https://lccn.loc.gov/2024047786

Printed in the United States of America on acid-free paper

1st Printing

First Edition

Book design by Elizabeth A. D. Eno

The authorized representative in the EU for product safety and
compliance is Penguin Random House Ireland, Morrison Chambers,
32 Nassau Street, Dublin D02 YH68, Ireland.
https://eu-contact.penguin.ie.

For Mike, Amida Care, and all seventeen minutes
of the full-length "MacArthur Park Suite"

We try to discover in things, which become precious to us on that account, the reflection of what our soul has projected on to them; we are disillusioned when we find that they are in reality devoid of the charm which they owed, in our minds, to the association of certain ideas.

—Marcel Proust

Where is the body?

—A'keria Chanel Davenport

CONTENTS

AGGREGATED
DISCONTENT

OBVIOUS COMMUNITY MEMBER

I t's not like I had the medical records of the other dozen or so people in the theater, which was about to screen *Monica,* the big trans movie of the summer. But as far as I could tell, my boyfriend, Mike, and I were the only actual trans people there to see it.

The lights were, of course, somewhat dimmed as we walked over to our seats, but on our way I didn't spot any "obvious community members," or OCMs, as my dear friend Lola likes to call them: those people who visually scream one or more letters of our clunky little acronym without having to actually say anything to make that affiliation known. Then again, Mike and I weren't exactly giving OCM either—or maybe we were? I mean, that's the thing about not being able to see yourself from an outside perspective: You can't see yourself from an outside perspective. Maybe everyone else in that theater was also trans themselves, silently remarking, just as I had moments before, that they were the only trans people there.

Monica, a 2022 Venice Film Festival favorite that enjoyed a wider release the following year, concerns a trans woman returning home for the first time in years to reconnect with her family of origin. I mostly liked it, especially the scene that plays just before the credits roll, in which the title character, played by Trace Lysette, kneels down to give her sensitive, creative, artistic nephew a word of advice before he sings the national anthem in front of his whole school:

> When you get on the stage, I want you to take a moment and think to yourself as you look at everybody, OK? And you say to yourself, "You lucky bastards, here I come," all right? And you slay that stage, and you make a moment. You got everything inside you, all right? OK, go get 'em.

In case the reason for my use of terms like "sensitive," "creative," and "artistic" weren't plainly apparent, Monica's nephew is probably gay, maybe even trans like his aunt is. She sees it. Her brother, the boy's father, sees it too—and, thankfully, doesn't seem to have a problem with it, whatever "it" ends up being, unlike his mother when Monica began to deviate from the norm. With this in mind, the scene reads like Monica is telling her nephew something that she wishes someone could've told her when she was his age. Her words are ones of encouragement derived from the wisdom that she'd been forced to learn in the years she was on her own, delivered to the boy by the kind of maternal figure that she herself never quite had, at least not in the house she grew up in. Monica ran away from home in her teens and has only returned now, some two decades later, to make peace with the dying, dementia-plagued mother who drove her away in the first place. She fails to rekindle that bond by film's end, but she does manage to forge an unexpected new one with her elementary school–age nephew. She sees herself in him and sticks around for his sake, as well as for her own, perhaps in an effort to heal her inner child while at the same time trying to shield him from getting hurt in quite the same way.

I cried during that final scene for all the obvious reasons: I'm an adult trans woman who'd been one of those "sensitive," "creative," "artistic" little boys herself, fighting the "faggot" allegations from the moment some bowl-cutted Prometheus in a Big Dog shirt introduced the word to the playground. As I watched the scene, something buried deep inside me, something long interred within that traumatized core whence all personal essay fodder springs eternal, burst open in yearning as it ached for a similarly healing exchange—and I'd never even been thrown out of the house! Nor lived through anything comparable to what Monica probably had to endure as a result of her mother's rejection.

The scene, in some ways, redeemed *Monica* for one of the issues that I'd had with the film up until that point, which was that its protagonist seemed to live in a world in which no other trans people existed. Even beyond the bounds of her family's stifling, hetero-suburban bubble, she didn't seem to have any friends at all, trans or otherwise. She never calls any of them, never texts them in distress or even to complain in some overly long voice memo, as I'm wont to do to a few different group chats at least forty-nine times a day.* In fact, her only confidante for most of the film is the voicemailbox of a shitty ex-

---

* Conservative estimate—shout-out to "Low Engagement, High Breasts," "Believe wxmen etc but," and all the rest.

boyfriend that she cries and screams into whenever she gets upset. She seems extremely isolated, which, I get it—that's the point: Monica feels more isolated than ever now that she's back in her childhood home, with her webcam clients and the men she flirts with online being her only points of connection beyond the family that threw her out. The enormously talented Lysette conveys that unspoken pain so well, but it nonetheless struck me as a bit unrealistic, that a woman like Monica, who'd had to learn how to survive on her own from such a young age, would now, as an adult living in a city on her own, have no friends or community to speak of, much less speak to.

Maybe that hadn't always been the case? Maybe, over the course of her relationship with that shitty ex-boyfriend, he'd isolated her from whatever family she'd cobbled together while in exile from suburbia, thereby leaving her with no one to turn to after they broke up, save for a crackling voicemail greeting that never says anything back. Or maybe that isolation was simply a narrative oversight on the part of the filmmakers, both of them queer though neither of them trans women. Perhaps they grasped the nuances of Monica's childhood, the part of her life that most resembled their own, far better than they did the years that followed, which could have led to such details escaping them.

That latter reading, of course, is pure speculation. But I thought it made sense, and as we shuffled out of the theater while the credits rolled, Mike said he did too. Mike and I had met about seven years ago, though we'd followed each other online for a bit longer than that. I'd been dating an acquaintance of his at the time, and he was dating Kay, someone who would later become a good friend of mine. I'm grateful to say that I'm still friends with Kay, given how easy it could've been for us to fall out in the wake of our boyfriend rehoming. The first time I ran into her after Mike and I started dating was at a trans fundraiser party held every month in Queens. We talked a little at the bar, though not about you-know-who, neither of us daring to broach that potentially vibe-killing subject before we'd downed a few drinks. It was only later, while smoking together in a quieter corner of the backyard, that we finally cleared the air, so to speak, and thank god we did. She didn't hate me, I was relieved to learn. Her main concern was maintaining our friendship; that was mine as well, and I told her as much.

The mood now lightened and much of the tension relieved, I'd joked that "it's like the writers of *Trans Brooklyn Sitcom* decided to shake things up for season five."

She'd laughed. "I mean, there's only so many characters." An ironic estimation, given the setting—a nightclub packed with a couple hundred other trans people—but beyond the four-block radius, not untrue.

After exiting the theater, Mike and I tossed our concessional detritus and parted ways to our respective restrooms. I reemerged first, so I stood by the door to the men's room while I waited for Mike to join me. The door swung open, and two older men who looked to be about in their sixties walked out, evidently in the middle of a conversation that they'd started on the other side of the door.

"—there was no scene where you see Monica when she was a man," one of them said to the other as they passed, "so it felt unfinished . . ."

It was, without a doubt, one of the stupidest things I've ever overheard in my life. His words were a cold slap of reality; while I was sitting there in that theater, engaging with the specifics of a film's depiction of contemporary trans life, some other guy sitting a few feet away had decided to give it, like, two or three stars because he didn't get to see a "before" pic. It was like he'd come into the theater with a hardwired idea of what a trans woman is and what her narrative should be. And when *Monica* failed to deliver on that, presenting instead a more intimate slice of one fictional trans woman's life, however flawed it might have been at times in its execution, he failed to see her entirely, just as he failed to notice the trans woman standing outside of the men's room, doing everything she could to not burst out laughing as she caught this rare glimpse of the cis mind at work.

When Mike walked out a minute later, I told him what I'd heard. Mike, too, had been eavesdropping on the two men while he was in the men's room, and after stitching his half of their exchange onto mine, we laughed our way out of the theater, lost in hysterics by the time we touched sunlight. It can be so frustrating, not being seen, whether literally or in that other, more annoying sense of the word. But it's times like these that remind me how much fun you can have away from the spotlight, cackling in obscurity with those others standing just out of frame.

PICK ME

The store was as busy as ever that morning, which is to say not very busy at all. I never expected any more than a few dozen people to walk through our doors on the average day, and only a third of them would actually buy something. The business model didn't really make sense to me, but that was for the married artist couple who ran the place to figure out, not me working part-time for $12.50 an hour.

They'd set up shop in a part of Manhattan that once was called the Tenderloin—or "Satan's Circus" among clergymen and reformers, per Lucy Sante's *Low Life*—just south of Herald Square and Koreatown. Because of the neighborhood's location—north of Madison Square Park—many had taken to calling it "NoMad." I had done this too when I'd first moved to New York, about a half decade earlier, but enough born-

and-raised New Yorkers corrected me, or simply scrunched their faces up in palpable disdain, that I was shamed out of it. They made it all too clear that "NoMad" stank of realtorspeak; apparently it had been coined only in the late 1990s, after wealthy new residents began to move in en masse. I much preferred the roster of nicknames that I'd come up with while working over there, anyway: the Bootleg Earbuds District, the Affordable Fake Necklaces That Will Break After Three Dates District, the $17 Salad Bowl District, the Boutique Hotel District.

Our store was connected to the lobby of one such boutique hotel, along with a pricey coffee shop, a Michelin-starred gastropub, a Tinder date–serviceable oyster bar, and the Midtown outpost of a pricey SoHo clothing store. We weren't officially affiliated with the hotel, but given our location, most guests naturally assumed that we were its gift shop. It's not like I didn't understand the confusion; we did stock many small tchotchkes that could serve as souvenirs, as well as various toiletries, albeit very expensive ones, for the hapless, unmoisturized traveler in need. Still, I held firm at what we were and what we weren't—not out of principle, but because I wasn't being paid enough to work that second, made-up job. Many times, for example, one of the hotel guests who'd bought something from me would then ask if I could watch their luggage for the day while they went out sightseeing. I would always tell them I was so sorry, but I couldn't. I'd smile at their disappointment and wish them a good rest of their day. I loved triggering that momentary reversal of power between us as I drew the limits on how far I would actually go to serve them. More than that, though, I just loved saying no when I could.

We did have some regulars, some of whom came in every

couple of months to buy one of our signature tongue-in-cheek key tags, designed by the married artist owners themselves. Many of those regulars would drop by every few months for the latest issue of their favorite art-world quarterly. Still others would return for one of our many esoteric soaps, or a tube of that Japanese moisturizer that no other store in the city would stock. We also carried a lot of what you might call "artisanal children's toys," like our hand-carved wooden block sets and a $16 piece of orange yarn that, the pamphlet claimed, would help kids "learn to visualize." Of the non-regular, onetime shoppers, my favorite might be this one woman who came in and beelined to a yellow-spined cookbook displayed in our front window. She asked me about our return policy, saying, "I just want to make sure it looks good in the stack." I had no idea what that meant. It wasn't until later, hours after she'd left, that it finally hit me: She didn't need the recipes; she just wanted a pop of yellow to offset her other décor choices. The next day she came back to return it, explaining, "It didn't look good in the stack."

The books in our window display lured in some decent foot traffic from time to time, as did a prominently displayed poster of a cartoon man's waistline, his wrinkled dress shirt haphazardly half-tucked in. Across the top and bottom of the poster screamed the words TUCK FRUMP in a blocky, all-caps font. We also sold stationery that carried the same message, though with the *T* and the *F* swapped. Such wares were a hit with much of our clientele, especially the older, moneyed liberals, the ones who still couldn't believe that Hillary had lost the election the year before and really seemed to want me, the visibly trans shopgirl, to know it. "Oh, that's great!" they'd say, laughing, upon spying the cards, before locking eyes with me to strike a sympathetic pose. "It's so awful, isn't it?" they'd lean in to tell me. I'd say that it was, and their smiles would reemerge, happy, I guess, to have been able to commiserate with someone they deemed so affected.

Months before I started working at the store, I might have been walking beside some of those customers at the satellite Women's March in New York, which took place in concert with others worldwide on January 21, 2017. Hundreds of thousands of people had flooded Midtown Manhattan to protest the inauguration of President Donald Trump the day prior. I don't remember much of the Women's March, despite having been one of those hundreds of thousands. I have no recollection of having held aloft a homemade sign that read LITERALLY GET AWAY FROM ME, for example, though I have since stumbled on a photo of me online in one of those "Signs from the Women's March" quickie-content slideshows in which I appear to be doing just that. I chalk up the holes in my memory—as well as my past self's cringey, misanthropic attempt at a cogent political message—to the fact that I would go on to transition only a few weeks after the Women's March. The girl was a little interrupted, shall we say, so I'm willing to cut her some slack.

I do remember finally finding my friend Tommy, after peeing at the Barnes & Noble on Forty-sixth and Fifth that day; I also recall my friend Tyler's sign: ABOLISH EVERYTHING, over and over in tiny red text. Though it was frankly illegible from more than a few feet away, I loved it for its clarity—rhetorical, if not literal—as well as for its directness and rigor. Surrounded by signs bearing *Harry Potter* puns and various references to Marvel's intellectual property, a lot of them calling for Trump's arrest or for some other top-down intervention from our demonstrably broken justice system, my friend's two-word call to action felt clear and simple. Its destructive implications also very much appealed to me, given my nihilistic bent in those final days of not-quite-manhood.

My clearest memory of that day concerns something that I saw at the end of the march's route, after my friends and I had peeled off from the other demonstrators to begin our return home to Brooklyn. We passed a group of men standing in a circle, furiously chanting, "HER BODY, HER CHOICE! HER BODY, HER CHOICE!" at one another. I couldn't help but note the irony as I tried to stifle my laughter. A group of men gathering to delineate the extent of a woman's bodily autonomy—wasn't that, in part, what we were all there marching against?

The following year, an estimated two hundred thousand people turned up for the city's second annual Women's March, about half as many as the year before. I did not count myself in their number that time—not because I was taking some pointed stance against it, but because I didn't even know it was happening. No one had mentioned it to me. I hadn't read about it online or seen anyone tweeting about it. I decided that my ignorance—my *exclusion*, better yet—had been due in some way to the fact of my transness. This was often my answer for a lot of things in that first year of my transition. My penchant for such conspiratorial thinking wasn't exactly unearned, of course. Trans people pretty famously face disproportionate levels of discrimination: in housing, in healthcare, in employment, in love. But then again, I was not "trans people," and "trans people" weren't all me; squares and rectangles—you know the drill. Still, in the case of that second Women's March, I could easily imagine that many concurrent forms of social segregation might have played a role in my not having gotten the memo. Perhaps discussions of the march had remained cloistered within the same cis, white, straight, and middle-to-upper-class milieu from which the first Women's March had sprung, ergo news of its follow-up never managed to reach the more diverse social circles I ran in. Self-serving? Sure. More convenient than true? Probably. But that reasoning still made sense to me. It wasn't so much that I wanted to go, but I wanted to have had the choice to go or not go, and I feared that I hadn't been given that choice precisely because of my gender, itself still a source of great insecurity for me. The perceived snub therefore was able to serve as yet another referendum on not only my womanhood but my tenuous relationship to womanhood writ large. Harron is excluded. Transphobia strikes again.

In any case, I couldn't have gone. I had to go work at the store.

• • •

Despite the petty annoyances and the low pay, I liked working at the store overall. It was one of my two jobs at the time—well, three, depending on how you would've divided up all my freelance work. I was also a journalist, working as a breaking news blogger for a queer content site two days a week and publishing about half a dozen one-off assignments every month outside of that, mostly interviews and midlength reportage that followed the same rote narrative structure: a character-driven lede that zooms out then zooms in then zooms out then zooms in and then closes with a quote. I learned that format, among other industry knowledge, from an ex who'd gone to J-school. Speaking of which, you're welcome: I just saved you a semester of J-school.

Working at the store meant that I'd get to take on fewer inconsequential assignments and focus my creative energy on pieces that I actually cared about, or at least mostly cared about. After ignoring our work for so long, so many editors in that early Trump era suddenly wanted trans content authored by trans writers, but their editorial vision was so often prescriptive. Many of them only sought the kind of work that adhered to a limited set of predetermined narratives: violence bad and representation good, unless representation also bad, in which case representation? Bad. If that story could be told by way of a vulnerable personal essay, then all the better, since they generally paid less for such writing than they would for reported editorial. I avoided first-person writing as much as I could be-cause of that—well, that and the fact that I had a whole complex around being taken seriously in the industry, a familiar struggle for anyone beset with so many capital-I Identities. Ironically, it was those very same identities that got many editors to notice our work in the first place, especially in the wake of some new horrifying legislative announcement that de-manded some kind of authentic response. It was like the worse we were targeted by the Trump administration, the better our chances were of getting published online. It was just like that O. Henry story. You know, the one about the man who got a hairbrush for a woman who sold her hair to buy a laptop so she could write for *I Have Hair Monthly,* which then shut down because that first guy was actually a venture capitalist who'd pulled all his funding from the site so that he could afford to buy her that hairbrush? It was all very that—very "Gift of the Magi."

I accepted that those editors were limited in their thinking, though it frustrated me to no end. Still, I kept on pitching in the hope of getting more interesting work out there—and while I sometimes succeeded, there was so much rejection too. Working at the store gave me a reprieve from all that—the rejection, the disappointment, the ever-present anxiety shared by many freelancers that I could always be working on *something*. And given how slow it usually was during my shifts, I had time to write and edit on the desktop computer we kept beside our register. Plus the job forced me out of the house, which prevented me from being as reclusive as I so often wanted to be in that early period of my transition. Before that, I'd navigated public space as a white man, which, for me at least, meant slipping through spaces unbothered and unnoticed at my discretion, unless there were cruisey gays present, which in New York there often were. I could feel like I was invisible when I wanted to be, something that I didn't come to appreciate until I no longer had that option. Now, as a white trans woman—or at the very least, this unmissable, gendery thing, depending on the trans literacy of whoever crossed my path—I couldn't evade the surveillance of strangers. Perhaps thanks to my race, this unwanted attention almost never escalated beyond words and stares, but receiving that attention every time I entered a subway car or having my genitals debated while I waited in line at the deli still, understandably, managed to add up. It would weigh on me preemptively anytime I had to leave the house, as I dreaded what new forms of dehumanization I might encounter. It was enough to stop me from leaving my room sometimes, except on those days when I had to go to the store. I couldn't call in dysphoric to work no matter how much I might have wanted to, but in commuting all that way, three trains from borough to borough, I maintained a connection with the world beyond my bedroom that helped mitigate the feeling that I had no business being there.

Sometimes during my shifts, I'd flirt with the men who came in—their gazes were the only strangers' gazes that I yearned for. While assisting them on the floor, I'd casually glean the most glamorous facts of their lives and throw them all in the pot with whatever fantasy I felt like cooking up. This one, an art director. That one, a photographer. I prayed that one would pluck me out of my dreary, loveless limbo—that he'd be so gobsmacked by the sight of me that he'd order me into his life, like that modeling scout who discovered Gisele Bündchen while she was scarfing down McDonald's at the mall. I dreamed of being discoverable. Would you discover me? I'd discover me. I was only a year into this second puberty of sorts, flooded with hormones and filled with delusion. I'd get a whiff of old cigar smoke while crossing the lobby to our stockroom and imagine the man that this scent belonged to: handsome, of course, and very wealthy, his suit jacket smelling of the finest tobacco as he wrapped me up in his strong, burly arms. He'd hold me tight, tighter than any of the faceless men from the apps ever wanted to, and for longer too. The fantasy of it all helped to mitigate the pain of getting misgendered by customers, which thankfully happened less and less frequently over the two years that I worked at the store. I changed the way I looked almost constantly in that time, often in response to having been so fundamentally misread by those very same men who I hoped might "discover" me. To sidestep how much that misreading hurt, I would turn it into a game. Would customers still greet me with a "Hey, man!" if I put my hair up? What if I changed up my part? What if I gave myself bangs?

What if I talked like this? Or what if I talked like *this*? What if I wore more makeup? What if I wore way too much makeup? What if I swapped the YouTuber drag beat for just a brow pencil, mascara, and ChapStick?

At least once I settled on a look and got myself to work, I'd get to see my friend Thora, as our shifts would often overlap, with one of us opening the store and the other staying on later to close it. She was a freelance writer as well. We'd often read over each other's drafts between rounds of edits and praise each other's work effusively. When an editor at a print magazine posted on Twitter that he wanted trans writers for a special assignment, we encouraged each other to reach out immediately. When Thora got a response from him, the assignment was something that neither of us could have anticipated, given all the exclamation points in his cheery call for writers. He was offering her the chance to contribute to "a package," as he called it, about the trans people, most of them Black trans women, who'd been senselessly murdered that year. We couldn't tell what offended us more: that he'd sprung such an evidently upsetting topic on who knows how many trans writers without warning, or that he didn't seem to be seeking out Black trans writers specifically to be the ones who told this story. Or maybe it was his shameless ignorance of trans writers in the industry—for what is an editor's call for trans writers but a public admission that they don't read our work?

Tokenization was something that we both often dealt with, Thora and I, though I didn't always reject it outright. Sometimes it was the only way to get work as a freelance writer. My transness rendered me visible to certain editors even as it obscured whatever craft or technique I tried to bring to my work. I hated that bargain but accepted it all the same, because in the end it meant I got paid.

Thora was the one who had gotten me the job at the store, thereby saving me from an increasingly torturous bagel-shop gig where I'd been pretending, for months, that I wasn't on estrogen, answering to a name that I no longer used, for minimum wage plus tips, to say nothing of the post-work panic attacks and all those backward baseball caps I had to wear for food-safety reasons, which only added to the masc-for-masquerade of it all. Working at the store with Thora meant that I got to be myself, the same me, all the time, not just at home or when I went out with friends. That self might not have been legible to every customer who walked in, but it was to Thora, and it was to me, and that on its own was life-changing.

Having transitioned around the same time, Thora and I shared a bond that was both instant and intense. If one of us was losing her mind, then both of us were losing our minds, and one of us was always losing her mind.

"When you talk, it's like a Chrome window," she once told me. "You're always opening new tabs as you go, just tabbing, tabbing, tabbing, but I know I can trust that you'll eventually X them all out and get back to the first tab you started with."

"When *you* talk, it's like you're on the beach," I responded, "dropping flower petals in the shape of your sign"—Cancer—"and then gasping and whispering, 'I've said too much.'" Like the time she asked if I'd read *The House on Mango Street,* because I reminded her of Marin, a girl I later learned was always "waiting for a car to stop, a star to fall, someone to change her life."

By 2018, though, Thora was gone, having taken a hostessing job at a chic, since-closed restaurant downtown. By then, I knew that I had to get out of there too. There were surgeries that I wanted, ones that I knew I could never afford on $12.50

an hour, even as my freelancer rates had risen from around $250 per piece to $350 on average. My best bet, I figured, would be to get another staff job in a newsroom, similar to the one that I'd left two years prior, so that I could change sexes in relative privacy. With a job like that, I'd have insurance again, and if the plan didn't cover it, I'd at least be making enough money to conceivably save up, something that I would never be able to do as a retail-working freelancer. Any savings that I ever did manage to amass was always gone by tax season. If you're a freelancer, remember: Try to pay quarterly taxes. There, I just saved you another semester of J-school.

While my plan made sense in theory, in practice I was getting nowhere. I would find a promising job prospect—a writing gig at a women's news site, a strategist position at a cringey queer nonprofit—then go through multiple rounds of interviews, edit tests, and references, only to find out after weeks, if not months, that I just wasn't right for the role. I felt like a beautiful yet embattled horse, chasing dangling carrots down a dusty old back road, too caught up in trying to catch those strung-up orange spoils to notice that I was trotting ever closer to a glue factory. I hoped that someone would swoop in and save me, a lover, maybe, or an employer. But neigh, no one did. Hey, man! Tuck frump.

• • •

One day I was working alone at the store, typing away in a Google doc while watching my inbox in a separate window, when a new email appeared.

I gave its bolded subject line a quick glance: "Lush Is Something Something Trans Employees Something Something."

What?

I read it one more time:

Lush Cosmetics Kicks Off Human Rights Campaign by
Elevating Voices of Trans Employees

Confused, I clicked it open. It was another press release, no
different from the dozens of others that I received every week
from publicists hoping that I might spare some coverage for
their clients, almost all of which I chose to ignore. But something about this release got under my skin. Maybe it was the
sloppy intro, which revealed its obvious fill-in-the-blank tem-
plate. "I caught your story about the daily things transgender
and queer people do to avoid violence," it began, before
launching into its deeply impersonal spiel about how the company had launched a new campaign. (They were selling a new
trans-themed bath bomb, half pink and half blue, to benefit a
handful of trans rights organizations.) Maybe it was the fact
that, as the attached image clearly showed, stores across the
country were going to replace their typical window displays
with LED screens bearing quotes from trans employees. ("This
is my identity, not a trend," read the one in the attached
image.) Maybe it was the rainbow capitalism of it all—using
the material realities of people like me to build up their brand
and sell more of their soaps. Maybe I just thought it was corny
that they'd named the transgender bath bomb "Inner Truth."
Whatever the reason, it pissed me off, and I spent the rest of
my shift fuming over it.

How many trans people were even working at Lush? I knew
firsthand just how difficult it was to get hired somewhere as a
trans woman, my employment at the store notwithstanding.
In the final hours of my shift, I decided to put my rage to good

use. I would go to every Lush in the city and find out for myself precisely how many trans employees were being elevated,
as the company's press release claimed. And then I'd go write
about it, pitch it to an editor, something! Anything! I don't
know, scene missing—I'd figure that part out later. It would all
come together. I was sure that it would. And with that, I was
off to Lush number one.

There were five Lush stores scattered throughout Manhattan, and the first one was only six blocks away from the shop.
It was still light out when I left work, though the sky had
clouded over toward the end of my shift. To my dismay, the
weather app on my phone said that it was likely to snow in the
evening. The air was already palpably humid, thicker than
usual with its garbage and gasoline smell, that particular eau de
Midtown that I'd mostly become inured to. I figured that I'd
have to be quick with my impromptu post-work reporting if I
wanted to make it home before the weather decided to change.

Arriving outside of the Herald Square storefront, I was
greeted by a bold purple LED screen in the window. It declared to me, in white Helvetica, that "30% of transgender
people have experienced homelessness."* A company I'd work
for six years later would put up similar signs in the break room
during Pride month. "More than 40% of trans adults in the
U.S. have attempted suicide." *Like, thank you, sign, that's great
to know, but I'm just trying to grab the oat milk.*

I understand the purpose of signs like that. Americans at
large don't like to think about people who are trans, much less
those who are also unhoused or unsuccessfully suicidal. (They

---

* I believe Lush got this number from the National Center for Transgender
Equality's 2015 survey examining the lives of trans Americans. The updated 2022
survey reports the same statistic.

do think about us quite a lot, especially as of late, but according to them they don't like it.) A sign like the one outside of Lush, for example, would theoretically force shoppers to consider some ugly truth that they'd rather not, as well as raise awareness of a major systemic issue faced by some of the most marginalized people who walk among us. But as I stood there staring at the window display, I noticed that I was the only person who'd actually stopped to read it, and that was only because I was making a point to do so. Besides, I wondered, what were the causes of this disproportionate experience of homelessness? A similarly disproportionate rate of employment discrimination, for one. And how can we counteract employment discrimination? By literally giving people jobs! The purple sign was cute, but I couldn't see its value if there was no one it described working in the store behind it.

The muggy stench outside gave way to sweeter, perfumed odors once I entered the store. It wasn't quite floral or citric but rather both at once, and even a little bit musky too, but what else should a room filled with soaps and scrubs and bath bombs smell like, all piled together on tables and shelves over every square inch of the room?

A few steps into the store, I scanned for trans employees and failed to spot any—a deranged thing for most people to do, but I wasn't most people; I was on assignment. And then I spotted her, stacked among the other bath bombs some ten feet from the door: the great transgender soap—or perhaps I should use her preferred name? I'm sorry, Inner Truth. There she was: Inner Truth. She was two-toned and shaped like a heart with beveled edges, about the size of my palm. Half of her was a cloudy neon blue. The rest of her was Starburst pink, a nod to the pastel pink, white, and blue of the transgender pride flag—"an abomination," aesthetically speaking, as the critic Andrea Long Chu once described it, that "looks like the banner of a nationalist party for children six and under." I then wondered if pairing the two colors that respectively represent "boys" and "girls" was kind of like saying that we're "the best of both worlds," a common line of chaser thought that also happens to be the title of *Hannah Montana*'s theme song, but decided that was a reach. It was probably just the flag thing.

I grabbed one of the bath bombs from the stack and brought it up to the cash register. On the walk over, I passed a bunch of little purple signs nestled in between the product piles, each one bearing some downer factoid or other. "Trans folks often face discrimination, affecting key areas: safety, employment, and housing," read one. For the second time that day I thought: *Thank you for that information, sign.* But I didn't need a sign to tell me how hard it was for trans people to get a job. The entirely cis workforce of the store had made that unfortunate stat clear enough. Were they an adequate sample size from which to determine anything? Were trans people even clamoring to get a job at Lush? I certainly wasn't, but there wasn't time to consider that. I had a bath bomb to buy and a narrative to build.

"That'll be $6.48," the cashier said after ringing me up.

I slid my card into the chip reader. "By the way, do you know any trans people that work here?"

"We've had some in the past, I think," she said. "We've also had people that are, um, genderqueer and ace, and I believe there's more on the corporate side of things." She handed me the bath bomb in a little paper baggie. "If you want to fill out an application, we've got it on our website."

Clocked yet again! As I moved on to the other locations

over the course of that afternoon, I got nearly identical responses from the employees I spoke to.

"Not at this location . . ."

"There are some who work in corporate . . ."

But never there in front of me—well, actually I did meet a nonbinary worker at one of the later stores. They asked me what my pronouns were. *I have a ponytail and tits,* I thought but answered, "She/her."

Nevertheless, I had my story. Rather than simply employing more trans people, the company had funneled who knows how much money into a seemingly well-intentioned campaign whose sole purpose was to raise awareness of the fact that trans people have a hard time getting jobs. I understood that the company was raising money on behalf of trans organizations, but according to its own press release, the one that I found in my inbox earlier that day, it would only be donating half a million dollars—a paltry fraction of the company's annual revenue, which tops out at more than half a billion every year. If they truly wanted to have an impact on these organizations, I thought, they would simply give those organizations money directly out of their own earnings. But that wasn't the point of the campaign, I concluded. The point was to capitalize on whatever goodwill "being pro-trans" carried in those early Trump administration days by very publicly doing something irrefutably pro-trans. Corporations are all about their bottom line, so raising money for trans-led groups and advertising that charity as loudly as possible must have been more profitable than it would have been unprofitable. Otherwise, the company wouldn't have done it at all. "Many corporations became public advocates for LGBTQ equality because doing so made a great deal of financial and business sense," writes Carlos A.

Ball in *The Queering of Corporate America*. "If large corporations had determined that publicly promoting LGBTQ rights would threaten their business interests and profits, they would not have engaged in political activism on behalf of LGBTQ causes." Similarly, if Lush truly cared about how jobless trans people were, the company would've simply given a bunch of us jobs. This was New York City, after all. Not everyone here is a transsexual, despite claims to the contrary from the fascist media crowd, but there are, suffice to say, plenty of us here. So why didn't I see more of us out there on the floor at any of the Lush stores I visited, selling their Inner Truth to every customer who walked in? I rushed to get home as the snow came down in slushy chunks. The story, my story, was writing itself.

I took the subway downtown and transferred at Fourteenth Street. While walking down the long corridor between the two trains, I saw a man who was walking toward me gesture in my direction while turning his head to his partner to tell her something—but what? Was he gesturing at me? I was probably just being paranoid, but *what if they were talking about me?* I'd been gawked at, mocked, berated, and worse, simply because somebody saw me and didn't like the fact that they had. I'd been hardwired to expect the worst while I was out in public, so even when that didn't happen, I'd stay anxious, on alert, imagining what might come next and seeing it everywhere I looked. The man I passed in the station might have been making fun of me. He might have just found the exit and was pointing his girlfriend toward it. Either way, I was spiraling, even as my feet kept moving, wondering what other people saw when they looked at me and whether it was the worst thing I could possibly imagine.

● ● ●

The unknown terrified me, and in that first year, I had nothing but unknown. When I tried to picture my future, what it might look like after changing sexes, I was seized by a mix of excitement and fear, a thrill of possibility that completely overwhelmed me. I knew many other trans women, but they were all around my age, give or take a few years in the game. I didn't know what my forties would look like, much less my fifties or sixties. There was no longer a set path laid out before me, which meant that, theoretically, anything could happen. But if anything could happen, then *anything could happen.* That open-endedness could energize me, or it could leave me debilitated. I could be anything I want, as the lyrics to Sophie's "Immaterial" go, but with no name and with no type of story, where do I live? Tell me, where do I exist?

In the absence of clear answers, I turned to others for what to do next. Maybe a man would save me, but what man? Who was he? And where? If I pulled up Grindr on my phone, sure, I'd be hit with a nonstop barrage of DMs from faceless torsos, all of which appeared to belong to men with limbs and faces. But where were the men beyond that screen? Where were they in real life? Harassing me, belittling me, or otherwise acting like I didn't exist, at least until they logged in to Grindr.

I only knew one girl at the time who had a man. I remember once how we locked ourselves into some Bushwick punk bar's graffiti-covered bathroom to dip into her coke. "That's, like, so amazing!" I gushed at her about her having a boyfriend. "It's just so beautiful to see you two in love." She smiled and responded, rather matter-of-factly, "Yeah, he's great," as she put the little baggie back in her purse, not waxing poetic for one second about it.

To me, they were evidence that the impossible wasn't quite so impossible.

They broke up six months later.

It still seemed like the best I could hope for.

Once back at my apartment, I surveyed the usual sights: the crusted-over frying pan left dirty on the stove, the pots and bowls jutting out of the sink, the half dozen vape pods that littered the floor. It was the work of some roommate or other, maybe the one who made sausages every morning, always cooking them on high till the windowless kitchen grew acrid and hazy with smoke. It was annoying, but at least I'd usually be awake by that point, thanks to another roommate, the one who'd always begin his day by making a smoothie in the loudest mini-blender imaginable.

In the bathroom, I undressed and lowered the heart-shaped soap into the tub. It began to fizz with pink and blue bubbles, radiating out from all sides. Soon it had dyed the water a smoky lavender, coating its surface with a slick, seminal sheen. Before it had fully dissolved, I slipped into the water and let the remains of my Inner Truth break down into nothing. I grabbed my phone from the rim of the tub and started to take some pictures, first of the dissolving bath bomb and then also of myself. I could use some of them in the story, I thought, should anyone care to run it. And all the pictures of me? I could always send those to some man. Someone out there would want me, I thought. There had to be someone who could tell me what to do next.

DISCONTENT

Before the elevator door could close, a disembodied hand thrust a silver laptop through the narrowing gap, activating the motion sensor to reopen the door. That hand, as I could now make out, belonged to Sara, one of my new co-workers in the newsroom at Free Surgery Depot Dot Com.

I'd started calling it that while interviewing for the job a few weeks before, in the summer of 2019. The reason was simple: The company's insurance plan was incredibly comprehensive, covering all forms of trans healthcare, from electrolysis to surgery—a victory hard-won by the union a few months before I got there. This wasn't the only reason why I wanted the job. For one thing, I'd been assigned to a desk that covered Healthcare and Identity, capital letters and all, so I'd be able to continue writing about gender-affirming care, one of my beats at the time. I was also excited to finally join a union, something I'd never been able to do in all my years of organizing with other media workers. But I had tentatively scheduled a surgery for the following year, surgery I wouldn't have been able to pay for out of pocket, so I can't overstate how major it was to land a job that would foot the entire bill. It's true that "healthcare in this country would be simpler and more humane if employers were simply removed from the equation," as the labor organizer Lena Ruth Solow once wrote, for the system we have in place pressures workers to "remain in workplaces that are actively *harming* their health" so that they don't lose access to their insurance coverage. But the paradigm was the paradigm. What could I do? I was just happy to have the insurance.

Sara, one of the Depot's editors, was one of the half dozen women who'd pulled me aside when I'd first started working there to surreptitiously inform me who I could and couldn't trust. She was also super active in helping lead our union. With her infectious, Valley girl lilt and an encyclopedic knowledge of our rights as workers, she was a lot like Elle Woods, but for media labor organizing. I'm sure if I asked her how she managed it all, she'd have cocked her head, faux-confused, and said, "What, like it's hard?"

After the door closed and our elevator began its ascent to the newsroom's floor, Sara handed me a flyer filled with information. "I'm just making sure everyone knows about their Weingarten rights," she explained, enthusiastically but hushed, as if she were blessing me with gossip. "If they ever pull you into a disciplinary meeting or some other kind of labor dispute, tell them you're invoking your Weingarten rights, and they'll have to wait until you have a guild representative with you before they can proceed."

"Oh my god," I said, slipping the flyer into my pocket. "Thanks!"

"J'adorrrrrrrre, right?"

That information would unfortunately come in quite handy, but let's table that for later. For now, let's say that my experience at Free Surgery Depot Dot Com became very fraught very quickly, and it all stemmed from my boss, who just so happened to have been one of those people I was told that I couldn't trust. Her pivotal offense that broke my trust for good happened when I was about a month in. I didn't respond to a Slack message fast enough for her liking, so she came up behind me at my desk and startled me, lowering her face a few inches from my own to demand that I answer her question—something about a draft, I think. Feeling cornered and intimidated, I sputtered out an answer and then beelined to the bathroom after she walked away, where I spent the next half hour hyperventilating in shock. I felt physically intimidated and thought about quitting my job on the spot, but I knew that leaving wasn't an option. If I quit, I'd lose my healthcare, and with no healthcare, there'd be no surgery.

In addition to that one distressing incident, which for me would prove irreconcilable, there were so many smaller things she did that made working at the Depot unbearable. Her management style was muddled, her editorial judgment baffling. She wanted us to work on ambitious, longform features but also wanted a steady stream of short-to-midlength articles riffing on that day's news—voicey blogs with a hint of reporting, like "I Made This NYU Professor Comment on Prince Harry's Sex Life" and "The Who-Gives-a-Fuck Reality Behind Some Shit That I Saw on TV." She would tell me that I should develop a beat while dismissing the ones I suggested. I'd try pitching coverage of gender-affirming care, access to which was just beginning to come under legislative fire in a few states nationwide, but she shot down most of those stories, only green-lighting a few. Eventually, she told me to shift focus entirely. When I asked her why, she flatly informed me, "Those stories don't do well." Traffic mattered most of all.

She'd kill stories I'd been working on after multiple rounds of edits and then criticize me for not producing as much as the other writers on my desk. One of those killed stories was a would-be exposé on the discriminatory hiring practices and unsafe working conditions at a trendy women's clothing store, one that trumpets its ethical business practices. I spent a couple of weeks interviewing former employees, one of whom sent me pictures of the stockroom basement as evidence of those unsafe conditions, only for my boss to spike it because, in her words, "there's no story there." A reported feature on trans women's reproductive care met with a similar fate. "We don't do motherhood," she decided one day, reversing course on a story that she'd green-lit herself. "Besides," another editor added, "I feel like that story's already been done." She Slacked me some articles about trans men giving birth—that is to say, trans fatherhood. Had either of them, these two cis women who seemed to feel so comfortable editing my coverage of trans issues, even known what I'd meant when I said the words "trans motherhood"? What led them to believe that this wasn't worth covering? Did they even know what a trans woman was?

For all that my boss did not quite grasp, she certainly understood what would get eyes on the page—like this one idea I discussed with her in one of our semi-regular one-on-one meetings. It concerned a reviled plastic surgeon in Florida who'd lost his job earlier that year after he was exposed for mocking his patients on an anonymous Instagram account. He'd posted nonconsensual pictures of their genitals and other bits of flesh, like a surgically dissected penis twisted into the shape of a heart, and mocked the patients those appendages belonged to with slurs and other cruel comments, hashtags like #RealDicksMatter and #WhatTheFuckIsThat. I'd learned from a source who worked in the field that the surgeon had started operating again under a new employer, a potential scoop that no other outlets had yet picked up on. My editor's eyes lit up when I let slip what I'd learned through the community grapevine, that patients sought him out for his phalloplasty results, that his work was said to put AriZona iced tea cans to shame. I was excited when she gave me the green light, as this would be a chance to produce the kind of hard-hitting, good-faith reportage that matters of trans healthcare so rarely receive. But that excitement plummeted as I walked out of her office and thought about how she'd responded, and what specifically about my pitch had elicited that response. I could already imagine how she might edit the piece, how in her hands it would turn into a subtextual sideshow, the kind I don't even want to read, much less write. She wanted the trans content, but only for the metrics: the views, the engagement, the time spent on page. Everything else about it was inconsequential, including the trans woman writing it.

• • •

To be a trans woman working in media is to find yourself trapped behind a one-way mirror, your limbs duct-taped to the back of it, as you're forced to observe what looks to be the dullest office party imaginable, attended by your so-called peers from other publications. There's a whole world that lies beyond the generic conference room they're huddled in, one filled with other people and free from overhead fluorescence. But none of the partygoers you're forced to observe show an interest in leaving the room. They're happy where they are, mingling with the other like-minded recluses, the hum of the lights above drowning out the outside world.

They're talking about you—their idea of you, really, because none of them have actually met you themselves, much less ever seen you in person, what with the mirror blocking their view. Still, they don't seem to like you, and they can't stop talking about why, swapping their rumor-mill stories about you, their half-truths they've embellished in bad faith. They're all experts, you see, having made you their beat for the past couple of years—not that they've spoken one word to you. But why would they need to? They've got articles for that, all of them written by others standing on their side of the mirror. They've also got op-eds. Newsletters. Studies they've misinterpreted. Reddit posts. Normal posts. Screenshots. Vibes.

You might want to stop them from talking, but really, what are your options so long as you're trapped behind the glass? Should you bang your head against it or make some other attempt to disrupt them, they'll either politely ignore the noise and carry on with their misleading discourse, or else they'll pull out their phones and start furiously typing up a draft of their next column—probably something about how the woke mirror agenda is trying to violently silence them with leftist campus rattling. Should you refuse to bang your head or do anything to disrupt them, they'll just keep on talking. Either way, you'll end up as content for them. Fodder for their bylines. Gristle for their paychecks—which are bigger than yours, by the way, given that a lot of them have been able to work on staff at the same publications for years, penning their little columns with absolute job security, something you've probably never known and will probably never know in this industry. But don't blame yourself. It's not all your fault. I mean, you're dealing with a lot. You're taped to a mirror.

It's embarrassing to watch them be so wrong, and sure, it's a blow to your ego. But you also can't stop thinking about the impact their words have had on the world beyond their conference room. Do they really not see the feedback loop between their "social contagion" exposés and "irreversible damage" polemics and the ongoing legislative assault on your continued access to healthcare? Do these partygoers really not know that their coverage has been used to defend those laws in court? You keep trying to ask them that via Morse code, whomping your head against the glass with varying force and frequency, but none of them hear you—oh, wait! One of them does. But instead of responding, he pulls out his phone and starts drafting his next column, "The Woke Mirror Is Giving Me Pronouns at Gunpoint."

Just when you think you've had enough, you hear the door behind you, on your side of the mirror, burst open as your saviors rush in to snip you free from the tape.

You're safe now, they tell you. They're here to interview you. They want to help you get your story out there. You tell them that you can actually tell your own story, that you're a writer like they are, that you know what to do.

One of them scoffs and mumbles, "My impact," and asks that you cite him in whatever you write.

Another one steps forward—oh god! You recognize her. She used to frequent the other side of the mirror, as you remember all too well, talking with the others about how crazy it was that saying the word "woman" was now punishable by death, and how relieved she was to finally be in a space with no men in it. (By which she meant trans women. The actual men didn't bother her.) She runs her own site now, one that only ever covers you in a positive light.

"You can pitch us, if you want," she says. "Maybe something that really sticks it to those people on the other side of the mirror."

You tell her no thank you, that you're looking for something more stable.

"How about a staff job?" offers a third.

You don't know her, but you do know that the site she works for used to publish stuff like "Why You Should Punch Trannies If They Don't Give You a Bump." The site has been trying to turn over a new leaf, though; like, for example, their latest article you read was called "Why You Shouldn't Punch Trannies Even If They Don't Give You a Bump."

"We're really trying to build out our Identity coverage," she says, the capital I in that word somehow audible to you. "It's a major focus of ours right now. Readers love this kind of content."

You're intrigued but still uncertain, so you ask her about the healthcare. "Honestly?" she says. "It's fab." You accept the job on the spot. Maybe you should have asked her more questions, but really, what's the worst that could happen?

• • •

It feels trivial to complain about a staff job I once had, given that those barely exist as it is. I don't just mean for trans media workers; even cis people can't catch a break. The United States lost between two and three local newspapers every week in 2023, according to a Northwestern University study, which also found that we've lost about a third of our newspapers total since the year 2005, as well as two-thirds of all newspaper journalism jobs in that same time span. The state of things is dire for all but the most insulated journalists, but "for trans writers," as Joan Summers once wrote, "it [is] the only sort of culture any of us have ever worked under." We've never had staff jobs, broadly speaking, save for a lucky and mostly white few, and even those of us who've landed them never last long in those roles. Of the very few trans women that I can think of who had staff jobs around the same time that I did, only one of them still has a staff job. The rest of us burned out, left the industry, or disappeared, or else we were laid off—and yes, I'm one of those "we."

Through our union, I tried addressing some of my problems with my boss, like the unrealistic article quotas she set. Neither I nor the other writers at my desk ever managed to meet them consistently—though only I seemed to be reprimanded for that on a regular basis, something I learned over after-work drinks with those two other writers, both of whom happened to be cis. But our discussions with management went nowhere. I tried going to Human Resources, but as far as I could tell, they never took my claims seriously. I never received a follow-up from my first meeting with HR, and the second time I contacted them, this time over email, I didn't even receive a response. I didn't have faith that they'd do anything; after dealing with sexual harassment at a previous workplace years earlier, I had come to conclude that workers are incidental to HR's true mission, at least in our industry, which is to protect a media company from any threat of litigation.

Still, I wanted some kind of documentation—that my boss had physically intimidated me a few months back, that she held me to higher standards than the other writers at our desk.

Other women in the union had suggested I create a paper trail of her mistreatment. My memories of working with the union are some of the only ones I cherish from my time at the Depot. It depresses me to think about how rare that is for trans media workers, the chance to actually work in a successfully unionized newsroom.[*] A wave of unionization has swept through the industry over the past decade, but what good does that do for the average trans media worker who, because of the broader issue of employment discrimination, can't even get hired on staff in the first place?

When I finally heard from HR in the spring of 2020, a month into working remotely on account of the COVID-19 pandemic, it was to invite me to a disciplinary meeting with my boss. After accepting the Zoom invite, I was greeted by both her and an HR representative in a separate square of the call.

"We want to talk about your performance," said the HR representative.

"Is this a disciplinary meeting?" I asked, trying to quell my mounting panic.

"Yes," said the rep.

"Then I'm invoking my Weingarten rights. I need a representative with me before we can continue."

When we resumed the meeting with my guild rep present, my boss told me that she was putting me on a probationary

---

[*]   Rare but not improbable, obviously, even in recent years. For example, Alma Avalle, James Factora, and Lex McMenamin—journalists at *Bon Appétit, them,* and *Teen Vogue,* respectively—helped lead the Condé Nast Union's ultimately successful effort to win its first contract in 2024.

"performance improvement plan" because of my low page-views and article count from the previous month. She left out that in that same month, an unprecedented pandemic had swept the globe, and that New York's governor had ordered a stop to all elective surgeries in an effort to stall the virus, which indefinitely delayed my own procedure, one I'd waited years to have, mere days before it was scheduled to happen. She also omitted that she'd encouraged me to take as many days as I needed to mentally recover after receiving that news, during which time I didn't publish any articles. You'd think that the woman who had edited my work about Healthcare and Identity, again with the capital letters, would have understood how these things might affect one's productivity and general ability to function—and yes, I think she did understand. I think she knew what she was doing.

The demands of my performance improvement plan were extreme, requiring that I double my weekly article count and my pageviews month over month. I knew from the start that I'd never be able to meet them; performance improvement plans are often a way to create just cause to fire someone, as a member of the union explained after the Zoom call. Still, I tried my best, however unsuccessfully, hoping against hope that I'd find a way to meet these demands and hold on to my healthcare until my surgery was rescheduled, whenever that would be. With no time for shame or impropriety, I wrote traffic-hungry listicles and gimmicky early-pandemic fluff about sourdough starters and things we missed about life before lockdown. I also took on longer, more personal assignments that I wouldn't have wanted to write for her otherwise, given how little I trusted my boss with the more vulnerable parts of myself. One of those pieces, an essay about men and the ways in which they've hurt me, ended up getting a lot of traffic and praise. Even my boss had nice things to say about it. She was also very pleased with my reporting on how COVID-related shutdowns had affected access to trans healthcare. As far as I could tell, she failed to note the irony. Or maybe she did? I never thought to ask.

My performance improvement plan had a thirty-day timeline, after which, had I not sufficiently improved my performance, my boss would've probably fired me. Before the end of those thirty days, though, I was laid off along with dozens of others, including the only other trans woman in our newsroom who covered trans issues—a fortunate turn of events, I guess, because a layoff at least meant I got severance. Plus, I got to keep my health insurance until the end of the calendar year, which meant I was still able to go forward with my surgery when it was rescheduled. Still, it was sad, to have my career in media derailed like that, seemingly permanently. Though I still occasionally freelance, I've given up on the idea that I'll ever work in a newsroom again.* Doesn't the world need more trans journalists? I certainly think that it does. So does Free Surgery Depot Dot Com, apparently. I mean, they published a whole article about why the world needs more trans journalists a year after I got laid off.

---

* Perhaps a blessing in disguise, given the transphobic "both sides" Zionist chokehold many of them seem to be locked in.

WHAT'S NEW AND DIFFERENT?

*T*he *Devil Wears Prada* has birthed a handful of memes that anyone stationed at a particular cross section of social media—the millennials, the gay guys, and the gay guy–adjacent—should be very familiar with, if not fully sick of, by now. There's the one where Emily asks Andy if she's wearing the Chanel boots—

"Are you wearing the—"

                              "The Chanel boots? Yeah, I am."

—only the memes have evolved, to swap out "the Chanel boots" for "the *Chromatica* jockstrap," "the masque of the Red Death," or what have you. There's the one that references Miranda Priestly's disinterested take on "florals for spring," as in "Referencing memes in your lede? Groundbreaking." But my absolute least favorite and perhaps most run-into-the-ground of these is the endlessly spawning, beyond incorrect take that the *real* villain of *The Devil Wears Prada* isn't actually Miranda, Andy's indisputably abusive boss, but her boyfriend, Nate, whose lack of enthusiastic support for his girlfriend's plainly exploitative labor conditions is thereby reframed as an implicitly sexist objection to both ambitious young women and older women in power.

It's a deranged reading of *The Devil Wears Prada,* albeit one that the film would support. For those who have not seen director David Frankel's 2006 adaptation of Lauren Weisberger's novel of the same name, it follows Anne Hathaway's Andrea Sachs, who also goes by Andy, as she ventures into the pre-Recession print-media world of New York, her journalism degree from Northwestern in hand. She aspires to become a serious journalist and to be taken seriously, period, and she has no reason to doubt that she will. Why should she? She's the kind of girl who was positioned to do well in life from the start, and then, lo and behold, she did. She got good marks in school, graduated from a prestigious university, one that's known for sending forth top talent in her desired professional field, and won't have to shoulder the financial burden of that education, crushed by student loans for decades to come, if the dinner scene where her dad insists on paying her rent for the month serves as any indication of which class she sprang out of.

I obviously don't know the girl—who, for the record, does not exist—but Andy strikes me as the type who might earnestly believe that her accomplishments in life have been entirely of her own making. The type who, no matter how well versed she might become on matters of oppression and privilege and structural blah blah blah, will always retain a vestigial conviction in not just her own potential but how much she deserves to realize it. Not everyone will have the opportunity to do so, but she does. So why should she waste it when so many others—so many undeserving others, so many undeserving *men*—would never dare question their own right to success?

I have no way of knowing how accurate this reading is. I can't go and ask her, what with her, again, being fictional and all. But if I am correct in my analysis, it would certainly help explain why she so disdains the one job that the media world is willing to give her: an entry-level position at the media giant Elias-Clark, an obvious Condé Nast stand-in, working as an assistant for *Runway* editor in chief Miranda Priestly, portrayed in the film by Meryl Streep. With its long hours, relatively low pay, and ruthlessly punitive supervisor, the job is undeniably horrible, but that's not why Andy looks down on it. Her resentment, in my view, is one that is rooted in class and a perceived upending of her rightful position therein. To put it another way, she's supposed to *drink* the coffee, not go fetch it for others! More than a source of money—and if she's lucky in America, healthcare—a job, for Andy, is first and foremost a matter of aesthetics: a means of confirming what she thinks to be true; a lens through which to see herself and to be seen by others. If this were not the case, then the following cautionary tale from Emily, Miranda's more senior assistant, about why they should never leave their desks wouldn't have landed so hard:

Emily: You are chained to that desk.

Andy: Well, what if I need to—

Emily: What? No. One time, an assistant left her desk because, you know, she sliced her hand open with a letter opener, and Miranda missed Lagerfeld just before he was about to board a seventeen-hour flight to Australia. She now works at *TV Guide*.

Andy (aghast): Man the desk at all times. Got it.

A different full-time job in her field? The shameful horror! The horrible shame. Even more terrifying is what this exchange tells us about Miranda. Before we've even met her, the audience understands that she's a corner-office tyrant whose word must be obeyed. The implications are equally clear for Andy. Her chance to become that serious journalist, and to be taken seriously, will entirely depend on doing everything that Miranda asks of her, no matter how sadistic, no matter how absurd, no matter who else might get hurt along the way.

Considering the many resemblances between *Runway* and its real-world counterpart—Weisberger worked at *Vogue* before penning the film's source material—it's impossible not to wonder whether the author's time under Anna Wintour was similarly brutal. And perhaps it was, although I should note that Weisberger has always maintained that *The Devil Wears Prada* is a work of fiction, not a thinly veiled tell-all, and that Miranda is not Anna. "It wasn't a one-to-one portrayal [of Wintour]," Weisberger once told *Event* magazine. "But of course my time at *Vogue* informed the book, there's no denying that." In other words, it's fiction. Fiction, Nancy Drew! Fiction! Good old-fashioned, NDA-respecting fiction—a text that neither discloses nor disparages, much less aims to convey some obfuscated truth. But what kind of fiction are we talking about here? Is this spaceships-and-dragons fiction, or fiction of the "fiction must stick to facts, and the truer the facts the better the fiction" variety, as Virginia Woolf once wrote in *A Room of One's Own*? That, my dear reader, is for all the little Andrea Sachses out there to decide, sitting side by side in their undergrad seminars, majoring in comp lit with a minor in looking for evidence. But for now? Let's say it's the latter: that fiction can be fact just as fact can, in turn, be fiction.

Now, where was I? Right. Miranda. As much as Miranda antagonizes Andy—and she *is* the antagonist of *The Devil Wears Prada*, despite those aforementioned viral claims to the contrary—the editrix also offers her new underling, Andy, a model for the kind of professional success that she craves, one that is explicitly gendered as well as implicitly raced and classed. Andy might not like working for Miranda—and who would, what with her cutthroat management style?—but she never questions whether her boss even deserves her position of authority, no matter how vindictively she wields it. When Andy discovers that Miranda might lose her job to a younger, Frencher white woman, she has sympathy for the titular devil; Miranda might be one of the most powerful women in fashion, if not all the cultural industries combined, but she's still just a woman, able to be cast aside when a man deems her disposable. The kind of misogyny that nearly topples Miranda from her perch at the top is so pedestrian, isn't it? It's garden-variety, honestly—so common, so quotidian, so, dare I say . . . relatable? Andy certainly thinks so. Behind those newly cropped bangs, the gears are starting to turn inside Andy's head, just as they might be within our own. Perhaps experiences such as this were what made Miranda the way she is: many such instances of misogynistic treatment that, while manageable in the moment, grew crushing in the aggregate? Who wouldn't harden to the point of unfeeling after decades of unprecedented success in a man's world, anticipating her downfall at every turn? Sure, it made her ruthless, but it was precisely that ruthlessness that made her so successful. I mean, you can't shatter a glass ceiling if you're afraid of a little blood.

Despite this newfound understanding, Andy still doesn't want to someday become just like Miranda herself, at least not exactly like her. She may covet the woman's power, but she doesn't want to do what that woman did to get it. She's different, you see—*very* different. To prove this, Andy quits her job after realizing that she's indulged in some deeply Priestlian behavior: A car struck Emily, the senior assistant, leaving her incapacitated with a broken leg and therefore unable to accompany Miranda on her trip to Paris Fashion Week; Andy doesn't hesitate to take advantage of Emily's predicament and jumps in to fill the vacancy at Miranda's side, where Emily once stood. Struck by the realization of what she has become, and viscerally averse to any further Mirandafication, Andy literally walks away from Miranda just as they're about to enter some big event at the Place de la Concorde, leaving her now-former boss helpless as a throng of lesser industry figures, whose names she never bothered to learn, swarm to kiss the ring. Andy click-clacks to the center of the cobblestone roundabout, tosses her T-Mobile Sidekick into the Fontaine des Fleuves, smiles, and breathes a sigh of relief. She's finally free—or is she? *The Devil Wears Prada*'s denouement suggests that Andy still respects Miranda, despite all that her boss put her through. The woman might have been abusive, there's no denying that. But with time and distance, Andy comes to embrace Miranda as a kind of flawed role model, one who might have made her workdays miserable but still helped make her career path possible. As she struts off to her next job, thanks to an unexpectedly glowing reference from Miranda, Andy does so feeling indebted to her predecessor, though determined to better wield such authority should she ever hold it herself.

OK, so I don't actually know what Andy's thinking as those credits roll, what with her not being real and all, and me not being her. But again, per Woolf, the truer the facts, the better the fiction. Or as the famed existentialist Albert Camus put it, "When I look back on my life, it's not that I don't want to see things exactly as they happened. It's just that I prefer to remember them in an artistic way, and truthfully the lie of it all is much more honest because I invented it." Or was that Lady Gaga? The point is that although I might have invented some pieces here and there, I feel that my version of events is plausible, if not exactly the truth, and the same goes for what I think happened next.

• • •

Things were looking up for Andy after stepping out of Miranda's shadow. She had landed a job in the newsroom of a new print publication that, despite its rookie status after only a year in circulation, had managed to accrue a hip reputation in New York media circles.

"So, what's this place's deal again?" Nate asked her from the bed, the right side of his face planted firmly in their pillows. His head was pounding after drinking all night with his bros the evening before. It was always the first thing he did after getting back into town from Boston—once he dropped his bags by the door of Andy's apartment, usually blocking her shoe rack.

Andy groaned. She felt like she'd explained this to Nate a million times already.

"I told you, babe! It's basically like a successor to *Spy* magazine."

"What the fuck is *Spy* magazine?"*

"I don't have time for this, Nate! I'm gonna be late!"

Andy flung her coat over her arm, grabbed her click-clackiest heels, and slammed every door she could before stomping her way down to the street. Why was he always questioning her like that? If it wasn't the specifics of her job that she'd already explained to him over and over, it was that she worked too many hours, or that she should be making more money. Had she thought about moving to a cheaper place? Or switching over to ad sales? He always had some kind of inquiry that served no real, constructive purpose other than to make her doubt herself and question her decisions. Could he not see the course she had charted for herself, much less where that path was taking her? Was he threatened by her focus and the fact that it wasn't set squarely on him?

She dumped him two months later.

Andy was sad about the breakup, but she didn't let that slow her down. Her career took precedence, just as her goals always had. After Jeremy, her boyfriend throughout most of undergrad, had dumped her a week before midterms in her senior year, thereby spurring a tear-strewn breakdown that had caused her to miss an entire night of studying, she swore to herself that she would never again let a man have that much power over her. Henceforth, she would prioritize her energy for that which was her own: her schoolwork, her career, her creative ambitions. A man could ruin any relationship without warning, without even consulting her. But her work, her goals,

---

* I'm always saying this.

her hopes, her dreams—they were hers and hers alone, and only she had the power to destroy them.

So, while a weaker Andy in some other timeline might have been found trudging through Nolita after her breakup with Nate, stifling her wails while that annoying song about big girls not crying looped on her iPod ad nauseam, this Andy, the strong Andy, the don't-need-a-man Andy simply kept on keeping on. She didn't have time to indulge in such nonsense. She had stories to write, media mixers to go to, and those childish bangs to grow out.

And then the Great Recession hit. The *Spy* wannabe print mag that Andy had started writing for post-*Runway* failed to weather the financial crisis, making her one of the more than fifty thousand media workers to lose her job between 2008 and 2009. Unlike her breakup with Nate, this loss truly devastated her. Cue Beyoncé's "If I Were a Boy," half sung, half wailed between swigs of wine straight out of the bottle on the couch she barely left for days on end. Thankfully, she had her new and much more supportive boyfriend, Matt, by her side. Thanks to his job in banking or marketing or whatever, he was more than able to provide for them both until the worst of the economic downturn had finally come to an end.

They had a daughter together, their precious little Paige, and *then* they got married. Andy's parents were, of course, uncomfortable with that order of operations, as they always were whenever anything even moderately scandal-adjacent managed to pierce through their otherwise pristine Midwestern bubble—so uncomfortable, in fact, that they waited until after the wedding to even mention their granddaughter to any of the neighbors. But Andy merely rolled her eyes at her parents' silent though legible discomfort and kept on moving forward. She knew what she was doing. Her intuition had never steered her wrong.

Still out of work, Andy, now living in a spacious Park Slope brownstone, assumed the role of the stay-at-home Brooklyn mom well enough, handling the literal and proverbial SUV-sized stroller with ease—at least at first. By the time Paige was five, Andy was dying to get back out there. But get back out to where? The media landscape had changed so much in her time away, which she gathered while scoping out the listings on Mediabistro during Paige's afternoon nap. Whatever the industry had turned into while she'd been on her hiatus, as she called it, didn't appear to be very welcoming to thirtysomething mothers with a half-decade gap in their résumés, much less women entering middle age with no social-media acumen. I mean, why would she go anywhere near Twitter? The site that had ruined her friend Justine's life?!

Realizing the depths of her predicament, she dramatically groaned for no one and slumped over her sprawling kitchen island, only to immediately rise back up, disgusted, as she brushed the sticky Kashi crumbs off her forehead. Ugh! She really wished that someone had warned her that toddlers leave a light crumb coating of cereal debris on every surface they come into contact with. Even if they barely touched it. Even if they so much as looked at it. Even when they weren't eating cereal at all.

When did her life get so gross?

It was at this moment that she heard a voice, one that came to her whenever she felt at her lowest. An unnerving mezzo soprano that always managed to say the exact horrible thing that was sure to hurt her most when she needed to hear it the least. It was the voice of Miranda Priestly, chiding her for her pitiful descent into ordinariness. Andy fingered the stem of her afternoon glass of sauvignon blanc as she cycled through all the meanest things that woman had ever said to her during her time at *Runway*. Even if Andy hadn't merited those insults at the time, she certainly did now, as she sat there sipping her wine in her kitchen, blanketed in a dusty patina of puffed rice and regret. She remembered the time when Miranda had called her "disappointing," the time she'd called her "fat," the time she'd brutally dressed her down for scoffing at a pair of seemingly identical blue belts and then launched into a crash course on fashion supply chains, and—

Oh my god! Inspiration! When she needed it most, it struck!

What if Andy created an e-commerce site that bought unsold garments from fast-fashion retailers and sold them, flash sale–style, to budget-conscious shoppers with disposable income to burn? The more she thought about it, the more it made sense. She thought back on all the moms she'd met through Paige's preschool. Every complaint they'd ever made about shopping for clothes now that they weren't lithe and childless. Every dollar of theirs that they'd left unspent despite their best efforts to spend them. Did she have the answer? She was sure that she did. There were so many women like her, a whole demographic with untapped market potential, and if the retail world wasn't smart enough to recognize it, then she, one of their own, would have to step in.

One night, as Paige slumbered on the top floor of their townhouse, Andy pitched the idea to Matt in the parlor room two stories down. "I have sacrificed so much for this family," she said in a heated stage whisper. "Don't you know what that would mean for her to see her mother build something like this? What kind of lesson are we teaching her if you force her closest female role model to give up on her dreams?"

Hearing his wife's pitch, her eyes alight with ambition like he hadn't seen them in years, Matt overcame his initial reticence and began to see her vision. The next morning, he put in his two weeks' notice and joined the ranks of Park Slope's growing number of stay-at-home dads.

At least, that's what he'd later tell everyone who asked him—and believe me, *everyone did ask*—why he had given up his lucrative career in banking or marketing or whatever to risk it all on his wife's unproven gamble. In reality, Matt continued to have his misgivings about the arrangement, but as often happened with his wife, he acquiesced to her will in order to keep the peace. To that end, he concocted that bullshit narrative about wanting to see Andy go after her dreams. As a reward for his compliance, Andy did more than merely corroborate his story. She expanded on it, telling everyone who asked—which, again, *everyone did ask*—that the swap had been Matt's idea to begin with. What a man she had! What a resentful, embittered man.

With that hurdle cleared, nothing stood in our heroine's way as she sprinted forth into Silicon Alley, ready to disrupt the world of online retail as she knew it. In four months, her site, which she dubbed About the Fit, was up and running. A little over a year later, the much-buzzed-about startup had more than two hundred employees in a converted Red Hook loft, working like one big happy family.

Some mornings, Andy felt like she didn't recognize herself anymore. She almost couldn't believe it. An out-of-work mother-turned-big-name tech founder—and it had only taken her about a year to achieve it!

And then one morning, as she caught her reflection in the mirror inside her medicine cabinet, she realized that she quite literally did not recognize herself. What had happened to the nearly imperceptible fear in her eyes? That once-legible anxiety that now appeared to have been erased from her brow? When she turned her head, so too did the woman in the mirror. She raised her right arm. So too did the woman in the mirror. She thought to scream and opened her mouth, but no sound came out of her gaping maw. She was as silent as the other woman; her maw gaped open too.

A knock at the door snapped her out of her fugue.

"Jules!" Matt called from the other side. "Remember, we've got Paige's interview at Saint Ann's this afternoon! Pleeeeease, please, please, please, please make sure to get there on time."

"Uhhhhhhh," she vamped for a second while her brain caught up to her mouth. "Yeah, no, of course."

Had he called her Jules? That wasn't her name, but something about it felt right.

"I'll see you there."

The phone nestled snugly in her skinny jeans buzzed. It was an email notification from someone named Lauren. She unlocked her phone to read it: "Hey Jules! Just wanted to touch base on ORDER #405595 with the bride who received the wrong color dresses for her bridesmaids. She's confirmed a successful return and exchange and sent over some honestly adorbs photos of the bridal party (see attached)."

"Thanks for circling back, Lauren!" she wrote back, not thinking twice about who Lauren was, what she was talking about, or why she was also calling her Jules. "Crushing it!!!!! Happy hour later? (Shots shots shots shots shots shots haha) I'll see you in an hour!"

She slipped her phone back into her pocket, looked up at her reflection, and felt a calm wash over her. The panic that had plagued her moments ago was now totally gone. This was her. This was right. This was how things should be.

She grabbed her canvas tote and ordered a car to work. She was ready to reign another day, not with an iron fist like some bosses would, but with a heart as open as About the Fit's floor plan, where everyone was welcome—except haters, of course.

•••

Jules Ostin, Anne Hathaway's protagonist from Nancy Meyers's *The Intern,* released in 2015, nine years after *The Devil Wears Prada* came out, is perhaps the best example of a girlboss to ever appear onscreen, at least among those films contemporaneous to the term's origins. Sophia Amoruso, the founder and former CEO of online fashion retailer Nasty Gal, coined the label in 2014 in an act of personal branding, as it was the title of her 2014 memoir. Well, technically it was *#GIRLBOSS,* with the hashtag, caps, and all, but that was the mid-2010s—we don't do that anymore.

Much has been made of the girlboss in the years since the term's advent, but if I may slip on my textual originalist bandage dress for a second, complete with studded Litas, Amoruso's memoir defines a girlboss as someone who:

- Is in charge of her own life

- Gets what she wants because she works for it

- Takes control and accepts responsibility

- Knows when to throw punches and when to roll with them

- Knows when to break rules and when to follow them because whatever she's doing, she's doing it on her own terms

- Knows where she's going

- Values honesty over perfection

- Asks questions

- Lets herself have fun

- Takes herself seriously but not too seriously

- And never gets caught when she commits homici—

—I'm so sorry. Oh my god. That's a typo, I swear. What Amoruso actually said is that a girlboss is a total badass. "You're going to take over the world, and change it in the process," she writes, noting that it won't be easy. "It takes a lot of hard work to get there, and then once you arrive, it takes even more hard work to stay there. But then, who's scared of hard work? I sure as hell am not, and I'm sure you aren't either."

The age of the girlboss has come and gone, and with it that particular devotion to "millennial-pink" capitalism "with a feminism-lite twist," as the writer Samhita Mukhopadhyay once put it. What has it wrought in the end, this project of "feminism's assimilation into the status quo," per the critic Jamie Hood? Further branding opportunities for women like Amoruso—and other seemingly unassailable "She-EOs" like

Miki Agrawal of Thinx and Tushy or the *Lean In* queen herself, former Facebook exec Sheryl Sandberg? A woman in the
White House who sits back and cackles while her government
funds the slaughter of an occupied people? The unemploy-
ment rate for American women dropped 1 percent over the
past decade, so at least there's that. But I don't know, the impact could've been bigger. I guess we'll just have to lean in
even harder.

In hindsight, the girlboss is more like a grifter, and also a
bit of a street-corner preacher. She blew into town, pried open
people's wallets with an alluring prosperity gospel, and slipped
away into a neighboring hamlet before anyone could uncover
the truth behind the lies she was peddling. But if we understand girlboss feminism to be a kind of grifter feminism, then
Amy Dunne, Rosamund Pike's homicidal liar in 2014's *Gone
Girl*, might make for the better cinematic example. She reflects that "no days off" mindset taken to its most ridiculous,
murderous, pathological extreme. She kills people, lies about
having suffered rape and abuse, and covers it all up by manipu-
lating the American public's well-documented credulity, deliv-
ering unto them an expert-level performance as the victimized
white woman they'll always rush to believe.

Still, I feel like Amy Dunne's version of the girlboss is more
in line with what the term has eventually come to mean after
years of ironic memeification—the "Gatekeep, Gaslight, Girlboss" shitposting that mocked the "Live, Laugh, Love" décor
found hanging in the proverbial white woman's home. Treating yourself to a $12 latte? Finally doing your skincare routine
after rotting in bed all weekend? The world has agreed these
are girlboss slays. But at the risk of taking the shitposts too
seriously, this evolution of the term has compromised the girlboss by extricating her from the very structure that gave her

power in the first place. Without a workplace to control, without employees under her thumb, a girlboss is simply a girl. A girl with clear skin and a $12 latte, but still just a girl. Any old girl can partake in socially unsanctioned sociopathic pastimes, as long as she, like the "Amazing" Amy Dunne, is willing to risk the consequences. But women like *The Intern*'s Jules Ostin, both real and fictional, have been granted the power to ruin lives and never deal with the fallout. Worse than that, they may even be celebrated for amassing the power needed to ruin those lives—sometimes even purely on account of their gender. Like a feudal baroness lording over her open-concept loft, Jules holds the power to grant salaries and dole out health insurance, just as she holds the power to take such things away. Although Amy has literally killed people, I find Jules's capacity for violence to be much more compelling precisely because of its everyday nature. I mean, there it is, hiding in plain sight, so normalized and mundane that even Jules has no clue she's the villain.

• • •

Though Jules continued to grow her company at a rapid pace, those early years of her tenure were not without their hardships. Most significantly, perhaps, was the time when she was being pressured to step down as CEO of her own company. Her investors thought that she had too much on her plate. But her company was her baby! And you don't just give up your baby—unless you're literally giving up your baby, which Jules obviously supported (unless she didn't). How could she give up her company? The same one that she'd birthed on the counter of her brownstone's kitchen island and raised up to staggering heights? She had always held her business close, supporting its neck with the tightest of grips. Who were they—those men on her board—to go and tell her otherwise?

Complicating matters was the fact that Matt was cheating on her. He really thought she was too stupid to notice all those texts he started getting, too dim to ever figure out the password for his phone (6-2-8-8, i.e., "MATT"). He was practically taunting her, leaving his phone out on the edge of the coffee table, its incessant buzz-buzz-buzz while he left to use the bathroom. Sure, it hurt to learn that he was sleeping with another mom from Paige's school, but what really stung was the inescapable truth that he'd dare underestimate her intelligence. Is that how he saw her? Some moron who couldn't tell her lapis from her cerulean? The thought shook her to her core, so much so that in her ego-bruised state, she accepted a meeting with her prospective replacement, handpicked by the men on her board.

She was faced with a choice: her family or her company. Either way, she was about to lose something of hers that she'd worked to build from the ground up. In the end, she chose her family—that is, until Ben intervened.

Ben was Jules's most trusted friend. He'd come into her life thanks to About the Fit's senior internship program, which employed literal senior citizens in unpaid roles. The program was short-lived, having been swiftly shut down under pressure from the company's newly formed union, which doggedly opposed the program's many labor violations. But Ben stuck around as her friend and mentor. He advised her on all sorts of things, and, quite unlike Miranda, always knew just what to say to lift her out of her various spirals, like what he'd told her in those final hours before she signed away her company. No one would ever care as much about her company as she would. About the Fit needed her, and no one, not even the men on her board of trustees, had the right to convince her otherwise. She'd stay on as CEO, no matter how much pushback she faced.

Ben was right, Jules decided. So she marched back home to confront Matt and demand, again in a heated stage whisper as Paige had gone down for a nap, that he stop fucking that other woman. If he didn't, she'd divorce him and fight for full custody.

"Jules, you can't do this. You can't threaten me like this."

"You have no idea what I'm capable of," she told him. Knowing she was right, Matt agreed to end the affair.

Jules would later tell Ben that she and Matt had come to this resolution in a more amicable fashion, crying on the stairs, smiling through their tears, affirming their love and commitment to each other in their kindest, gentlest voices. She repeated that lie to her marriage counselor. Matt corroborated her story.

Reinvigorated by these back-to-back wins—keeping her company and her family intact—Jules set out to claim a third. She dusted off an old dream of hers, that of becoming a serious journalist, and launched About the Fit's very first venture into content production. It was an editorial platform that published articles and videos about fitness, gender, bodies, and sex from a distinctly female perspective, all of it funded through collaborations with About the Fit's various ad partners. Workout apparel had become one of the site's top-selling categories of merchandise, and with the president and #MeToo and everything else going on, Jules had come to understand just how important it was—"now more than ever," as she was quoted in the press release disseminated at launch—for women to speak up and share their experiences with the male-dominated world that worked to keep them down. She called the new vertical *Fit Bitch,* and she was its HFBIC.

Jules was in her "having it all" era, her Helen Gurley Brown era. (She couldn't stop saying the word "era.") No desire was off-limits, no goal beyond her reach. She indulged herself every chance she got, like when she started sleeping with Ben on a whim. What else was she supposed to do with her time? Go keto? Join CrossFit? "Discover herself" or whatever on an ayahuasca retreat? Well, yes, she did, in fact, do all those things—*and* she'd started sleeping with Ben. Having it all meant having it all, so the father figure became a daddy—well, she was the daddy, obviously, but you get it. They were fucking.

"Yoga pants for work?" he asked one morning, half under the covers, as he watched Jules get dressed.

"It's called *athleisure,* Ben," she corrected him with an ironic juvenile disdain, smiling as she swiveled her ass to face him.

"Well, it athlei-*sure* is giving me a boner."

"Oh my god." She rolled her eyes in mock annoyance before hopping back into bed with him. "I guess I can miss the nine A.M. pitch meeting."

The old Jules never would have uttered such blasphemy. But the new Jules? She was in therapy. Thanks to her sessions, she realized that her obsessive, micromanagerial relationship with her company was a maladaptive expression of the trauma that she had sustained through working for Miranda at *Runway.* Also, it was her parents' fault, though she hadn't quite figured out why yet. She never used to miss a day of work, much less skip a meeting, but not because she cared too much—instead, it was because she was paranoid someone beneath her might overthrow her if given the opportunity. It was a breakthrough for Jules. She didn't want to be like Miranda, so she started doing things that Miranda would never do, like missing meetings or trusting her employees to carry out tasks without insisting on final approval over every minor detail. They were a team, she realized, and she'd hired them for a reason. Jenna in marketing, Lauren in customer satisfaction, Craig in product, and Helen in editorial, her newest staff writer.

Jules was beyond thrilled to welcome Helen into her newsroom of badass women with something to say. Helen was transgender, though you really couldn't tell, except for when she spoke, and Jules recognized how valuable that kind of lived experience was. Women needed to stand with trans women. They were her sisters too. The world—no, *the patriarchy*—could be so cruel to trans women, *especially* trans women of color, according to some article that she'd seen retweeted onto her feed. She looked forward to taking Helen under her wing, mentoring her as a writer—maybe even as a woman, or even an entrepreneur! The fantasy thrilled her, and she plunged herself into it, just as she plunged her silicone cock right back into Ben.

• • •

This little fan-fictional cinematic universe wherein *The Intern* serves as a direct sequel to *The Devil Wears Prada* provides a representation of how the whole "lean in" boardroom feminist ethos can poison a woman against her broader class interests. Like, imagine if the latter film kept running past its end credits, and we learned that Andy's big takeaway from working for an abusive woman in power was simply that the wrong woman had been granted the power to abuse, rather than the inevitable fact that, regardless of sex, such abuses of power come as no surprise—something else that I think Lady Gaga once said. If only that movie were real!

Oh, wait.

It kind of is.

Working Girl, directed by Mike Nichols, follows Melanie Griffith's Tess McGill as she works her way up the corporate ladder from lowly exploited secretary to a potential exploiter of secretaries herself. Along the way, she sheds her crimped and piled-high mane of hair, her garish makeup and clacking gold bangles, the harsher angles of her Staten Island accent, and most every other marker of her working-class background, all to better blend in among the WASPs of mergers and acquisitions. Her role model in this transition is her boss, Katharine Parker, played by Sigourney Weaver. Katharine at first appears to be a major improvement over Tess's previous boss, a man who sexually harassed her so much she quit. Katharine, by contrast, encourages Tess to speak up and contribute her own ideas—you know, just like they are equals. Later, however, Tess learns that Katharine is in fact repackaging all those contributions and passing them off as her own. It might not be the kind of exploitation that Tess experienced from her previous boss, but it is exploitation all the same.

Tess emerges triumphant toward the 1988 film's end, having not only reclaimed her stolen ideas but snatched Katharine's man away from her too. She even gets a job offer at another company, for a position with an office and a secretary of her own.

When the secretarial pool at her old gig gets word that Tess is moving up in the world, they all cheer for her. This throng of nameless, faceless, heavily made-up women with ozone-killing hairstyles have waited their whole life, it seems, for a woman—any woman!—to become a boss, despite the fact that, as the movie has already demonstrated quite plainly through Weaver's Katharine Parker, a boss is still a boss, regardless of her sex. Perhaps their joy stems not from the fact of Tess's gender but rather from her working-class origins. Could a boss of two marginalized identities succeed at being a good boss where a boss with only one such identity might fail? In other words, was it the silver spoon in Katharine's mouth, the same one shared by every other boss on Wall Street, that made her so awful that her gender could do little to mitigate the dynamic? If so, then surely Tess's class solidarity would thereby extend past her leaving the literal class that she came from. Tess certainly seems to think it will, though the film conveniently cuts off just before she can prove herself right.

In the absence of celluloid, I must consult the almighty head canon—which, again, I have fully made up. Hmm, I can see it now: Tess reminds Alice, her secretary introduced in the film's denouement, "I get it, I get it" and "I know what it's like." She tilts her face with a knowing glance as she tells Alice for the second or third time this week about how "I used to be a secretary, you know?" Tess tells her, "Oh, thank you!" and "You don't have to do that!" But then as the clock strikes 5:42 on a Friday afternoon, she says, "Can you take care of this before you head out for the weekend?" as she herself is breezing out the door, her houndstooth trench trailing off one shoulder. Alice smiles and nods and says, "Yes, Tess, you got it," then rolls her eyes as soon as Tess leaves. "Why does she think we're buddies?" Alice writes to a friend over Gchat. (This unauthorized sequel takes place in a world where Gchat had already been invented in 1988. Everything else in the timeline's the same. The only difference is they have Gchat.) Tess, meanwhile, is out on the street, stepping into her limo. After hearing her driver speak, she asks, "What part of New York are you from?" "Staten Island," he tells her. She smiles. "Me too," she tells him. "Me too."

Lizzie Borden's *Working Girls*—plural, not singular— provides an interesting counterpoint to Nichols's *Working Girl*—singular, not plural—and not just because of their similar titles. Released two years earlier, in 1986, Borden's film follows Louise Smith's Molly, one of the film's titular sex workers, as she drags herself through an exhausting shift at an upscale Manhattan brothel. Her clients are not the architects of that exhaustion, at least not primarily; she might find some of them draining, but the money she earns while hiding that fact seems to feel, to her, a fair exchange. The worst of those men is probably Jerry—or "Fagbag Jerry," as Gina, one of the other sex workers, calls him. He's a sleazy, wealthy creep who makes his money through construction. Still sloughing off the sunburn from his last exotic trip, he's about to jet off to another locale, but not before paying some beautiful women to laugh at his hooker jokes and tongue what I can only presume is his equally sunburnt asshole—a little "around the world" action, as he calls his anilingual request.

In bed with Molly and Gina, midway through the act of penetration, Jerry springs the idea of "no rubbers" on the women, something that they had not previously discussed. "Thirty extra," Gina tells him, to which he acquiesces. Borden then cuts from a close-up shot of Jerry's hands gripping Gina's hips, his fingers digging into her flesh, to one of Gina's hands grabbing the edge of the bed for support before it slips off entirely. The music intensifies as if to suggest that he is hurting her, perhaps even raping her. But then the music suddenly stops, and we find ourselves in the bathroom with Molly and Gina, who are cleaning up after the session. Gina is washing out her diaphragm in the sink. Molly, seeing the blood, is immediately concerned.

"My god, Gina, what did he do to you?"

"Nothing," Gina answers, thoroughly untraumatized. "I have my period."

"Well, at least you made a lot of money," Molly tells her.

In other words, don't let the Dutch angles fool you. What the viewer just witnessed wasn't a man transgressing a woman's boundaries but a customer receiving a service after negotiating its terms with the worker providing it.

Borden seems to delight in the intentional bait and switch, anticipating that any viewer who's never done full-service sex work might misread the scene as an instance of sexual assault. She plays with the misconception that sex work is uniquely exploitative in order to demonstrate how it is merely exploitative in the way that all labor is.

This becomes even clearer once Molly's boss, Lucy, arrives.

A strict authoritarian in an alabaster power suit, Lucy is the brothel's madam. She used to work at one of these upscale brothels herself, but now she's the boss—and a benevolent one at that, as she reminds her "girls" in furious tones whenever they step out of line.

The character of Lucy is based on an actual madam who ran the brothel where Borden worked in the early 1980s. At the time, the filmmaker was still waiting to secure funding to continue work on *Born in Flames,* her 1983 film about multiracial coalitions of working-class women banding together to ensure their survival after a socialist revolution fails to improve their conditions. In an early cut of *Working Girls,* Lucy had a different name, Borden once told me in a phone interview. I won't repeat it here because it was also the name of the actual madam she worked for. "I had to very cheaply dub the name Lucy over [the real madam's name] last minute," she said. "I almost got in trouble because of that. The madam found out I was making this movie and that I'd used her name. She was flipping out and threatening me, leaving messages on my answering machine very Mob-like, telling me she'd shoot my kneecaps off."

Though the real madam's name was removed from the final cut, her mannerisms remain, right down to her tyrannical management style. She's always demanding things of her girls, asking them to hold things, like they're flesh-and-blood coat hooks. Nothing is ever clean enough, no one sorry enough for her liking. "This place is a mess!" she scolds them within seconds of entering the apartment. "Why can't I *ever* come in and find it nice and tidy?" Molly, Gina, and the other women get to work straightening things up. When they're done, Lucy beams at them as if she hadn't just dressed them down. She asks her girls to sit with her on the couch so they can ooh and aah at all the fancy new stuff that she bought for an upcoming ski trip with her boyfriend. (*Working Girl*'s Katharine also goes on a ski trip. The parallels between the two are honestly wild.) After flaunting a few of her new acquisitions, Lucy holds up a pair of silky pink underwear, which she dubs the "pièce de résistance." Her persona has now switched from the disappointed mother to the gossiping girlfriend, further blurring the boundaries between her and her girls with every new face she puts on, each of these shifts more jarring than the last.

Hours into Molly's never-ending day at the brothel, Lucy's boyfriend, Miles, arrives, as does a new hire, Debbie. Miles, like Lucy, is white, while Debbie is Black. She's only there for an interview, but within minutes of bringing her on, Lucy is already asking Debbie to stay and work for the next hour, until the evening shift starts. "Oh, please! I know it's late," she begs, like a child who's spotted a well-stocked cookie jar, before Debbie can give her an answer. Eventually, Debbie acquiesces, and Lucy's reign of terror begins.

Lucy remains friendly throughout their first exchange. Like many narcissistic white people who'd like to think of themselves as not racist, she very clearly wants Debbie to like her. At the same time, she wants Debbie to know her place. We can discern that there will be consequences should she forget her position, as we see the first frisson of mistrust ripple across Lucy's face. It's a perfect illustration of how Black women can go from "pet to threat" in the workplace, as the writer Erika Stallings has described this dynamic—like when Miles, who has been eyeing Debbie since he first saw her, cracks a flirtatious joke.

"Oh, Debbie, I love your shoes!" Lucy cuts in, changing the subject. "They're almost like mine. Charles Jourdan?"

"No, they're Vittorio Ricci."

"Oh." Lucy's smile fades, then returns when she suggests that the two of them go shopping together.

Before Debbie leaves, a regular arrives, though when he learns that only Debbie and Molly are available, he leaves, telling Lucy that he'll come back in a couple of hours. His rejection wasn't pointed at Debbie, but what Lucy says next sure is. "I'm just gonna be frank with you. Don't be hurt if you don't make as much money as the other girls." Debbie's eyes narrow, though she maintains her composure as she braces for whatever the hell Lucy's about to say next. "We've had some very attractive Black women working here before, and, I don't know, for some reason our customers just prefer the white girls, even if they're not as pretty."

"We'll see." Debbie smiles assuredly, brushing off the slight.

"Debbie," Miles interjects, "would you like to go upstairs?"

"Oh, Miles!" Lucy nervously sings, then flashes a gritted smile. "He's just kidding," she tells Debbie in a territorial contralto.

As the film continues, Lucy's demands grow bigger, her changes in disposition even more abrasive. When her financial adviser arrives for a session with her girls, Lucy asks Molly to do some light dominance for him, even though, as Lucy herself notes, they don't do that at the brothel.

"He's an old friend," Lucy pleads, now playing the helpless girl in need. "You don't mind, do you?"

Molly says that she doesn't, though it's not like she has a choice. She'll lose her job if she tells Lucy no, and unlike the men who pay Molly for sex, Lucy never takes no for an answer.

We see this clearly toward the end of the film, when Lucy asks Molly to stay on past her shift. Molly says no, and so Lucy begs, her manicured hand nearly clutching her pearls in a pathetic display meant to convey desperation. Molly holds firm, so Lucy shifts tactics, guilt-tripping Molly, as if her desire to go home were a sign of ingratitude.

"I try to accommodate you. You are the *only* girl here with a regular schedule. You are the *only* girl here who doesn't work weekends," Lucy scolds. "The *least* you could do is help me out just this once"—though the viewer can surmise that it's not just this once.

"All right," says Molly, relenting. "Can you call and have somebody replace me, and I'll stay till she gets here?"

Lucy tells Molly that she will.

She never makes the call.

• • •

"Now, calm down, Jules, calm down. There's no need to get so upset."

But Jules had every reason to get this upset. Helen had deliberately gone behind Jules's back to ask Jason, one of her literal employees—a man who, only a few years ago, had been one of her coffee-fetching interns—if she could be transferred to his team instead of continuing to work directly under Jules. Apparently, Helen didn't "feel utilized to the best of her ability" in her current position, writing content for *Fit Bitch*. Why? Because her boss—that is, Jules—"doesn't seem to know how to best utilize her."

"Just . . . Get out of my office," Jules told Jason.

"Wait, are you mad at—"

"No! Get out!"

She watched him as he walked out of her glass-paneled office. She made a mental note to root through his file later, the one she kept in that Google Drive folder that documented all sorts of minor infractions that she could use as fodder to build a case for firing him, should the need ever arise. She had one for everyone who worked for her, or at least all the people whose names she remembered, and even a few that she didn't. "Jason in Creative: 23 minutes late on April 13—fourth time he's been late this month." "Cheap jewelry in HR: Stole paper towel roll from the kitchen, March 10." Jules had the greatest joke about the dossiers too. "Why do you keep these files, Jules? I don't know . . . Just 'cause!" What a tragedy that she had no one to share it with. At least she could crack herself up.

Her gaze followed Jason as he walked away, then it landed on the back of Helen's head. Helen was animated, waving her hands—talking to the girl who sits in front of her, it seems. What the fuck was she even talking about? How she wasn't "being utilized to the best of her ability"? If anything, *Helen* was the one who didn't know how to utilize herself to the best of her ability. *She* was the one who kept pitching these completely off-brand stories that veered so far away from the vertical's focus. *Fit Bitch* had always been committed to telling women's authentic stories about health, wellness, and identity— a very simple mission statement that even the dimmest sales reps seemed to comprehend. But Helen couldn't even get that right, even when she pitched something that was actually on topic, like that one piece that was supposed to be about trans mothers navigating childcare at the gym. The draft that Helen filed had barely resembled her pitch. Instead of a fairly standard "here's what it's like . . . ," she'd gotten all meta in her lede, writing about how troubling it was to not find any sources, and then how she realized that this was probably because trans women were "gatekept" out of motherhood itself. Forced sterilization, healthcare discrimination, "cultural transmisogyny," as Helen had termed it—how was Jules supposed to sell Lululemon ads next to this? Who'd even want to read this? Where was the gym?! When Jules brought it up, Helen had defended the piece, claiming it was an important story. That may be true, Jules had conceded, but it still wasn't the story Jules had assigned.

"You really need to find some trans mothers to talk to," she had explained to Helen very patiently at the time. "Without the fitness element, this is just a story about motherhood, and *Fit Bitch* doesn't *do* motherhood."

"But that's the problem," Helen told her. "This piece is about *trans* motherhood. It's incredibly underdiscussed, and I think this would be a great angle to open that up for our—"

"Is it, though?" Jules cut her off. "I feel like that story's been done before." She pulled up a handful of articles from a few years back about trans men getting pregnant. "See? 2015. 2015. 2016. It's been done."

When she first took Helen under her wing, Jules had delighted in the idea of mentoring the girl, much as Ben had once done for her. Even Miranda, long since dead, after the tragic 2017 crash of the *Hindenburg II,* in which she had been burned alive, had played a pivotal role in molding Jules into the woman that she had become. She had learned so much over her years in business—as a woman, as a businesswoman— and had so much to teach Helen, so many hard-won lessons that she would have given away so freely. But the young writer didn't seem to want them. She continued to reject them outright. So why, then, Jules wondered, was she even here in the first place? The gears began turning in Jules's head as the answer, or at least *an* answer, revealed itself: Helen was using Jules for her company's healthcare benefits. She'd already taken advantage of About the Fit's incredible insurance package to cover the cost of her facial feminization surgery the previous fall. It was such an unthinkably expensive procedure without insurance that most transgender women, *especially* transgender women of color, would never be able to afford it out of pocket. Jules had read that in an article. Or had it been a tweet? Either way, she knew that Helen wouldn't have been able to pay for it otherwise, just like she wouldn't be able to afford whatever surgery she was supposed to get the following month. Jules didn't know what procedure it was. Helen hadn't yet told her, not even when she asked Jules about taking time off to recover. Her withholding of that information had felt so pointed at the time, and now Jules understood why. Well, Jules was nobody's fool. Not her husband's, not Ben's, not her board of trustees', not Jason's in Creative, and certainly not Helen's. She'd spend all night poring over Helen's file to build the necessary case to begin termination proceedings. She would stay up all night if she had to.

•••

It had been nearly an hour since we closed down the diner, and I still had so many eggs left to crack. I didn't understand why it had taken so long to knock things off the closing checklist. Usually by three o'clock, I'd have prepped our three butter tubs with seven sticks apiece, restocked all our dozen-or-so squeeze bottles with their respective jams and aiolis, cracked close to two hundred eggs into five or six pitchers, and blended their yolks and whites into a viscous pool of tangerine—what I liked to call "the forbidden Tang."

By this time of day, I would normally expect to be tossing my dirty, avocado-smeared rag into the appropriate bucket, taking off my apron, and sitting down for my shift meal before clocking out. But on that day I was so behind, and I had no idea why. Maybe it was because we were so busy that day? There had not been a slow moment, always at least a few tickets I was working on at any given time. I had plans to meet my boyfriend for a movie at six o'clock, and I knew I wouldn't make it if I didn't leave soon. I needed to go home in the next hour, or else I wouldn't have time to wash off the day's grease and that dull stench of latex that would cling to my hands if left unattended. Then I'd have to be back out the door again by five o'clock, maybe quarter after at the latest, if I hoped to make it on time.

I needed to leave, which meant I'd have to ask my boss if I could clock out without finishing my share of the closing duties. My heart started to race. My breathing grew shallow. I clenched and unclenched my jaw as my anxiety ran wild, forcing me to envision all the ways that this could go wrong. Maybe she'd be mad, or maybe she'd fire me. I'd miss my movie, and my night would be ruined, and—

"Of course, m'dear," she said with a smile. "Say hi to Mike for me!"

She'd apparently missed the memo that my request had been life or death.

Those stakes, of course, were never there—just something that I'd projected based on past experiences with unyielding managers and bosses who asked for too much. At work I've been threatened, berated, belittled, propositioned, pelted with merchandise, and worse. But those experiences with customers, readers, and others are not what I worry about when I start a new job. Rather, it's the memory of every old boss that haunts me to this day. The smiles on their faces when they told me they were leaving and that I couldn't follow suit until my work was done, even though it was already six o'clock on a Friday and that work might take hours to complete. I remember the ease with which they recast us in intimate familial terms, calling themselves "mom" and the rest of us "kids," or else claiming the role of the big sister, perhaps as a necessary precondition for the kind of mistreatment that intimacy breeds. I remember when my bosses pressured me to write things I didn't actually believe even after I resisted and said I didn't want to, only folding in the end because I couldn't lose my healthcare, not with my surgery date only a few months away. I remember their disconnect between content and reality: their public support of, say, Google's union, while making our lives hell from the other end of the bargaining table; assigning a late-in-the-day op-ed about the benefits of a four-day workweek, which kept me from leaving my desk until it was fully nighttime; their lust for trans content, and their disdain for the

trans women writing it, how they treated us like we were difficult until we became what they claimed we were; the way that
they never addressed me by name except to admonish me for
things I hadn't done wrong; their decision to lock up my
phone, like I was a child in detention; their physical aggres-
sion; their hostile stares.

Their cruelties, big and small, seem unthinkable to me. I
don't think I could ever treat someone who was working for
me that way. Then again, I have never exactly been in the position to know if that is true. Every time a new client arrives at
the brothel in Borden's *Working Girls,* Lucy greets him with
the same four words: "What's new and different?" Were I ever
to find myself sitting in Lucy's position—or Katharine's, or
Jules's, or Miranda's—what *would* be different, besides the
obvious, about my having a seat at the table? Despite what
separates me from that quartet of fictional women, would anything have changed? My presence there would be new, but
what would be meaningfully different? It's unlikely that I'll
ever have the chance to find out, but a part of me takes com-
fort in that prospect's unlikelihood, for a part of me fears the
truth I would then uncover, that what would change would
be: nothing at all.

•••

With one foot propped up on the bathroom sink and the other
planted firmly on her black chenille bath mat, Helen pulled her
outer lips upward until they were taut. She admired her reflection. Her labia minora looked so delicate, slack with a small
ripple at its edges, like the pastry dough's excess draping over
the edge of a pie tin. She couldn't believe how convinced she'd
once been that a result like this was impossible. For weeks after

her surgery, she had avoided looking directly at the postoperative site, afraid to confirm what she feared to be true—that she
had flown too close to the sun, that no one would ever want
her now, that her sexed body would have been better left in-
congruous than rendered illegible through surgical recon-
struction. How silly she had been to envision the worst for
herself. If only she could have had faith that sometimes you
do, in fact, get what you want—like a book deal after losing
your job. Sometimes? You get what you want.

Her book, as yet entirely unwritten, was to be a full-length
work of character-driven, narrative nonfiction that concerned
the ways in which discrimination and exorbitant costs had
pushed trans women into underground economies to meet
their medical needs. At the center of her book would be Mar-
celine DuPré, the little-known author of the even-less-known
1988 novel, *The Amaretto Mule,* a lurid tale of vicious transsexuals and black-market silicone set in the 1970s, which
Helen was certain was a work of thinly veiled autofiction, inspired by DuPré's years as a nurse in San Francisco. Helen's
working title was *Beneath the Amaretto Mule,* and yes, she
fucking hated it, but the people with the money didn't. She
could always change the title later, she figured, when she signed
her contract.

Black-market hormones, back-alley silicone—Helen considered herself lucky to have only ever encountered such things
in news coverage, authored by herself and others, as well as in
books that she'd read. Thank god she'd never had to actually
stroll down those avenues herself. Through a string of back-
to-back corporate jobs, she'd been able to get access to top-
tier health insurance that covered even the most expensive of
her gender-affirming needs. She'd been able to get her breasts
done while writing sponsored content for *Gay* magazine's

marketing team, and then *Fit Bitch* paid for her face as well as her vaginoplasty. Harron, on the other hand, covered that latter procedure through Medicaid. They're very different people, you see. Their names even sound pretty different.

Twelve procedures in total, performed over three separate surgeries, and Helen hadn't paid a dime, though she'd come close with her vaginoplasty. Jules, her now-former boss at *Fit Bitch,* had summoned her to her office and fired her just a few weeks before that procedure was scheduled to take place. While Jules listed the reasons why Helen wasn't working out, Helen had realized that in losing her job she'd also lose access to her surgery, one that she'd been waiting years for. All that time spent writing soulless copy for shitty transphobic bosses had been a waste, and now she was back at square one. She started to tear up and began pleading with Jules: "I just— I can't— My surgery— It's—" To which Jules responded by crying as well. Bewildered, Helen snapped out of her spiral, completely nonplussed at her boss's display. Through sobs, Jules assured Helen that she would personally see to it that Helen retained her insurance coverage.

"I'm so sorry that this happened," Jules told her as she pulled Helen in for a hug.

"Thanks," said Helen, who at this point was simply saying words.

The following day, Helen had received an email from HR with a severance agreement attached. If she signed it, she would receive the standard six weeks of severance pay plus the equivalent of twelve weeks of paid medical leave—more than four months of income in total, amounting to just over $25,000 by the time that it was all paid. All she had to do was sign a statement swearing that she wouldn't disclose anything about her experiences at *Fit Bitch* publicly nor disparage any-one who'd ever worked at the company, past or present. She knew that it was hush money, an extra security measure to avoid the discrimination lawsuit that Helen could probably build as a mistreated employee of transgender experience. Her union rep certainly thought so. Jules *had* gotten all up in her face and physically intimidated an answer out of her that one time she hadn't responded fast enough on Slack, and Helen *had* reported the incident to HR and never heard anything back. There was also the fact that Jules held Helen to a higher standard than she did her co-workers. They all produced the same amount of work, yet Helen had been the only one ad-monished for not doing more—another thing she went to HR about, though again to no avail. Jules had also fired her mere days—weeks, really, but what are weeks if not collections of days—before she was scheduled to undergo a major transgen-der surgery. Her case seemed pretty buildable! But the thought of getting paid not to work for nearly five months, especially at a time when she'd be recovering from a surgery that even made sitting uncomfortable, was far more appealing. She had signed the NDA, gotten her long-awaited sex change, and spent the next few months blowing her severance on various SSENSE sales and every frivolous goo that Drunk Elephant ever produced.

Bizarrely enough, getting fired from *Fit Bitch* might've been the best thing that had ever happened to Helen. As she spent her recovery in bed, dilating every few hours, she real-ized how disempowering her experiences with the healthcare system had been over the past few years. So much of that dis-empowerment had been directly tied to the fact that her access to gender-affirming care was directly tied to employment. She decided to pitch a lengthy personal essay to *Straight People* magazine about how psychologically damaging those myriad experiences had been. Having her access to life-saving, medically necessary care be decided for her by bosses, surgeons, insurance agents, and other authority figures who only viewed her as a source of new revenue had honestly been traumatic. At any moment, any of them could have betrayed her. Of course, none of them did in the end—even Jules had seen to it that Helen got her surgery—but the threat was real, and very psychologically damaging.

The resulting piece for *Straight People* mag had proven to be a hit, garnering more shares and engagement than anything she'd written before. The discourse mill churned for weeks in response to its publication, in part thanks to a misstep by the since-disgraced editor in chief of *The Private Equity Press*. His praise for her piece on Twitter prompted one of his disgruntled employees to reveal that this editor had threatened to take away his staff's gender-affirming healthcare benefits during their union's most recent bargaining session. Helen didn't have anything to do with that debacle, but she delighted in the attention it sustained for her, even as it made her anxious. She knew full well how risky success could be for girls like her— that the higher she rose, the farther she could fall. The spotlight had been so many trans women's undoing, but she still wondered if it might shine more favorably on her. Her wondering only intensified when an editor from a big publishing house emailed her, telling her that he was a big fan of her work. "Have you ever thought about writing a book?" Yes, she had told him—obviously. The opportunity was simply too good to pass up.

Now, a few months later and her pussy all healed up, she

was interviewing candidates for an assistant-type role—
someone who could set up her interviews, do her transcrip-
tions, and eventually help handle her press. The prospective
assistants had mostly disappointed her, but Sylphie, the one
she was about to do a Zoom interview with, seemed promising. They were younger than Helen, looked edgier, had chop-
pier bangs than she'd ever felt drawn to. They had the necessary
work experience as well, but Helen was far more interested in
how connected they seemed to be with other trans folks nationwide, something she'd gleaned through a cursory scroll of
Sylphie's TikTok and Instagram. Helen had mostly retreated
from the scene over the past couple of years. Getting the co-
sign of someone like Sylphie could really help out her sales.

Helen sat at her desk and opened Zoom on her laptop. She
looked at herself in the preview screen and took down her
messy bun, finger-combing her day-after hair to a state of sat-
isfactory faux effortlessness.

She entered the meeting. "Hi, Sylphie!"

"Hi! That's me. I'm Sylphie."

"I'm Helen! It's so great to meet you. How's your day
going?"

"Well," they laughed nervously. "It's kind of been a night-
mare so far. My boss was just being her usual micromanagerial
self, and— Oh god, I'm sorry. I really shouldn't be talking
about this in a job interview. I swear I'm not just, like, this big
hater or something. I really do care about the work I do,
and—"

"Don't worry." Helen smiled, seeing something of herself
in their nerves. "I get it. Trust me. You wouldn't *believe* the
kind of bosses I've had."

MONKEY'S PAW GIRL EDITION

*P*lease *be misogyny, please be misogyny, please be misogyny, please be misogyny. . . .*

The words echoed in my head as I approached them on the sidewalk: this group of about half a dozen men standing around and lounging in lawn chairs in front of the raised garage door of a metal shop in Williamsburg.

This was about eight years ago, at a time that I'd consider the tail end of my transition. My second puberty. My trans adolescence. Whatever you want to call it—that.

It was the middle of the day in the hottest, sweatiest stretch of the summer, so naturally I was wearing very little clothing. Just some blue denim cutoffs hiked up and cuffed as much as humanly possible, a mauve tank top worn and washed to the point of semi-transparency, and a slate-gray bra semi-visible underneath. I had also tied a hoodie around my waist—not because it covered me up, which it certainly did not, but because I felt insecure about the breadth of my shoulders in proportion to my hips. I hoped that adding an extra layer of fabric might give me a more balanced, traditionally feminine hourglass frame. As the prophet Jade Jolie once said on an old episode of *RuPaul's Drag Race,* "The shoulders should match them hips, but they don't." With the hoodie around my waist, I could at least make it look like they did.

I didn't mind exposing so much of my body like that. Like a lot of adolescents—which I basically was again, at least emotionally and in some ways physically—I took every opportunity that I could to dress inappropriately, even when that opportunity was just "walking to my friend Tommy's apartment." Exposing my body through the clothes that I wore—or on days like this, the clothes that I didn't—never gave me pause when I was getting dressed at home. Alone in my bedroom, I could confidently cycle through looks, like Alicia Silverstone in *Clueless,* no matter how impractical each individual piece was, before finally settling on the outfit du jour and leaving my apartment. Whatever I had on only ever became a concern when someone else in the world would insist on making it theirs, which would then leave me feeling exposed, but not in the way that I wanted.

On that sweaty summer day, my intuition told me that this group of guys on the sidewalk were about to make me their concern. I sensed that they were going to say something to me—or say something *about* me to each other, rather, as if I had been put on that sidewalk solely for their entertainment. I knew that, whatever it was, I wasn't going to like it. Experience had taught me that with a group of guys like this, a group whose collective presence exponentially emboldens each individual member to talk whatever shit they want about anyone unlucky enough to walk into their crosshairs, I was all but guaranteed to hear one of two things: something homophobic, or something misogynistic. In other words, one of them was probably going to call me a faggot, or they were going to objectify me, maybe reducing me to a body part—though not *that* body part, of course. The typical rules of catcalling strictly forbid it, even when the catcaller in question is fully aware of *that* body part's presence.

Though, can you imagine? Like, you're just walking down the street and some dude's like, "Hey, girthy . . ." or "I know she's swinging down there."

Anyway, whichever option they'd go with, I knew what role I'd play. I'd keep on walking without slowing down or acknowledging that they'd spoken a word to me at all. I had no desire to participate in my own humiliation. Thankfully, I wouldn't be expected to. Whatever they'd end up saying, they wouldn't be saying it for my benefit but rather for their own. I was merely a canvas on which they could splatter their ego for a gallery of eager onlookers. The field they could play their games on. A screen for their shared projections. A pair of tin cans strung up between tree houses. A hole through which to fuck each other.

Still, when it came to which disgusting game they'd end up choosing to play on me, homophobia or misogyny, I definitely had my preference. Whichever man would go on to open his mouth, I hoped that he would catcall me. In an ideal world, I wouldn't have to choose between being told I'm not a woman or being treated like I am, either encounter heightened with at least a low-level threat of violence. But I don't live in an ideal world. So I silently prayed that whoever spoke up would read me as a cis woman and disrespect me accordingly.

Please be misogyny, please be misogyny, please be misogyny, please be misogyny. . . .

I walked as calmly as I could through the narrow strip of sidewalk that the men had allotted for pedestrians. I fixed my gaze on the horizon as if I was Orpheus on his way out of Hades.

"You see the ass on her?" one of the men said to the others.

Thank god, I thought. *Misogyny.*

• • •

The Canadian performance artist Nina Arsenault once said that when people ask her if she wants to be "treated as a 'normal' woman," that is to say, a cis woman, she always tells them no. "I see the way you treat them, too."

It's a rhetorical sleight of hand that cleverly draws a distinction between being treated like a woman and *being treated like a woman*—that is to say, the difference between having one's womanhood recognized by others in our society and experiencing firsthand the ways in which women are treated within that society's bounds. Though intended to call into question the limited understanding of transition as it exists within the cis imagination, Arsenault's words also reveal the limited aims of many trans people when it comes to our transitions— especially, at least in my own lived experience, those of us who are white.

When I initially came out as trans—first with a new set of pronouns shared with an ever-broadening circle, then shortly after, with a new name—the idea of passing as female didn't matter to me at all. I knew that I was a woman, and everyone who mattered to me agreed. So who cared if some stranger on the street thought I wasn't?

Well . . . me, apparently, as it would turn out. I quickly discovered that I cared about being read as a woman quite a bit.

The way I found that out was all very "chicken or the egg." Random people I'd encounter who didn't know my full backstory—friends of friends, customers at the store I worked at, strangers on the street—would still see me as a man. Though they never directly confessed it to me, they made their oblivious misread all too clear through a stray "he" or "him" or some other verbal clue. I would then get upset, which helped clarify for me that I did want everyone, even strangers, to see me for the woman I was. To put it more simply, I was upset about being seen as a man, because you know who hates being seen as a man? Somebody who isn't one. A woman, for example. Maybe even some of the "men" reading this.

That pattern of misreading prompted me to work on changing my appearance to prevent that misperception as much as I possibly could. The thought of passing soon consumed me. On the sidewalk, on the subway, I would wonder what everyone around me saw when they looked at me, never considering for a second that most of them probably didn't care. I treated my part-time retail job like it was some kind of game, in which the only way to win was by making it through the day without any customers calling me "dude." I amped up my makeup and then toned it down after realizing that none of the other women on the subway were heading to work in the morning with a full-coverage beat. I changed my hair, adjusted my wardrobe, and continued to fine-tune my presentation until gradually the world began to greet me as I was.

When I said that I wanted those men on the sidewalk to catcall me, I didn't mean that encountering such a basic, everyday reminder of the patriarchy's existence was something of an end goal of mine. It wasn't. What I meant was, well—let's say that I'm a woman. (Please say that I'm a woman.) As a woman, I wanted the rest of the world to treat me like a woman too. But if (a) I wanted to be treated like a woman, and (b) to be a woman under patriarchy means dealing with misogyny, then by the transitive property, etc., etc., (c) I must have wanted everything that womanhood entails—regrettably, misogyny and all.

Does being treated like a woman necessarily have to mean that one is *treated like a woman,* whatever that might mean for each of us individually with respect to race, class, and other factors that shape our respective material realities? At present, I'd say yes, though I'm loath to admit it. It feels terrible and regressive, politically speaking, to link my experience of womanhood to my experience of gender-based suffering—exactly the kind of reactionary self-sabotage that transphobic radical feminists have been perfecting now for decades. It's more that I have accepted, however reluctantly, that I won't be free from sexism or misogyny until we are, all of us, free from the patriarchy itself. I can curate my bubbles as best as I can. I can surround myself with people who only see me for who I am while cutting all ties with those who don't. I can stick to those spaces where nobody present would ever call the basic facts of my body into question and avoid those that bar my entry on account of those same basic facts. But there is still so much that I don't control—so much that I *can't* control. Like random men on the sidewalk and the things that strangers say to me. It might have made me cynical, but I just can't mask that cynicism. I accept the reality of my day-to-day, even though I don't, of course, endorse it. I hate that I've now even clarified that—that, of course, I don't like misogyny—and hate that I feel compelled to, knowing, as I do, what kind of bad-faith readings that my writing on this subject is sure to attract.

Eight years ago, though, that catcall provided me with some twisted sense of relief. It meant that I'd achieved something—cracked the code, gamed the system. I thought that was enough at the time. On some days, I still do.

• • •

I used to go out dancing at least once a week, sometimes more. It all depended on what parties I'd heard about that week, whether someone I knew was working the door somewhere, or if a DJ friend had booked a weeknight gig at a bar that wasn't known for its dance floor. They'd always want a familiar face or two in front of them, or maybe even a dozen, especially if there weren't going to be that many people out there. I loved showing up and being one of those faces, especially on those quieter nights. With all that space and only a few of us making use of it, it would feel so free and intimate, like dancing in a friend's room or some other homespun afters, like the kind we'd inevitably end up at as the night wore on.

There was the occasional rave, the parties at punk lofts, the shows at DIY spots that have long since shut down, plowed and then buried under the since-built foundations of massive apartment buildings that now span entire blocks. If nothing else, I knew that I could always go to a friend's Wednesday-night residency at a bar popular with Brooklyn's techno crowd on a strip of Bushwick just east of Bed-Stuy, an area that *New York* magazine once called "Stuyshwick" (thank god that didn't catch on). I almost never went by myself, but even when I did, I knew I wouldn't be alone once I got inside, because it was always well attended for a weeknight. I was surrounded by friends and the friends of my friends, and all the other regulars I only saw when I went out, whose faces I remembered, if not always their names.

It wasn't some idyllic chosen-family playscape, far from it. In fact, the crowd was usually more than half people I had never met. Stepping out of the venue's long, narrow entryway and into the dark, neon-lit room beyond, I would sometimes feel anxious, like I had no right to be there simply by dint of having walked in. There were no laurels to rest on, no scripts to follow, only the memory of the last great time that I'd had out there on the dance floor and the drive to go feel it all over again. The only way to do so, at that place or anywhere else, was to push through the discomfort, throw myself into the throng, and make myself dance until something finally clicked. I liked that about techno and other similar kinds of dance music, how chasing their high demanded some skin in the game from me. They weren't genres that I'd generally listen to otherwise, while cleaning my apartment or riding the train to work. To properly experience them, I felt that I had to hear them in person surrounded by other people who were also sharing that experience with me, with the DJ perched up in their booth just letting us have it in every sense of the word.

At the back of that checkered dance floor, when it wasn't totally shrouded in fog, you could make out a message, painted in big white letters, that spanned more than half the wall: "If you touch a woman against her will in this establishment, we will literally ruin your life." I remember it so clearly because, ironically, that was always the spot, by the back wall under those words, where I happened to be dancing the handful of times I was violently groped.

It was always the same kind of guy too: a sweaty, wasted zombie of a man in his semi-unbuttoned professional garb, deciding to close out his after-work drinks by ruining some woman's night. It always felt so sickly intentional, their decision to come here of all places, like their drunken autopilot had set their destination to "tranny" and called up an Uber to Shemale Cove. At that time in my life, six or seven years ago, I would turn neurotic when I'd notice that a guy was looking at me. I'd get so hung up on whether he thought I was hot or if he'd merely clocked me. It was some time before I realized none of that mattered, that sometimes it was both, and he'd harass me all the same if he felt like it.

They'd lurch toward me in a horror movie slo-mo, blocking my view as they began to touch me. I'd shove them off and tell them to stop, but they'd keep coming at me. I'd shove harder and yell at them louder, but still they would keep coming. One time, I managed to extricate myself, find one of my friends, and cling to their side until I was sure that he had left. Another time, I was saved by this one heroic masc I'd never met before. They put themselves between us, started talking to me like they knew me, and led me away to another side of the bar where they knew that I'd be safe.

I was grateful for their care and the protection that they'd offered me, all without me even having to ask them for it. They just saw someone who needed help and paused their good time to give it. I was also moved by my friends who, when I'd tell them about these encounters after the fact, would promise to fuck up anyone they saw doing that to me. I feel an impulse to frame this vignette as a testament to community, or to the power of looking out for one another—the whole "we keep us safe" thing—but I can't. It feels dishonest, too eager to pacify. I don't dream of ruining lives after the fact. I just wish they'd never touched me at all.

● ● ●

Back when I wrote full-time, I'd periodically find myself in the online crosshairs of some anonymous transmisogynists who'd decided to take aim at me over something that I'd written. On one such occasion, in the fall of 2020, it was over the lead item in a celebrity news roundup that I'd blogged for a website that I wrote for on the weekends. I'd covered a recent interview with the novelist Chimamanda Ngozi Adichie in which she, not for the first time, publicly undermined trans women's claim to womanhood. She also voiced her support for J. K. Rowling, who was at the time, and I guess will be forevermore, under fire for making transphobic statements of her own. I felt a sting of disappointment, just as I had the last time Adichie had made such hateful statements, so I channeled that disappointment into a breezy three paragraphs, hit publish, and went on with the rest of my blogging shift.

Later in the evening, I was watching *Glitter*—unthinkably, miraculously—for the first time. Mariah was performing her cover of "Didn't Mean to Turn You On" in her sleek, aughtsy take on outré '80s fashions when my phone started blowing up with Twitter notifications. The online onslaught was happening again! I had to laugh, but then it kept coming, and I couldn't laugh anymore.

For the first few hours of the pile-on, the faceless horde accused me of being an imperialist Western white woman, guilty of the crime of trying to silence a Nigerian feminist writer—ignoring, obviously, for the sake of rhetorical efficacy that trans

Nigerian writers like Akwaeke Emezi as well as other writers throughout the global Black diaspora had also posited such critiques in the past. But then, after realizing that I was trans, they regrouped and refocused. I was no longer a Western white woman guilty of imperialist blogging, but a man, point-blank— a prime example of that empty, manipulative mode of debate that sees people "treating privilege politics like a Pokémon card game," as the critic Jae Bearhat once put it.* The horde dug up some old photos of me from before I had transitioned, along with some others from my first few months in the game, back when I was looking—well, what's a nicer way of saying "a mess"? Creative? Rococo? When I was looking a little more rococo. It felt like they were trying to out me for something that I wasn't even hiding in the first place, or trying to make me feel shame over something that I wasn't ashamed about. They hadn't known I was trans, despite the massive online paper trail I've left for anyone who knows how to google; not six months earlier, I'd written at length for *Esquire* about how my facial feminization surgery had been delayed due to the coronavirus pandemic. But each of them had not been personally informed before they read my blog about Adichie, and somehow that was my fault, like I'd set out to deceive them. I wonder if they thought that I was stealth, or that my success as a writer had been contingent on keeping my transness a secret—a totally plausible conclusion, if you ignore all the thousands of words I've blogged about being a fucking transsexual. It's somewhat funny in hindsight, that their best line of

---

* I'd heard Kay Gabriel, the poet and critic, say this a few times in the years that I've known her, such that I always associated it with her. When I asked her if it had ever appeared in her writing, as I wanted to cite it here, she clarified that it was the work of Jae Bearhat, who's graciously allowed me to quote it.

attack was to do the equivalent of outing me as a brunette. But as much as I didn't want to admit it then, or even admit it now, their shaming campaign sort of worked. Because of their hateful efforts, I felt worse about myself and retreated from public view on social media for a while.

The experience oddly mirrored the one I was having on dating apps at the time. Though I always disclosed that I was trans in my profile, I didn't like doing it, as I felt as if frontloading that aspect of myself, not to mention taking up so much of the limited character space to do so, made it look like being trans was my lone, defining trait. But I did so because there was a very real chance that whichever man had expressed interest in me would then rescind his interest, a process I had no interest in witnessing. To be a little playful with that obligated disclosure, I liked to preface my bios by writing, "I should probably disclose that . . . I like Lana Del Rey. Also I'm trans." It was always up top, so I naturally assumed that no one could miss it. Yet miss it so many of those men did—especially, I noticed, after I'd gotten my face done. After setting a date with someone I'd been chatting with, I'd ask them to confirm that they'd read my profile, a roundabout way of asking them to confirm that they knew I was trans. At that point, some guys would come back to me surprised, confused, even angry sometimes. Some would launch into listing their trans ally bona fides immediately after rejecting me, as if to convince me, though I think mostly themselves, that they were good guys, that they were definitely not transphobic. Others would still try to rope me into getting drinks with them so they might talk through their discomfort in person, as if I were simply dying to plead with someone to sleep with me. A few guys actually accused me of having added that disclosure after they'd already matched with me, as if I had set out to trick them. It all got very tiring, their projected shame and confusion. Some of them were simply putting on an act, feigning ignorance that they knew I was trans in order to excuse themselves for wanting to sleep with me, a favorite script among straight men. Others, I believe, simply didn't think of themselves as people who were attracted to trans women, and through no fault of my own I had shattered that illusion, one they apparently held very dear. I didn't know what to tell them when they reacted like that, so I'd just block them as fast as I could. I mean, what was I supposed to say? I didn't mean to turn you on?

• • •

"Ma'am, he'll have to come in and pick up the car himself."

It took me a second to register what the agent behind the counter at the rental-car agency was telling me.

When I'd handed her my driver's license—outdated but not expired, bearing my old name, an "M" for male, and an unrecognizable picture of me that was taken close to a decade earlier—I expected some uncomfortable silence, maybe a wary look, but nothing that I couldn't defuse with a self-deprecating line about how "It's an old picture" or "Yeah, I've changed a bit." That was usually how the interaction would go when my ID caused confusion, an L I always took because, hey, I was the F with the M on her license. It's not like a bouncer could update it for me on my way into a bar. Thanks to my penchant for procrastination, as well as some untreated executive dysfunction, I hadn't yet updated it myself, despite living in a city where it's relatively easy to get one's documents sorted out. If only we could strike the gender markers from our licenses entirely. I obviously support efforts to add a nonbinary gender marker like "X" to various identity documents, efforts that have succeeded in twenty-two states and counting. But I personally yearn for fewer bureaucratic hurdles, rather than more, however gender-affirming it might feel in the end to have cleared them. In the meantime, all I had was my unchanged ID and all the invasive, unnecessary questions that it provoked, along with the occasional uncomfortable compliment about my "before and after."

I thought that I'd be ready for whatever the rental-car agent might say. I even steeled myself for the possibility that, at worst, she'd go out of her way to start calling me "Mr. Walker" or punctuate each sentence with "Sir," veiling her transphobic disgust with displays of ostensible courtesy. What I hadn't anticipated when I handed her my ID was that she would somehow conclude that the "man" on my license was somebody else entirely—a boyfriend or a husband I must have left outside, perhaps leashed up to a lamppost like a dog. She couldn't fathom that the license I had handed her was, in fact, mine. I was almost impressed by her subconscious acrobatics, amused, and for a moment quietly flattered, by her instinctive refusal to read me as anything but female.

"No," I corrected her, as I attempted a knowing smile. "That's *my* ID."

She stared at me, confused.

"Only the person who made the reservation can pick up the car," she said, doubling down on her initial assumption. "He'll have to come inside."

My amusement quickly faded as our horrible, twenty-first-century remake of the "Who's on First?" bit dragged on and on. I pulled out my credit card, an expired AAA card—anything in my wallet that bore the same name as the one that I had on my license, but it wasn't clicking for her. She kept telling me to go get the man who'd made my reservation for me—the man who, again, didn't exist—then she called over another agent who told me the same thing. I tried to explain to them that "I am transgender," a word that I literally never say in full because, I don't know, the mouthfeel just isn't great. And in this particular instance, I didn't want to out myself in front of the people waiting behind me, given all the unsavory ways that they might have reacted to that disclosure; I was thousands of miles from home, on the western edge of America's heartland, and I didn't have a clear idea how wary I should be. To my dismay, however, that disclosure only spurred more confusion, as if whatever idea she had of a trans person did not match the person in front of her. If only my nonexistent husband would stop barking outside, slip off his collar, and come in and clear things up!

Increasingly frayed and distressed over being repeatedly and aggressively gendered correctly (a true top-tier *Twilight Zone* moment of my life—I mean, seriously, what the hell?), I began to panic, worried that the misunderstanding between us might prove insurmountable. How would I explain myself to someone who simply refused to hear me? Someone who not only couldn't see me but couldn't see that people like me existed? Thankfully, a third agent came over to assist the other two, and eventually the process got going. I managed to hold it together until I got into my rental, a truly massive Yukon Denali, taller and longer than anything I'd ever driven, and promptly burst into tears. I then tried to back the car out of the lot and started crying all over again about how big and scary the car was. Looking back as I reversed into a three-point turn, I saw the rear windshield receding endlessly before me, like when someone in a horror movie looks down a spooky hallway. Why was it so big? I couldn't even see the pavement. I could've backed right over my dog husband. Thank god he didn't exist.

Four days and an exchange for a much smaller rental vehicle later, I found myself back at the airport, waiting in line to go through security for my flight back to New York. I realized I was getting progressively more anxious as the queue shuffled toward TSA a few lurching steps at a time. My breathing had grown shallower and my habitual jaw-clenching had intensified as I approached what I feared would be yet another instance of public gendered humiliation. The experience with the rental car might have shaken my confidence, but honestly, the worst that those agents could have done to me would have been denying me my rightful SUV. But the TSA agents I was inching toward were different. If they proved to be in some way confused by my gender, the consequences could be so much worse. So much more physically violating, and so much more humiliating.

The line snaked through the terminal's atrium as one by one we flashed our IDs and approached the cylindrical full-body scanner. After taking off my shoes and placing my bag on the belt, I was signaled to step in. I raised my arms then lowered them and stepped out on the other side. A male agent motioned for me to stop walking and told me to raise my arms up perpendicular to my body, kind of like *The Vitruvian Man*—after the operations, I mean. Another agent, a woman, then approached me and asked if I was wearing a bra. I told her I wasn't. She placed the side of her hand perpendicular to my chest, right in the center of my solar plexus, and slid it down and around the underside of my right breast. She then repeated the motion with her other hand, on the left side. She cleared me to leave, so I did.

As a TSA experience, it obviously didn't compare to the worst that Muslim and Arab fliers have been forced to endure in the wake of the so-called War on Terror, which has largely rendered their rights conditional, in and out of the airport. Nor did it stack up against the usual mistreatment that trans people have grown to expect when going through security. I mean, I wasn't misgendered or made a public spectacle, nor was I literally manhandled by a male agent. If anything, I realized as I laced up my sneakers, my state-sanctioned groping had been totally gender-affirming. Something about my body had set off the scanner—probably just a few droplets of sweat puddling in the fold of my breast—so those agents of the state had tasked a woman with figuring out what the problem was. She hadn't questioned my gender. None of those agents had. If anything, the TSA had given my womanhood a governmental seal of approval. They'd seen a woman set off their surveillance, so they dispatched another woman to go check her out. It didn't even feel like a *Twilight Zone* moment: the ironic validation of being so affirmed it hurts. It just felt sad. Depressing, in fact. Even a little bit horrifying. The limits of validation, of simply having one's gender affirmed, had never been so clear to me than in that moment, in that hollow little victory I'd worked so hard to win.

TRANSGENDER SURGERY REGRET

I used to be able to change my pillowcases with such ease. After peeling off the dirty sham and tossing it in the hamper, I would clamp the fluffed-up pillow between my neck and chin, its broad side unfurled down my chest like a cotton-stuffed cravat, and slide the new case up and around it with both hands. Ever since I got facial feminization surgery, though, I've had trouble doing this. So often now, the pillow will slip right out from under my whittled-away mandible and flop down softly onto the bed below. It can take me as many as three or four tries to get it right, though usually still just one. No one told me this could happen, not my friends, not my surgeon. Yes, he might have hit the slay button, but I ask you: at what cost?

SHE WANTS, SHE TAKES,
SHE PRETENDS

"Is that Kurt Cobain?" I ask.

I make my way across the tiny, low-ceilinged room, my shoes crunching across the Astroturf flooring, to get a better look at the picture. It is indeed a headshot of the late Nirvana frontman—a headshot of a headshot, really, as Greer Lankton, the artist who created the installation that I'm slowly crunching my way through, has painted, in the same muted sage as the wall behind it, a dime-sized splatter above her subject's right temple. She also made the would-be bullet wound bleed out in messy streams with what appears to be red marker, one dribbling down his face, past his chin, and the rest exploding out the back of him. Adding even more color to what was originally a black-and-white portrait—taken by the photographer Mark Seliger in October 1993 for *Rolling Stone*, mere months before the musician's untimely death by suicide—

Lankton has given Cobain a bright yellow balayage, added blue to his irises, and dabbed his eyelids and lips with a rosy, cosmetic pink. Across the bottom of the picture, she has scrawled a macabre reference to his band's breakthrough album: "OOPS!! NEVERMIND."

"It's weird, I don't think of Greer as someone who outlived Kurt," I tell the two archivists standing behind me; they're guiding me through the installation, titled *It's all about ME, Not You*, which Lankton first staged here at the Mattress Factory, an art museum in Pittsburgh, in 1996. "I usually only see Greer being historicized in this eighties East Village scene kind of way, so that's how I always think of her," I say, stepping back to join them at the center of the room.

"Greer was living in Chicago when she made this," says Sinéad, one of the two archivists. "She moved there in the nineties. She couldn't take it, I think, everybody passing away in New York, all of her friends."

Lankton, who died a few weeks after the opening due to a drug overdose, which was ruled a suicide, modeled her installation after her actual apartment at the time. Her home was understandably cluttered, as she not only lived there but also made and displayed her work there. Standing at the center of the installation, I'm reminded of a teenager's bedroom, one whose owner hasn't yet cleansed it of its vestigial childish trappings. There's celebrity iconography—posters and sculptures—plastered all over the walls and shelves. Drug paraphernalia spills out from under the bed. On the wall, art is tiled together in a *Tetris*-like mess, evoking that specific kind of haphazard maximalism commonly found in teenage décor, when all you might have are posters and thumbtacks to tell everyone who you are. "One communicates with whatever one has at one's disposeall [*sic*]," Lankton wrote in a sketchbook of hers from 1977, which Primary Information published as a book in 2023.

And, of course, there are the dolls. They're strewn over every inch of the room, some posed in what look to be their proper spots, while others form disorderly piles on various parts of the floor. It's the dolls that steal focus, as the dolls often do. (So much so, that, in hindsight, I'm surprised that I even noticed that Cobain portrait at all, buried as it was behind all that soft sculpture.) Pop idolatry might be a throughline in Lankton's body of work, but when I think of Greer Lankton, I tend to think first of the medium rather than themes: dolls like the two-foot figurine of Blondie singer Debbie Harry posing on a nightstand in Lankton's installation, or the groom-and-bride cake topper standing at her feet, modeled after Lankton and Paul Monroe, her green-haired onetime husband, on the day of their wedding. Beneath them swarms a nest of troll dolls—Lankton's favorite mass-produced doll, as she once said.

A large, emaciated doll with a pained expression on her face lies beside the nightstand tableau in a chaise longue, buried under blankets and prescription pill bottles—all of them Lankton's, as the labels plainly read. A life-size industrial goth, corseted and painted from hairline to clavicle, hovers over the emaciated doll's bedside with a needle in her hand. She reads like an angel of mercy, or perhaps an angel of further misery, come to save the other from whatever pain she's in. Maybe the pair are two sides of the same doll: the nightlife queen and the thing she shrivels into once struck by dawn's first light; think *Swan Lake* for club kids or "Dracula goes to the Limelight." It makes me think about Lankton's later years, after moving back to the Midwest, going out to Chicago gay clubs like Roscoe's and refinding her people after leaving New York behind. She'd often question her surgical transition, as politically inconvenient as that may be for us to acknowledge, and would sometimes yearn for a timeline in which she hadn't gone "full-time," as the queens and transsexuals used to say, given the complications that stemmed from that decision.

In one corner of the room sits a figure whose feet Lankton molded into permanent stilettos, as if reinterpreting Barbie's terminally arched feet through the lens of extreme body modification. In another corner stands a bust of Candy Darling, the actress and transsexual icon who starred in Andy Warhol's *Women in Revolt*. She looks mournfully to the side, "her thoracic cavity open to view," in the words of the poet Kay Gabriel, "crammed with cosmetics next to the swollen ventricles of her heart." On the statue's back, the archivists told me, for I couldn't see it myself, an inscription quotes Patti Smith's 1975 cover of "Gloria": "Jesus died for somebody's sins but not mine," a provocative citation for the daughter of a Presbyterian minister. Even more so was Lankton's decision to give as much wall space to pictures of Smith and Darling as she does to her collection of Jesus and Mary iconography. The mother and child cling to each other in every one of these images as if they were a singular dyadic being, one capable of "SWITCHING BETWEEN 1ST AND 3RD PERSON PERSPECTIVE," as the artist Juliana Huxtable once described the ability to give birth to oneself, and isn't that what this installation amounts to? What all of Lankton's work is about? The dolls. The pill bottles. All that death and Astroturf. It's quite literally a body of work, and like any body, so ripe for projection.

"They always end up looking like me," Greer once said of her dolls, but when we look at her body of work, who exactly do we see?

• • •

I first learned about Greer Lankton in 2019 while interviewing Zackary Drucker, the Emmy Award–winning filmmaker and *Transparent* producer who starred in the 2022 Sundance favorite *Framing Agnes*. I was working as a staff writer for *Out* at the time, though my tenure there would be brief, only about eight months in total—just long enough, thankfully, to get two surgeries covered before the magazine's owners, who drastically shrunk our budget after news broke that they owed six figures in unpaid freelancer payments, could create any more trouble for us or anyone else.

I had contacted Drucker in the hope of interviewing her as a source for a reported feature on trans women visual artists and the self-portraiture they create in opposition to the cis gaze, which would, as per tradition in the Western art canon, rather see them as muses than as artists in their own right. By the time I filed the story, though, it had become more of a straight profile of Río Sofia, a visual artist and community organizer in Brooklyn who has since become a close friend, and *Forced Womanhood!*, her series of mixed-media self-portraits inspired by an erotica magazine of the same name. The series drew on motifs from Frida Kahlo and Caravaggio, as well as the illustrated covers of its namesake porno mag, which devoted its pages to various forced-feminization fantasies. In doing so, Río hoped to speak to the ways in which she'd found transitioning to be limiting rather than flatly liberating, as the loudest pro-trans messaging of the mid-2010s would insist.

Looking back on that piece, I'm proud of how trans-centric it was in its perspective, as it had not only a trans subject and author but a trans editor, in the writer and activist Raquel Willis, who would later author the 2023 memoir *The Risk It Takes to Bloom.* More so, however, I'm proud that, with this story, I was able to get a trans woman's naked body on newsstands nationwide, presented on her own terms, unmediated by conservative glossy-mag sensibilities, much less an outsider's fetishizing lens. Still, it's true that "visibility won't save us," as the Canadian journalist Alex V. Green once wrote. All the trans representation in the world won't change the fact that, Green continued, "most trans people are still living under precarious and profoundly unequal conditions. Most urgently, Black and brown trans women are dying in record numbers, and many more are suffering on the streets." Yet there is still a "formative and transformative power" in that representation, as the filmmaker Tourmaline notes in the introduction to *Trap Door,* a 2017 critical anthology on trans cultural production, and that power can assist in "making new futures possible" simply through the act of presenting them for public view. A trans woman's body holds a similar power. The sight of it can inspire intense lust or hatred, even violence, but it can also make living seem possible for someone who thought that it wasn't. It is proof that "a body can be otherwise," as the theorist McKenzie Wark writes in her 2023 memoir, *Love and Money, Sex and Death,* as it demonstrates through its very existence that the "powers of creation go beyond mere procreation." But creation, of course, often requires destruction in order for it to take place. I can imagine that this implication might be scary for some, but as Cecilia Gentili, the late author, activist, and much-heralded Mother of All Whores, once instructed us to do in her one-woman show, *Red Ink,* "Always terrorize cisgender people. It doesn't take much. Sometimes you just have to show up." I can only hope that in forcing transfeminine nudes onto the shelves of even the most remote Barnes & Noble, the issue of *Out* that carried my profile managed to terrorize as many people as it may have inspired.

Anyway, before I reframed the story around Río, I had approached Drucker for an interview. She was a worthy source for the piece as *You Will Never Be a Woman . . .*, her aggressively t4t experimental short film co-directed with Van Barnes and Mariah Garnett, was exactly the kind of authentic self-portraiture I hoped to examine. Though I ultimately had to cut Drucker's quotes from the piece—my first draft was severely over word count—our conversation proved transformative, opening my eyes to the breadth of trans women artists, most of whose work I'd never encountered before: International Chrysis, Nina Arsenault, Keioui Keijaun Thomas—and, of course, Greer Lankton.

"Even through decades of time passing, I am still so inspired by her work," Drucker said as we sat at the table in her hotel room, coincidentally six floors up from the boutique where I used to work. "Speaking of artists who were able to represent gender dysphoria without internalizing the shame of being trans, I think that her work has withstood the test of time. It's also undeniably captivating, you know?"

After learning more about her, I did. Her dolls struck me as so morose and yet so full of life, their bodies and poses as alternately grotesque as they were utterly, disarmingly beautiful. Theirs was a kind of beauty that I hadn't yet grasped at that point in my life, a time when I still understood beauty more as a cudgel to beat myself with whenever I felt I'd failed to achieve it. Lankton presented something else entirely. But as much as her dolls transfixed me, I was also drawn to Lankton herself. I felt in some ways connected to her on account of the shared facts of our bodies. I decided that the next chance I got, I would drive to Pittsburgh to see *It's all about ME, Not You* in person. I started to plan a birthday road trip with some friends and the guy I was seeing, but then I got stuck on jury duty on my literal birthday and had to postpone it. I tried to pitch a story about Lankton, but every editor passed, given its lack of a "timely news peg." (Translation: "I don't know who that is.") Pandemic restrictions and an intensive period of postoperative recovery further pushed back my pilgrimage, but I finally made it down to the Mattress Factory in March 2022. The dolls, unsurprisingly, did not disappoint, but it was Lankton's personal scrapbooks that stuck with me the most—specifically her photo-booth pictures.

• • •

"I'm going slightly cross-eyed and very insane," reads the caption underneath the photograph in front of me, its subject staring past me at a limp three-quarter angle.

It's a picture of Lankton, taken in a photo booth when she was eighteen years old, just a few months before she transitioned. The caption is handwritten—all the captions are—though I'm not sure when she wrote them or when she compiled these scrapbooks, which the Mattress Factory archivists have left me to explore in a back room, provided that I wear the pair of white cotton gloves they gave me. The mementos contained within the books—pictures, news clippings, artist statements, résumés, business records, and other effects—comprise only a fraction of the museum's Greer Lankton Collection, which numbers about fifteen thousand objects in total and has since been fully digitized and made accessible online.

With a lot of the captions, there's a sense that Lankton's using them to craft a cohesive narrative of her life, especially with these earlier photos, which would suggest to me some distance between the younger Greer in the photos and the perhaps older Greer who's writing them in. As time goes on, the captions begin to feel more immediate. Less cohesive, and less interested in cohesion.

The first album I flip through is all pictures, most of them taken in photo booths. There must be hundreds of these strips, all cut up and collaged over every page with names and dates and other details written beside them, almost always by Lankton herself. Most are black-and-white. Some of them sport color, though usually because Greer appears to have added that color later with what looks like markers and pens, much like she did with the Kurt Cobain portrait in *It's all about ME, Not You.*

As I delve further into this diaristic log of self-portraiture, I feel a growing kinship. I, too, spent the early years of my transition visiting photo booths to document how I'd changed. I used booths all over New York City—film only, *never* digital—though mostly the one in the back of Bushwick Country Club. The lens of an old-school photo booth will always find the glamour, even when the subject thinks that there's none to be found. Striking a dramatic pose before its coin-operated lens, waiting for it to spit out that still-sticky strip, its headshots all blown out to the point of silent film stardom—it was, and remains, one of my favorite ways to see myself, to get a sense of what I look like, to record my shifting form. I can't believe Greer did this too. I can't believe she got it.

The captions give context to the imagery: which photo booth, where; various medical updates; brief missives about her life and how she was feeling. They also help expand on other preexisting biographical material, which sometimes proves conflicting, though maybe she would have liked the lack of total legibility. Some of those sources, like her baby book, state that she was born in Flint, Michigan, while others, like the *New York Times* obituary authored by photographer Nan Goldin, say Holly, a nearby village; a 1992 profile even claimed that Lankton was born in Chicago. She definitely spent her earliest years in the suburban enclave of Holly, before her parents moved the family to Park Forest, Illinois, a postwar planned community in the orbit of Chicagoland. The geographical trajectory of her life mirrored that of many white Americans of her generation, as the children of white flight who'd grown up in the suburbs returned to the cities that their forebears had fled. Lankton herself was born in 1958, a year before Barbie and the original, gemless troll dolls hit the market. The earliest photo-booth picture shows Greer at eight years old, vying for space in the frame with her older brother and sister. Her caption says that they took it at the Goldblatt's department store that once anchored the Park Forest Plaza, an outdoor shopping center that has since closed.

Though young, she was already making her own dolls at this point, and had been doing so from at least as early as preschool. Like many children before her in the long history of DIY doll-making, she constructed them out of everyday items found around the house: dried apples, corn husks, hollyhock blooms, pipe cleaners, clothesline pegs, and rope she'd fray to resemble hair. She always focused on making their bodies; their faces were incidental. "The body is more interesting in the way it's put together," she once told a reporter.

Making these dolls might have been a way for Lankton to express her femininity before she felt able to dress as she wanted, as the writer and filmmaker Morgan M. Page once suggested in an episode of her fabulous trans history podcast, *One from the Vaults.* Greer's hometown was not exactly forgiving of gender-nonconformity. Her peers bullied her, both verbally and physically, for being, in Page's words, "a dress-up-loving, doll-playing feminine child." That harassment only continued as she grew into her teens.

Some sources claim her parents posed a similar resistance to both her gender-nonconformity and her interest in making dolls, but Lankton's own words refute that on several occasions. In a news clipping preserved in the Mattress Factory's archive, she tells an interviewer that her parents were, in fact, very supportive of her doll-making, adding that her father, a Presbyterian minister and amateur woodworker who later ran a church camp out in Michigan, had an appreciation for the arts and liked to make puppets himself. Her mother, who later worked as the cook at said camp, taught Lankton to sew and, according to a 1974 article in the local newspaper, assisted her teenage daughter with her earliest soft-sculptural work, some of which was displayed at her local library while she was still a student. An article in her high school newspaper, also published in 1974, mentions that Lankton liked to wear a washcloth on her head as a kid and pretend that it was her hair. What this had to do with the actual subject of the piece, Lankton's achievements on her varsity gymnastics team, is anyone's guess, but the feature does go on to note that her parents "never turned off [her] will to express [her]self," even permitting her to wear that little scrap of haircloth during her dad's Sunday services.

Elsewhere in that same interview, Lankton alludes to the fact that she had dolls as a kid, presumably purchased for her by her parents. "I didn't like the ones I had," she tells the interviewer. "I didn't like their hair, or they didn't move right." So perhaps her problem wasn't a lack of dolls or parental homophobia that deprived her of such things. Maybe it was that she found all the store-bought ones lacking and thought she could make something better.

Then again, as the Mattress Factory's archivists told me during our walk-through of her work, Lankton was apparently known to share contradictory narratives when discussing her life in the press, particularly when it came to her gender. "Depending on her mood, depending on her audience," Sarah, one of the archivists, told me, "probably because everyone always wanted to know about her trans identity. She never tried to hide it ever, but she didn't want to be talking about it all the time." She could have been just as mercurial when talking about her relationship with her parents, especially in a public setting. Privately, especially in her teens, she struggled with gaining her mother's approval, "trying to win back [her] love because of guilt over my reality," as she wrote in one of her sketchbooks; she then compares this dynamic to *The Best Little Boy in the World*, Andrew Tobias's 1973 memoir about being a closeted teen who tried to compensate for his latent deviance by excelling at everything he could. Jojo Baby, the late icon of queer Chicago nightlife and Lankton's artistic mentee, shared some additional insights with the writer Grace Byron in 2022: "Her parents gave her an ultimatum one summer. They said either you get a job or you get a sex change and she's like, 'I hate to work, so I got the sex change.'" Lankton herself said something similar, and similarly flippant, in a 1992 interview with the *Lincoln-Belmont Booster:* "[My father] was in favor of anything that would straighten me out."

In my estimation, many things can be true at once. Parents

are often fine with their sensitive, artistic sons being so sensitive and artistic, at least in the privacy of their own home. But when those sons start to channel all that sensitive artistry into becoming a freaky, preoperative daughter, their parents often grow significantly less fine, to put it mildly, whether in public or in private. Where absolute clarity evades us, I think common sense might prevail: The transsexual artist from fifty years ago probably had a complicated relationship with her parents, however accepting of her they might have been or later grew to be. In the 1970s, gendered indeterminacy generally proved more disturbing than a presentation that aligned with either pole of the binary, as is still often the case today. This attitude was certainly held by most providers of trans medical care at the time. Their goal was not the provision of that treatment in and of itself, much less the "affirmation" of their patients' genders. Rather, they aimed to eliminate gender-nonconformity, whether that meant giving hormones and surgery to those who could pass as cis and assimilate into mainstream society unnoticed—those who, essentially, proved more disruptive in their unaltered state—or withholding that care from those whose transsexuality would always remain evident on their bodies, often subjecting that latter group to conversion therapy instead.

Whatever the climate within the Lankton family home, the culture of Greer's suburban hometown was no doubt smothering. "[The] American middle class aims at taming the wild beast to be best used for the corporations' interest and the chosen few," she writes in that teenage sketchbook from 1977. Even that aforementioned 1974 profile in Lankton's high school newspaper, the one that spotlights her achievements on the gymnastics team, undercuts its praise with homophobic concessions. "One may giggle, weep, or grunt," it reads. "But for sure one must admit that [Lankton] certainly delivers well." It is easy to understand why the word "suburban" eventually took on a derogatory connotation in Lankton's adult lexicon. (Goldin, a close friend of Lankton's, recalls her own postwar suburban upbringing as similarly suffocating in her Oscar-nominated documentary, *All the Beauty and the Bloodshed*.) In one interview with *i-D* from the mid-1980s, Greer bemoaned how "suburban" Barbie had become over the years. "Oh, I love Barbie," she clarified. "But I think she's gotten really bad. . . . She was really cool from '59 to '65, but then she got too blonde, too tanned and too rich." For Lankton, the suburb was a suffocating place, one that had no place for her. "She was anxious to get out of high school," writes her childhood friend Joyce Randall Senechal in the afterword to that 1977 sketchbook.

In 1975, Lankton left high school early to study textiles at the School of the Art Institute of Chicago. She moved out of her family's home and into the city proper, with her parents' and psychoanalyst's support. Her photo-booth pictures from this time, many of which she took at the now-demolished Randolph/Wabash L station that once stood in the Loop, show a more exuberant, outwardly feminine Lankton, one who'd only just started to reveal herself while living in Park Forest. The concept of transsexualism was not foreign to her; Senechal recalls Lankton scouring her local library for books about trans women—Harry Benjamin's *The Transsexual Phenomenon*, memoirs by Canary Conn, Renée Richards, and Christine Jorgensen. But a brief summer fling with a transsexual named Lisa, who told Lankton that "sex change was the only answer," intensified her long-held questions over how she wanted to be in the world. "As David and Lee's friend said last year, 'You'd be the perfect transsexual,'" she writes in her 1977 sketchbook. "One doesn't need the operation always. Hormones may be enough." Later, she makes a promise: "I swear to become my body."

In the meantime, she dove headfirst into Chicago's local gay scene while she continued to experiment with her look, as documented in her photo-booth strips: She tweezed her eyebrows super thin, grew out her hair, dyed it orange and then black. "As the late, great Candy said, 'I've got a right to live,'" she writes, promising to herself, "I will not die. I will become." She's wearing makeup in most of these photos, though sometimes she's beaten her mug after the fact with, again, her markers and pens. These mixed-media edits lend some of the images a certain pop art effect, no doubt inspired by Warhol's portraiture. Lankton adored Warhol when she was growing up—even more so, his various Superstars like Candy Darling. She hung pictures of Darling and fellow Superstars Jackie Curtis and Holly Woodlawn on the walls of her teenage bedroom, as well as a framed still of Divine in the 1972 John Waters film, *Pink Flamingos,* when she's aiming her pistol in that red fishtail gown right after declaring, "Filth is my life!" Lankton considered Warhol an early influence on her work, though after making his acquaintance many years later, she remarked that he was the dullest person she'd ever met. She remained enamored with Candy Darling to the end of her life, though, crafting many dolls and other sculptures in Candy's likeness. Flipping through one of her photo albums, I notice that Lankton appears to have paid homage to Darling's iconic deathbed portrait by Peter Hujar. Under a Polaroid of Lankton draped sideways on a hospital bed, her arms positioned exactly like Candy's, she writes that she was being treated for lung failure at Beth Israel Hospital following a "huge coke binge" in 1990. "BONEHEAD," she scrawled next to it in shaky caps.

A triptych of photo-booth portraits from early 1977 show Lankton all dolled up. "I pretend to be pretty," she captioned them. But the following month, she again "become[s] the boy," cropping her hair, growing out her eyebrows, and adopting a more somber, vacant expression. She doesn't smile in any of the images that follow, nor put much of an effort into her poses either. In most of them, she's either staring blankly away from the camera or confronting the aperture head-on in palpable resignation. "Forever forgetting to eat," she captioned another set of photos. Her dysphoria and disordered eating seem to have been closely intertwined, as they are for so many others. But her anorexia also stemmed from her anxieties about maintaining control—of herself, of her body—which, to Lankton, felt like matters of life or death. "Control is survival," she notes in her sketchbook, the early pages of which double as a food journal, noting what she ate and when she didn't. "I'm tired of all this destruction to bring on the new when the new just repeats the same fucked up cycle. I do believe there's something beyond," and she wonders if transitioning might be what leads her to it. "I'll still be doing what I'm doing"—that is, taking active steps to remold her body—"only happily and constructively." It's an optimistic view, though one that later proved naïve. "I will not solve this for a long time," she writes. "But alas transsexualism will ease the fear to at least allow me to function."

Five days after taking those joyless photos, she was admitted to Riverside Hospital's psychiatric ward in nearby Kankakee, Illinois. She was suffering from a nervous breakdown as well as what she called "psychotic depression." In a 1978 interview with the *Suburban Trib,* she said that she tried to tell her doctors in the psych ward that she was a woman, but none of them had listened. "They put me on antipsychotic drugs and told me that if I was born a boy I should be a boy," she recalled. "I told them I wanted a sex change and they said that wasn't the issue."

After five weeks of this conversion therapy, Lankton left the hospital and returned to her daily life. "I am told I am a boy regardless of how I actually feel and make a feeble attempt at growing a beard," she captions another sad attempt at would-be masculine portraiture. She's wearing a flannel button-up shirt under an unzipped black hoodie. These pictures are depressing to look at, filling me with despair for all the obvious reasons—though Lankton's Warholian edits do manage to lighten the mood some, like how she's used marker to give herself an ugly beard, much as she markered in eye shadow and rouge on earlier photos. A bit of camp in the bleakness.

Her captions from March 1979 say that she made her "final attempts at boyhood," but she soon admitted defeat. The following month, her makeup returns and her hair grows back in, now once again long enough to feather out at the ends. I turn the page to find a four-by-four grid of sixteen photos; each looks more severe than the last. In a more legible penmanship than the shaky, all-caps one that she'd later adopt, Lankton captions the photo set, "Back to normal."

• • •

Though her first dolls were made out of flowers and food, by the time she hit high school, Lankton had upgraded her materials. The scale of her creations had also grown more ambitious. Her first attempt at a larger work was a life-size soft sculpture of a stoner with a handlebar mustache. She fashioned his skin out of T-shirts that she'd dyed a pale beige. To fill out his cotton-blend flesh and provide it with some mobility, she stuffed him with the innards of old mattresses and gave him a jointed skeleton devised of wire hangers. His eyelids hang heavy. His hair, made of yarn, falls to his chest. His shirt says STONED AGE. She hated him. As she told the Park Forest *Star* in 1974, "There's nothing different or exciting about him." The paper had run a profile on the burgeoning young artist because her town library was displaying some of her work. She much preferred the exhibition's smaller pieces, also made from stuffed T-shirts with articulated wire skeletons, to her larger, slumped-over stoner. One of these smaller dolls, svelte and meant to resemble a fashionably evil society woman like Disney's Cruella de Vil, wore a handmade gold lamé dress, a spindly cigarette holder, and furious eyebrows that met in a "V." Another, sporting glasses and with hair made from dyed-orange mop tassels, Lankton said she had modeled after some fat women she had observed at her local laundromat.

These early pieces gesture at where Lankton's practice was heading in terms of both content and form. She would continue building dolls of all sizes as the years wore on, from figurines to posable mannequins, and she would always do so layer by layer, starting from the inside out. Her wire-hanger skeletons gave way to jointed metal and wood, complete with rib cages, encased in various substances meant to mimic soft tissue, all of which would end up invisible to the outside viewer. Moving past T-shirts, she would eventually transform plaster and old fabrics into skin, painted and dyed to her liking, and complete them with dolls' teeth, human teeth, human hair, and glass eyes, sourcing these last items from a taxidermist on Thirty-first Street in New York.

These sculptures, and specifically her reactions to them, signal a growing interest in only depicting those bodies that she found to be "exciting" and "different." Rather than more sculptures like the life-size stoner—that is to say, just some guy—she made fat women, skinny women, the world's Candy Darlings and its various Divines. She was interested in bodies, period—what they looked like, how they moved, which bodies were deemed unfit for society—but she was most interested in bodies that captured her attention or spoke to her in some way. She wasn't very interested in "pretty" people, by which she meant palatable or conventionally attractive in a way that might appeal to those detestable "suburban" tastes, and so she didn't make that many "pretty" dolls—her words, not mine. "The most tasteful doll I've made is a real pretty one, but I don't like him too much 'cause the pretty ones aren't very interesting," she once told *i-D*. "It's like with people. The prettiest people are the blandest." She did, however, think that most of her dolls were beautiful, with the most beautiful of all being the most interesting, the most eye-catching, different, and unique. "They're all freaks," she told the *East Village Eye* in 1984. "Outsiders, untouchables. They're like biographies, the kind of people you'd like to know about. Really interesting and fucked-up. It's what you want to read, the kind of people you stop and notice."

While Lankton framed her artistic interest in terms of appreciation, her sculptures of such bodies do lend themselves to an obvious paranoid reading—that is, one that analyzes a work first and foremost based on the ways in which it appears to reflect, resist, or recapitulate broader systems of oppression, per queer theorist Eve Kosofsky Sedgwick: "In a world where no one need be delusional to find evidence of systemic oppression, to theorize out of anything *but* a paranoid critical stance has come to seem naïve, pious, or complaisant." As an anorexic, drug-using, postoperative transsexual, Lankton would have readily included herself in that group of societal outsiders, but it's still a sideshow of her own making, one that people might see themselves in, but not necessarily care to star in. But the further I parsed her old interview clippings, the more reductive that reading began to feel. "If you look at any dolls, you can sort of see how people saw themselves at a particular time," Lankton once said in an interview. When asked whether her spindly-limbed dolls were inspired by "Giacometti's elongated figures," she said rather matter-of-factly, perhaps even a bit annoyed: "No, I used to be anorexic, so I made them like that. They kept getting thinner and thinner and thinner, and then the ones that I had made, I made thinner, too. I needed their bodies." But what did she need them for? Monuments to a past that she no longer wished to embody? Aspirational figures, not unlike the "thinspo" found online today? And if that latter reading were in fact the case, what of the sculptures of fat bodies that she made in tandem? If she needed those thinner sculptures, then she must have needed the fat ones too. In the same interview, Lankton told the reporter that her sculptures didn't solely reflect what she'd experienced firsthand, like anorexia and surgery, but also "things that I would have liked to look like or be. Just fantasies." When I look at *Blue Babe,* a zaftig bust with Old Hollywood eyebrows and a cerulean finger wave to match, all I see is fantasy. To reframe *Blue Babe* as anything else feels willfully dishonest, an attempt to see something other than what my eyes can plainly tell me.

Consider, as well, *Madame Eadie,* the "wearable doll" Lankton made while studying at SAIC, which gave her the appearance of an otherworldly fat woman. While there's something undeniably fatphobic about it—the piece is, quite literally, a fat suit—I think it's too interesting to outright dismiss on those grounds alone. For, as *Manhunt* author Gretchen Felker-Martin once said of Lankton's work, "I think [it's] so fascinating for someone who so publicly struggled with anorexia to covet fatness and to use it to protect herself in public." Why did she want to wear that doll? What might she have hoped to embody, and how would Madame Eadie allow her to do so? Another of Lankton's wearable dolls, this one headless and made of sheer nylon, hangs in one of the corners of *It's all about ME, Not You.* It is baggy and loose, as if semi-deflated, which makes me wonder if Lankton might have stuffed it when she wore it, expanding her frame to whatever size she wanted, even when she was physically unable to do so.

What helped me come to this conclusion was the realization that I've never encountered a paranoid reading of Lankton's transsexual dolls—a non-transphobic one, I mean—that specifically took issue with her interest in representing preoperative trans women's bodies. (Or should I say nonoperative?) I would imagine that I've never seen such a reading because Lankton is trans herself. No one thinks to question why a trans woman would sculpt so many women with penises, despite the fact that this particular trans woman's body looked nothing like that for most of her adult life. We don't accuse her of fetishizing her transsexual subjects' bodies, in part because of our own projections onto the bodies of trans women—yes, even Lankton's. But there's also no question that these dolls, like the nude Candy Darling draped in a pink feather boa, are giving us a fantasy, even in their abjection. Given the artist's oft-stated regrets about having undergone vaginoplasty, her sculptures of trans women, much like her sculptures of fat women, might have allowed her to imagine herself with a body that she'd never have.

In thinking about this, I'm remembering an all-trans tribute to *Hair* that I saw in 2019, produced and directed by Charlene Incarnate, a pillar of Brooklyn's drag scene and star of the HBO documentary *Wig*. Though not promoted by name but rather in vague terms as "a night of classical musical theater numbers," the performance, staged as part of La MaMa's annual Squirts showcase for up-and-coming New York talent, revealed itself, once the metaphorical curtain went up, to be none other than an abridged version of the famed hippie musical. Perhaps Charlene had chosen to obfuscate what exactly the evening entailed in order to preserve some element of surprise, as *Hair* is famous for its onstage nudity, and her production upheld that tradition. Not only that, she upped the ante by having her cast—which included Remy Black and Image Object, also Brooklyn nightlife fixtures—perform the entire show fully naked. (She also made other updates, like swapping out lyrics from "Initials" so the zeitgeisty number would concern not LBJ but HRT.) I found the decision to showcase a range of trans bodies neither covered nor adorned to be so impactful, ironically because it allowed its performers' talents to take center stage. By displaying those bodies exactly as they are, thereby negating any fixation on what their nonexistent clothing concealed, the production destigmatized the naked trans body for me in a way that I desperately needed, given that I had a "trans body" myself.

Remembering that Lankton once described her dolls as fantasies, I wonder if her nude sculptures of transsexuals also allowed her to demystify bodies, both her own and those of others. Just as she'd once told a reporter, they were things she would have liked to look like or be. "Sometimes they end up looking like me," she said, "but they're more like people I'd like to see. Or sometimes I'm thinking of the way I'd like to look." She was twenty-one when she underwent sex reassignment surgery, about a year after she started hormone replacement therapy, and she did all this within close proximity of her parents, who covered the costs of the procedure through her father's church's health insurance. I wonder how that influenced the way that she transitioned, involving her parents in the process to such a degree. Also, as previously mentioned, Lankton experienced complications from the procedure, which would sometimes make her wish that she'd never had it done. In interviews conducted years after her surgery, Lankton would express that she didn't feel like a woman or a man but rather some other third gender. She would also sometimes fantasize about how her life might have been different had she decided to live as a drag queen rather than as "a sex change," that is, a post-op transsexual. What she meant by "drag queen," though, might be different from what it means now. Four decades ago, a "drag queen" could have also referred to someone who lived a feminine life in the gay world—someone who had, in many ways, transitioned but would not have been deemed a woman in the eyes of straight society. To "be" or "become" a woman was also a commonly used euphemism at the time to say, without saying, that you'd undergone bottom surgery. "I've had a transsexualism operation," says Brooke Xtravaganza in a memorable beach scene from the 1990 documentary *Paris Is Burning*. "That means I've had a sex change. I'm no longer a man. I am a woman . . . and now I'm as free as the beach." She skips off toward the water. "And yet that voice is still there," says her house sister, Carmen Xtravaganza, turning to the camera and flashing a sly grin.

It was by design that there were so few accessible paths to womanhood for transsexuals of Lankton's generation. There were even fewer for those who lacked supportive parents, much less adequate health insurance. Mardi Pieronek, a TikTok creator who has gained popularity in recent years for talking about what it was like to transition as a teenager in the 1970s, really emphasized her lack of options in an interview that I conducted a few years ago. "With kids back then in the seventies, with me, finding the doctors who would get you hormones was like trying to find a back-alley abortion," she told me. "Only certain psychiatrists would get you the letters. You had to work the streets to make the money to go to the one surgeon in Toronto, or you went to Dr. Biber in Trinidad, Colorado. We had no support whatsoever." Pieronek wasn't the only teenager to tread that particular path, but, as she explained, "the only reason you don't see these stories is because of how marginalized we were. None of us made it here to tell you we've always been here." Most other teenage transitioners of her time, she said, were "either murdered or killed themselves." Cecilia Gentili, the late Argentine artist and activist, experienced transition as similarly restrictive when she did so in her late teens in the 1980s. "I was living in Rosario, which is where I met trans people and started doing sex work," she explained to me in an interview for *New York* magazine. "I tried to go to college, but I had to give that up when I transitioned. It was not something you could do at the same time. I had to choose between being miserable as a person and being trans and losing all of that. As you can see, the choice was clear."

As young transsexual women who lacked financial resources, Pieronek and Gentili were, despite having grown up in opposite hemispheres, not to mention a decade apart, presented with a parallel limited set of options. They were shut out of most labor markets, only able to make money through sex work and nightlife, and they were expected to pursue medical interventions as a part of their transitions—hormones and surgery, with feminization being the goal—because doing so was also a matter of safety and achieving some semblance of financial security. On that latter point, Gentili told me it wasn't until decades later that she began to unpack the rigid understanding of transness she'd internalized as a result of her lived experience. As the coordinator of the Apicha Community Health Center's trans health program, she would always assume that every new patient who came to see her not only wanted hormones and surgery but wanted them as soon as possible. "I didn't know that some trans people don't want hormones and some trans people don't want to be a man or a woman. So at first I was like, 'OK, this is what you're gonna do,'" she said. "'I'm gonna get you on hormones, and I'm gonna get you letters for your breast augmentation, and I'm gonna make you a woman,' and they were like, 'Oh no!' I learned a lot from my community. I learned with them." Pieronek went through a similar process of unlearning when she joined social media in 2017. "I was in that 'Harry Benjamin standards of care' brain," she said, referring to the American doctor whose postwar medical practices determined, for decades, who was allowed to transition in many countries, or at least who was able to access that care under direct, professional supervision.

Lankton, a slender white teenager from a middle-class background, androgynous even before HRT, was deemed a worthy candidate for medical transition. Still, despite the advantages that helped her receive that care, which, again, included support from her family and insurance that would cover her surgery, I can't stop thinking about how her life might have been different had her parents not been so imbricated in the process of changing her sex, or if she'd been born a few decades later and benefited from the rise of the informed-consent model of trans healthcare, which could've given her more autonomy in choosing the care she received. I share similar concerns about young transitioners today, not because they're able to access gender-affirming care with relative ease, at least in comparison with decades past—which, to be glib, I think is fab—but because they, like Greer, might have so many cis authority figures in their ear—their parents, their doctors, their surgeons—determining for them what their gender will look like. I wonder if that might have been a part of what Lankton meant when she talked about regretting her surgery, her regrets of becoming "a sex change" instead of becoming "a drag queen." When she began to disidentify with womanhood in the later years of her life, perhaps what she rejected was not necessarily transsexual womanhood itself but the transsexual womanhood that had been constructed for her—by her parents, by her doctors, by a stringent model of care that cared little for its patients' autonomy—rather than one she constructed on her own terms. But of course that's all speculation on my part. Speculation and projection. Reasoned and warranted, I would hope, but speculation and projection all the same.

In any case, Lankton had a habit of fixating on an alternate reality where she never consented to surgery, much as she would fixate on her weight and the difficulty that she faced in maintaining it. Maybe she questioned whether she would've made a different decision were she able to go back in time. Maybe she would've waited until later to make that same choice if her parents and doctors had not intervened, perhaps when she was older and living on her own, away from her family and whatever "suburban" sensibilities they might have imposed on her medical transition. I can relate to that fixation, in part. I have no regrets over bottom surgery, but now, even a few years out from the procedure, I sometimes catch myself feeling nostalgic for my preoperative body and its particular planes of sensation, and then I grow a bit wistful knowing I'll never traverse them again. I can imagine that Lankton, in building transsexual dolls like her Candy Darling nude, might have been able to confront, and perhaps even soothe, her neurotic fixation on the body she'd never get back. Perhaps these figures collapsed the difference between the two bodies for her. Perhaps they rendered that difference mundane, for herself and also for others.

"If I make a beautiful female doll then put a penis on it, some people will complain that I've ruined it," she once wrote. "Yet, that's the truth—there are people out there like that. The work forces people to deal with issues they'd rather not face—to talk about something instead of around it. Maybe they'll see the differences aren't that great; that it's not really that bad."

• • •

Throughout the '80s and '90s, many critics and journalists tasked with writing about Lankton's art would get so hung up on Lankton's own body and the fact of its being transsexual that they could barely engage with her work in any meaningful, substantive way.

Many writers of her time, particularly those who were also enmeshed in the same East Village art scene, would call attention to Lankton's transsexuality through verbal winks and nods—subtle, euphemistic references for readers already in the know. One such journalist wrote about "Greer Lankton's exhibit of life-sized, anatomically correct soft sculpture" in 1984—apparently a favorite phrase, as another individual wrote that same year, "As for Greer Lankton's marvelous work, let me simply say that it was anatomically correct."

When it comes to those who confronted the matter head-on—well, I, for one, wish that a lot of them hadn't. In an *i-D* interview published not long after Lankton's first solo show at the East Village gallery Civilian Warfare, the British journalist Dylan Jones introduces his subject first as "a transsexual" and then as "a transsexual that makes dolls." He then goes on to describe her voice, writing that it "hovers somewhere between Liberace, Linda Blair and Molly Parkin." It's like reading the transcription of a carnival barker, shouting lurid claims about his newest freak. The banner across the top of the page is somehow even worse: BIG COCKS, BIG WILLIES, TITS, TRANNIES, DRAG QUEENS.

The critic Sylvia Falcon found herself similarly stuck on Lankton's physical form, unable to look at the artist's body of work without first scrutinizing the body of the artist. "Transsexuality is a subject I approach with marked skepticism," begins her 1983 piece for the *East Village Eye,* and it's only downhill from there. Falcon goes on to say that she views trans women as stereotypical simulacra of her sex: a man's idea of a woman. As such, she initially views Lankton's dolls as a misogynistic "burlesque of femaleness." She even likens the work to a patriarchal psyop: "the perfect act of sabotage—a pseudo-woman castigating her adopted sex." She then describes how meeting Lankton, whom Falcon graciously agrees is "a woman," changed her perception of the dolls. Her words, while no less transmisogynistic, then take on a softer, benevolent tone. "Her women look horribly victimized because to a certain extent she feels victimized," writes Falcon. "Lankton's work represents the struggle with her new persona, and as such it is valid. To her credit, Lankton doesn't deny that she was socialized as a male and she recognizes the adjustment to being female as twofold. Her biological rebirth has been realized; her psychological development is still being actualized through her art." We can only hope the same for the critic's psychological development.

Though I obviously loathe the conclusions she draws, Falcon isn't exactly wrong to note that Lankton's art often evokes suffering in its depictions of womanhood, however much I disagree with her interpretation of that choice. Even the critic Hilton Als, who admired Lankton's work, was not immune from the occasional paranoid reading, writing in 2014 that he "had to turn away [from her dolls, sometimes], they bordered on a kind of drag that I don't particularly feel comfortable with—women as an object of ridicule rather than celebration."

Depictions of suffering abound in Lankton's body of work. She created many feminized Christs, for example, whose narratives of gendered pain feel much too obvious to warrant explanation. Among them is a bust from 1988 titled *Jesus/ Mary*. Sporting a full beat and pencil-thin eyebrows à la Madge Bellamy, the androgynous figure stares off to her left as blood drips from the thorny crown piercing her forehead. Another smaller figure, a doll from 1983 called *Drag Queen Jesus,* is posed for a crucifixion, only she's missing her cross— humiliating! She has on red pumps, black evening gloves, a strip of black tulle around her chest, and nothing else—except for, again, a full face of makeup. Her bright-red lips appear upturned at the corners, as if wearing a painted-on smile to mask her pain and sacrifice. Or maybe it's camp? A separate piece, *Jesus's Cha-Cha Heels,* makes a good case for that reading. The 1986 sculpture, whose title references an iconic scene from the John Waters classic *Female Trouble,* resembles a pair of red pumps with golden crosses on their heels; from where the balls of one's feet would rest, bloody nails point skyward. It obviously speaks to pain and femininity, but to claim that it's simply about victimization, as Falcon does, means willfully overlooking the agency Lankton implies with the piece, not to mention her wicked humor. After all, to paraphrase Divine from that scene in *Female Trouble,* she wanted cha-cha heels! She might very well have been laughing at the fact that her martyrdom was, in many ways, of her own making.

Another sculpture that I would hazard speaks to Lankton's thoughts on pain and womanhood is a doll she named *Charred Woman,* constructed no later than 1981, after she suffered a nervous breakdown, according to the Mattress Factory archivists, Sarah and Sinéad. My immediate reaction to the piece—or rather, a photograph of it, as I've yet to see it in person—is that it recalls the motifs of minstrel imagery. The life-size figure, feminine in shape, is all black from head to toe, with parts of her body painted red: her vulva, her belly button, her nipples, and her lips. The red lips on black skin made me initially think of blackface, which felt out of place with Lankton's broader body of work, which, at least to my knowledge, is otherwise devoid of such racist imagery. Other photos of the piece revealed its details: the corset, garter belt, and remnants of a bra that strap the figure into her pin-up hourglass shape. I also noticed the rouge on her cheeks, which whooshes up to her temples in that decidedly '80s style. After taking the title into consideration, I began to see Lankton might have likely intended it literally: a woman burned alive, with only her markers of womanhood—her genitals, breasts, and makeup—left unscathed by the fire. It could very well reflect her feelings about how she arrived at her own womanhood, as if to say, yes, she got what she wanted, but at what cost?

In an interview from later in the decade, Lankton describes all of her earlier work that pertained to her transness as "tortured and mutilated" because that was how she felt at the time. "If I feel more tortured, [my dolls] come out more tortured," she explains, adding that she no longer feels that way, at least with respect to her gender. The interviewer then asks if that means she will stop making art about transness and changing sexes. "No, I think it will just keep changing," she says. "I think they already have. The acrobats are about the latest," she adds, referring to a set of nude dolls posed in various positions, hanging from the ceiling, their painted fabric genitals flapping in the air at all sorts of angles. "They're pretty happy," she says. "They're healthy."

Not everyone agreed. The acrobats and other nude artwork featured in her 1984 solo show at the East Village art gallery Civilian Warfare drew criticism from some local community members. Their objection was twofold: They felt that Lankton's work, a lot of which was visible from the sidewalk, was inappropriate for children who might be walking by, and this tension reflected their broader concerns about gentrification and displacement, which was already impacting the neighborhood's multiethnic working-class communities.

"We felt it was a lot of pornographic art," Esther Cartagena, coordinator of community services for a local housing group, told *The Village Voice* in 1984. "The majority of people here are Hispanic . . . and the art doesn't relate to them." She added that she had no problem with new galleries opening up in her neighborhood. "We like art down here," she said. She just didn't want those new galleries, restaurants, bars, and cafés to displace longtime residents or drive up rents.

These new establishments would end up doing exactly that, though it was New York City's government that laid the groundwork for that demographic shift in race and class. In a deliberate effort to convert low-income housing to condos and luxury rentals—and thus replace poor and working-class New Yorkers with wealthier residents—the city enacted tax breaks and other profit-driven policy changes in the 1970s to bring real estate developers into neighborhoods like the East Village. Developers also took advantage of the HIV/AIDS epidemic's massive death toll in the '80s and '90s to seize even more low-income housing, which had been left vacant by those who had died from the virus, as Sarah Schulman documents in *The Gentrification of the Mind.*

Lankton made her living in the art world, in part because her transness prevented her from finding stable employment in other industries. "When I tried to be a waitress, I'd go up to a table and take their order, and they couldn't get over the fact that I had such a deep voice," she once said. She made money from selling her art, sometimes more than she would've otherwise earned trying to wait tables. Art galleries that sold her work priced smaller pieces anywhere between $75 and $500, while life-size sculptures like the lavender-skinned *Princess Pamela,* purchased by the rock star Iggy Pop and possibly named after the downtown soul food restaurateur Pamela Strobel, could go for many thousands. Lankton also spent her twenties working as an assistant for various artists, like the sculptor Mary Ann Unger and the photographer Geoffrey Biddle. She

was employed as a seamstress for the fashion designer Robert
Molnar and worked as an assistant to Kermit Love, the puppet
builder and longtime collaborator with the Muppets creator
Jim Henson; Lankton even helped Love construct one of the
first Big Bird suits, according to one of her old CVs. She would
later display and sell her dolls at Einstein's, a boutique in the
East Village owned and operated by Paul Monroe, her husband at the time and who remained in close contact even after
their marriage ended in the early 1990s.

As for whether her work was inappropriate, for neighborhood kids or anyone else, Lankton herself disagreed. Some
found her work shocking on account of its nudity, or the fact
that it showcased bodies that would often go unseen, but shallow provocation was never her intention.

"It's just anatomy," she said. "Like everybody always thinks
if you put a vagina on it, it's really sexual, but it's just part of
the anatomy."

• • •

Sitting in that back office of the museum, flipping through
Lankton's old photo albums, I am utterly captivated as I watch
her make, unmake, and remake herself one portrait at a time.
Her physical mutability seems fitting, given how interested she
was in bodies and the ways in which we shape them. "My work
is figurative, but not just about the figure," Lankton once said.
"I am interested in the body; the whole idea of contortion and
balancing, what the body can and cannot do (as well as what
we as individuals believe we can and cannot do)—but I'm concerned with the creation of a person, rather than merely a figure, concerned with what it means to be a person."

In a set of photo-booth pictures taken in 1978, a twenty-year-old Lankton poses in a plain white tank top with minimal daytime makeup, which she has enhanced after the fact with warm-hued markers in that pop art style she favored. Her hair is longer. She's plucked her eyebrows and shaved her underarms bare. "I decide I will become a woman," she captions the set. "I begin to concentrate on the change." Ten days later, according to another caption, she decides to name herself Greer.

Her style shifts rapidly in the pictures that follow, morphing through an array of eclectic, decade-clashing fashions. She plays around with her makeup too, favoring a bold lip to match her dramatic, smoky eyes. Her poses turn similarly theatrical, a kind of editorial camp, with her arms jutting out taut against the walls and ceiling of the photo booth, as if the kiosk itself were collapsing in on her. I turn the page and find Lankton, suddenly topless, smiling all wide-eyed and ecstatic in a four-panel photo strip collaged into a square. In the first picture, she's holding a pill bottle, and then in the next one, the camera has caught her popping something into her mouth. "My very first estinyl pill," reads the caption. "I obtained the estrogen from a friend."

The start of her medical transition coincided with her last day of classes at SAIC. That summer, she would undergo surgery in Ohio before heading off to Brooklyn to continue her studies at the Pratt Institute, where she would go on to earn her bachelor of fine arts in 1981.

It was the end of an era for Lankton—the end of many eras, in fact—and the start of whatever came next. "She wants," reads a caption. "She takes."

I am delighted by the pictures that she took during her first

year living in New York, some of them at the McCrory's on
Fulton Street, which she dubbed "the K-Mart of Brooklyn,"
others at a Manhattan Woolworth's. She appears to have liked
going to this one photo booth in Midtown, located in an ar-
cade on Forty-second Street; she even once sneaked off from a
school trip to a museum to snap some more pictures in it. The
photographs themselves, as well as their captions, document
the various physical aspects of her medical transition in minute, familiar detail. She tracks how many months that she's
been on hormones, how many hours of electrolysis that she's
completed. "Waiting for hair and tits," she writes in one of the
captions. The picture, snapped at an undisclosed photo booth,
shows Lankton posed in mock agony with one breast exposed
as she tugs at her hair with both hands. In another caption, she
notes how many weeks out from surgery she is, as well as other
changes that she has made to her look. "Blonde hair," she
writes under one such picture. "NEW BANGS," she captions
another.

Looking at them, I feel like I'm lurking through some
younger trans girl's Instagram feed, scrolling past HRT updates and selfie after selfie: an anxious record to prove one's
existence before you've quite come into being. "She pre-
tends," Lankton captions a photo on the next page. Have any
of us ever done anything new? She's even using the third person to caption her own photos. How beautifully unoriginal we
trans women are, that for as long as we've been able to document these changes, we've done so obsessively through whatever means we've had, enraptured by it all, even if only in
private, as Lankton has done here. Looking at the pictures, I
see a part of myself, the girl I was many years ago.

Lankton drops the transition updates from her captions
after 1980, though the photo-booth visits continue. Occa-

sional nudity, impromptu make-out sessions, pictures with friends, sometimes playful groping. There are a lot of solo shots of Lankton posing like a model; in a later album, I learn that she modeled a little in the early 1980s, some print and commercial work here and there. There are also plenty of "bodychecks," as the good people of TikTok might call them: pictures that seem to showcase how small her waist is, how visible her ribs are. The captions occasionally note how thin she's gotten, sometimes listing her exact weight in pounds. It's hard not to notice the parallels between these captions and the ones about her transition. Again, as she herself says in her sketchbook, "I'll still be doing what I'm doing."

The photo-booth strips abruptly disappear in 1986. I don't know why she stopped, or even if she stopped. The truth could simply be that one of her photo albums got lost, misplaced perhaps somewhere between Chicago, New York, and Pittsburgh. Still, the shift seems sudden and strange, and I wonder what might have caused it. Later, while sifting through her press clippings, I notice that a journalist asked if her art was all fueled by anguish. No, Greer says, telling him that his analysis is reductive. But while her work isn't directly about anguish, per se, she does admit that anguish sometimes plays a key role in her practice. "When you are really anguished, you don't go out a lot," she says. "You don't want to see people. So you end up in your apartment making things."

Lankton was grappling with plenty of anguish by 1986. She'd lost many friends and community members in the East Village art scene, and that number would only continue to rise until her own death, ten years later. Robert Vitale, a longtime friend and former boyfriend who often accompanied her to the photo booths, died of AIDS-related complications in 1989, as did the writer and actress Cookie Mueller in that same year. The artist David Wojnarowicz, Lankton's friend and sometimes collaborator, died of AIDS in 1992. In a letter to Lankton's parents sent in 1987, Paul Monroe, still her husband at the time, expressed concern for his wife. "I'm really worried about Greer," he writes. "She has been having trouble sleeping and gaining weight. She is constantly talking about being a failure. I think most of it has to do with a lot of our friends being sick and . . . Greer has lost six close friends this past summer. And when [the artist] Ann Craig recently passed on it really hit Greer hard."

Amid all this death, she was also grappling with addiction, and her anorexia had once again grown quite severe. Her finances worsened, and her marriage to Monroe, whom she'd wed in a ceremony officiated by her father, seemed to be falling apart. It's easy to imagine the toll that all this must have taken on Lankton, who was already prone to depression and self-imposed isolation when she wasn't doing well.

In 1989, she temporarily moved back to her parents' house in Illinois to detox and gain some weight. She succeeded in doing that, so she flew back to New York, where she ended up relapsing. The following summer, she traveled back to Park Forest to enter treatment at a rehab facility not far from her hometown. Eventually, she moved back to Chicago, where she found refuge in the gay scene and made friends with some of the club kids and queens, much as she had in her youth. She had trouble breaking into the city's art world and felt frustrated by the disconnect between her past notoriety in New York and this newfound sense that she was a nobody. She continued making her dolls, though at a more languid pace than before; maintaining sobriety sapped her energy, which understandably slowed her rate of production. After some time, her dolls began to garner notice again. She'd been displaying them at the Alley, Chicago's legendary punk and goth boutique that opened in 1976, constructing custom window displays as she once did at her ex-husband's boutique in New York.

After four years of absence, the photo-booth pictures return, starting with a single self-portrait in 1990 and then a flood of others after 1992. Over the next few years, Greer's look changes consistently. Her blown-out blonde bob becomes a chin-length black shag, which she then crops even shorter, like Mia Farrow in *Rosemary's Baby*. She grins. She poses seductively. She gets naked and handsy with her friends, just like she used to do in her older photos. I'm happy to see this side of her return. It feels like she's found herself again—though, again, as I've said before, this might be projection, a willful submission to the pacifying allure of a simplistic, self-serving frame.

A local reporter profiled Lankton for the *Lincoln-Belmont Booster* in 1992. In the picture of her that ran alongside the piece, which she took at the photo booth at Roscoe's, she's staring down the camera in front of a Chanel scarf, which she's draped behind herself to create a makeshift backdrop. She's drawn her eyebrows high and wide, curving them into an unflappable arch in a way that's a little bit Dietrich but also by way of Divine. Her handwritten caption reveals that she didn't care for the *Booster* profile, especially the part in which the reporter called her a "34-year-old soon-to-be-divorced transsexual recovering dope addict." I also notice, in reading the profile, he smoothed down the rougher edges of her life story, minus that one "dope addict" line. The version of her life that he presents to his readers is very much a butterfly narrative, one that includes all the clichés that you might expect to find in the average trans-authored memoir: Lankton had a troubled childhood and always felt different, but then she transitioned, and look at her now, she's a beautiful woman and wonderful artist, and now she's finding success. Never mind the fact that her transition was by that point long in the past, about a decade and a half, to be exact, or the fact that changing sexes hadn't solved all her problems, much as he seems to suggest that it had.

Lankton's was a life that defied clean resolution, and that defiance continued through her final years. By the mid-1990s, she was once again on a professional upswing. She exhibited work at both the Whitney Biennial and the Venice Biennale in 1995, before opening *It's all about ME, Not You* in Pittsburgh the following year. But in her artist statement for the 1996 opening of that installation, she refused any rose-tinted frame. "Have been Anorexic since 19 and plan to continue," she wrote. "FUCK Recovery, FUCK PSYCHIATRY Fuck it all because I'm over it."

At times, I worry that the affinity I feel for Lankton, not only on account of her body of work but also on account of the shared facts of our bodies, isn't as genuine as I'd like it to be. That I'm just another writer like the one who wrote for the *Booster,* telling herself a story because it's the one she wants to hear. Ultimately, I don't think that's true, but here's what I can say for certain: Greer Lankton was a person and an artist, not a mirror. I might see myself when I look at her, but, as she said: Oops! Nevermind.

TALES FROM THE
HOSIERY COUNTER

Much like Jia Qing Wilson-Yang's 2016 novel, *Small Beauty*, in which a Chinese Canadian trans woman unexpectedly discovers through the death of a cousin that her late aunt was also queer like herself, Casey Plett's novel *Little Fish*, published in 2018, is propelled by its protagonist's suspicion that her grandfather might have also been trans. Throughout the course of *Little Fish*, however, Wendy, a white Canadian trans woman who was raised Mennonite, continually loses track of this thread. The mundane difficulties of being a trans woman in the present—financial instability, survival sex work, the suicide of a close friend—repeatedly stop her from pursuing her quest to dig up the trans woman she thinks might be buried deep in her family's past. In many ways, her ontological fixation is a red herring, for Wendy as well as the reader. Faced with a difficult present and an even more terrifying, uncertain future, she's trying to figure out how she got here, many years out from transitioning, and what she's supposed to do next, with no models for what the rest of her life could look like. Even if her Opa did turn out to be trans, she would still have to answer those questions for herself, but it's tempting for both Wendy and the reader to wonder: What if someone has already answered them for her?

The possibility of having a trans ancestor—not in the sense of those community elders who paved the way for us in years past but a literal ancestor perched a few branches up one's family tree—is a thought that's captivated me too. With all the secrets that my mother's side of the family has kept hidden from one another for decades, for example, a bit of gender-nonconformity might very well have been one of them. The biggest of those big reveals—well, more of an open secret, but only confirmed by my mom and other relatives of her generation when I was in my teens—has been that my great-grandmother only immigrated to the United States from Ireland in the 1920s because her father, my great-great-grandfather, forced her to. Apparently, my great-grandma had gotten pregnant out of wedlock, so her dad sent her away to marry a friend of his who lived in Brooklyn instead of letting her stay with the biological father, who might have had ties to the IRA, according to my aunt Siobhan, though I don't know that for sure. One of her twin girls grew up to be my grandmother, which meant that the man who ended up raising her, the great-grandfather I never met, wasn't actually biologically related to her or my mother, or to me. With that kind of family history kept secret for decades, anything could be possible, right?

In the early weeks of my transition, I spent a ton of time sifting through my memories, searching for some kind of evidence that I was always this way, whether or not I or anyone else had recognized it. The movies I used to watch, the toys I used to play with—all of it flashed through my mind, anything that might have helped me shore up my burgeoning woman-hood when it was all still very theoretical and incredibly easy to question. Deep in the pits of those memory holes, looking back on my younger self, I would think about my earliest experiences with depression and how young I had been when it first manifested. Third grade? Maybe earlier? Could that have been related to everything I'd been taught to suppress? I mean, maybe, but I don't think the truth is quite that cut-and-dried. Depression is recurrent on one side of my family. I've dealt with it, my mother has, and so did her dad before her. She and her younger sister, Siobhan, have told me all about it.

In the 1960s, my mom's family was living in central Connecticut, in a town just east of Hartford. Like many white American families after World War II, they'd been able to move out of New York City and into the suburbs thanks to the G.I. Bill, which promised cheap home loans and low-interest mortgage rates for veterans, among other benefits. Unfortunately, the government failed to provide any nondiscrimination protections for Black Americans and other people of color, who were largely unable to take full advantage of the G.I. Bill due to the racist practices of the very same financial institutions needed to buy a house. As a result, this governmental assistance served to benefit white Americans almost exclusively—people like my mother's parents, neither of whom were college graduates—lifting them into the middle class and allowing them to build wealth at a disproportionate rate.

As the white middle class expanded throughout the United States, so too did small networks within it of gender-nonconforming individuals, who called themselves transvestites as well as cross-dressers. These were people who lived their lives as heterosexual men, many of them with wives and kids. They largely disdained homosexuals and transsexuals and were often eager to distinguish themselves from either group—in hindsight, an ironic bid for respectability, given that some of them, I'm sure, would later transition and live out the rest of their lives as out and proud lesbians. But back in the '60s, they found one another by word of mouth and with help from publications like *Transvestia,* a newsletter-turned-magazine that became the first long-running trans-oriented periodical of its kind. It published social commentary, self-help, erotica, and true-life stories from readers and from its editor, Virginia Prince—as well as social listings to facilitate real-world subscriber meetups. The figureheads of these publications are difficult to square with present-day trans politics. On the one hand, as historian Jules Gill-Peterson has observed, they presented one of the earliest critiques of compulsory medicalization coming from within the community, but they formulated those critiques within tight-knit correspondence circles and clandestine, invite-only gatherings that were generally just as segregated as the suburbs that many of them called home. I did spot one Asian American person in the pages of *Casa Susanna,* Michel Hurst and Robert Swope's 2004 collection of photos taken at the titular cross-dressing resort that operated in the Catskills in the 1960s, and Susanna herself was a Chilean immigrant—who, sidenote, worked as a radio DJ for one of New York's Latin music stations. But these interconnected communities were otherwise totally WASPy, cloistering themselves and their writings within circles of white college graduates and their white-collar peers, taking pains to exclude gays, transsexuals, people assigned female at birth, and even sometimes unmarried straight men.

As it turns out, a member of my family did encounter some of the cross-dressers of that era. None of my relatives were doing the literal cross-dressing themselves, at least as far as I know. But according to my aunt Siobhan, my grandmother, who worked at a bustling department store on the other side of Hartford for the last couple decades of her life, helped quite a few of those individuals with their covert shopping needs.

I never got to know my grandma, having only met her once when I was just a few months old, so I love hearing stories about her, this woman I'll never know. And, of course, I love any anecdote that would shatter the illusion of postwar America's so-called golden age, or whatever the revanchists among us would claim. White suburbia has never been as pristine as it would like to present—but, hello, I already knew that. I mean, I came out as gay while living in one such enclave and spent all four years of high school hooking up with strangers throughout the county, most of whom I met online, and that was back when George W. Bush was in office. The knowledge that deviance lurks behind even the whitest of picket fences wasn't, like, new information for me. What *was* new was what I learned about my grandma. And through a gossipy, thirdhand account that's probably unfit for a rigorous peer review? What's not to love!

What follows is a transcription of the story that my aunt Siobhan told me, which has been lightly edited and condensed for clarity's sake, with minimal interjections from me added in italics.

● ● ●

Grandma worked at the store from when I was ten or eleven years old, which would've been fifty-eight years ago, so 1965. She worked there until you were born.

—*So, 1988?*

Yes. The store was called D&L, which stood for Davidson and Leventhal. It was their main store in New Britain, Connecticut. She started out working in jewelry and cosmetics but would also cover hosiery and lingerie.

I don't know how it happened that she and I were talking about this, or what led to this conversation. Maybe it was when she was forced to retire because she was sick. We would have a lot of very interesting conversations at the time, some of them were very funny, others very heartfelt. Whatever led up to it, she told me about how, when she worked at D&L, she had a lot of male customers who would come in to buy jewelry for their wives. Grandma would always ask, "What's the occasion?" or "What are they gonna wear this jewelry with?" so she could decide on the style and design and the colors, and how their wives might want to coordinate it—her conversations with customers would always start that way. These men became repeat customers. After a while, she had built up a lot of these repeat customers, men who came in to buy jewelry for their wives. One of them would refer another male customer to her, who would refer another male customer to come in. They'd tell 'em, "Go see Mary." Some of them would say to her, "Well, your coloring is the same as my wife's. Would you mind putting the necklace on?"—or the bracelet or whatever it was. She would accommodate them—not a big deal—and help them look at a variety of merchandise they had for sale, make recommendations, and then help them decide.

Somewhere along the way, there was this one particular customer who said to her, "Well, my wife's coloring is very much like my own," and she said he wanted to hold it up to himself and see how it looked.* One thing led to another, I'm not sure exactly what—I suppose he either confided in my mother or she figured it out on her own without him having to tell her, or her having to tell him that she figured it all out—but she figured out that this piece of jewelry was actually for him. So, time went on, and, well, I'm not sure if that same customer ever came back, but she built up a bit of a following of . . . cross-dressing men? Is that the right, uh, statement to make?

—I mean, they were claiming to be men, and they were literally cross-dressing! I don't know if they would've necessarily called themselves cross-dressers, though. Like, I don't want to assume. Transvestites, maybe?

"Transvestite" may have been a little too sophisticated at the time. A little too exotic a term for our little town. Anyway, one thing led to another, and somebody finally confided in my mother, "I need a dress to go to a particular type of occasion." I don't know what kind of occasion it was, but they said, "I need a dress. Would you help me pick one out?" She said, "Of course."

Just like with the jewelry, she went through everything with him. "I see your coloring is this," blah blah blah, "I'll show you what we've got in your size," all that sort of stuff.

---

* Covert cross-dressers and closeted trans women presenting themselves to the world as men continued to use this gambit for decades to meet their shopping needs, as a 2016 *Broadly* interview with Monica Prata, a feminine image consultant who works with newly out trans women who want to refine their personal style, would suggest. "When I was in high school, I got a job working for Nordstrom," she told the defunct women's website. "Pretty regularly around 8:30, 8:45, close to closing, guys would come in, and they would say that they're shopping for their girlfriend. . . . They would describe her to me, and for whatever reason something just didn't really ring true. I thought to myself, maybe this person is uncomfortable, perhaps they're shopping for themselves. So I would select clothing that I knew would fit this individual, that would ultimately feminize his shape, and I would put them in a fitting room. Within the ninety days that I worked at Nordstrom, I was the number one salesperson in the store."

That was my mother. She said, "Look, if you're going to wear that dress, you've gotta wear the right lingerie. You've got to have the proper foundations"—as we said back then—"because you can't"—well, my mother was not as graphic as I am. She wouldn't have said, "You can't have your chest hair hanging out! You better shave if you want to make the dress really work!" She would've been more tactful, but it was something to that effect. Her goal was for him to look good in the dress. To do that, he'd need the proper lingerie, so she took him to the lingerie department, stuck him in a dressing room, and said, "Just stay there. I'll hand you a bunch of stuff to try on with the dress so we can see how it works." He would try the stuff on, open the door and let her see how things fit so that she could make the proper adjustments to every piece he was wearing. With pantyhose, I'm not sure if bigger size ranges would've been available at all the stores back then, but I know my mother well enough to know that she would have told them to go to the pharmacy and buy L'eggs.

—*Gleg's?*

L'eggs. L-apostrophe-E-G-G-S. They came in a little egg-shaped container.

—*Ohhh, yeah, they had those on an episode of* Mad Men, *I think. Sorry, you were saying that Grandma was helping them figure out their "foundations."*

My mother was really big on foundation garments for us girls growing up, and for herself, if any of us were going to wear a dress. Let me tell you, there was a lot of polyester going on back then, a lot of clingy fabrics just coming out on the market that were not as subtle as they are today. They didn't have a whole lot of drape and sure showed off everything wrong on your figure. If you had a slight bulge somewhere? Man, that baby was all over it.

So she would recommend the best products that they had available, including the best undergarments, to make any customer, man or woman—or, I should say, woman or man—look their absolute best. The other thing is she would do their makeup, or at least she would recommend makeup to them. I'm not sure if she would actually put the makeup on the customer, but she would show them how to apply it and find the absolute right tones, the right blushes. Whatever you wanted, if they sold it, she could show you. For her, it was really all about getting the whole look together and making sure that the customer was happy and dignified and that their look was subtle. It had to be head to toe. If the customer had questions about what shoes to buy, she would have the answer. I don't know if the store necessarily sold shoes, but I think she would've at least made some recommendations. In that era, it was always about the entire outfit, head to toe, and that included getting a manicure, getting your nails done—it had to be the whole thing. Whoever the customer was, it was important to my mother that they left the store feeling completely satisfied and that they looked their absolute best. Even though she never saw them in that final look, she wanted them to have everything they needed to look their absolute best.

When I was starting to prepare my mother's wake, I was worried that no one would show up because my mother wasn't working any longer, and a lot of her friends weren't really around anymore. I knew the core group of neighbors and friends and relatives would be there, at least. But I was stunned, just blown away by the number of people who attended. The line was out the door! And among those people were some of those customers. One of them I spoke to because I was asking everyone, "Oh, how did you know my mother?" I could not tell you that person's name. I don't know how that person identified themselves, but they said to me, "She was my best friend!" A total stranger! I would never forget that moment. I knew she was great at her job, I knew that she loved what she did and liked the social aspect of it and all of the friends that she made on the job, but I had no idea of the impact she had on her customers. I just wish she knew that. I wish she could have heard that. My little mother, we always called her "small but mighty."

—*I wish I could've actually, like, met her, or remembered meeting her, I mean.*

She was so thrilled about you. She would love you so much today.

• • •

The first time my aunt told me a version of this story was close to a decade ago, the first time I saw her in person after I had transitioned. A lot of the details escape me, but I remember we were sitting in the otherwise empty back patio of a Japanese restaurant, both of us bawling by the end of it. I don't know how my grandma would have felt about me, if she would have been "so thrilled" to see me today, but since I'll never know, I'll take my aunt at her word. Besides, I think that what she was trying to tell me, at least in part, was that *she,* my aunt, was thrilled about me, that *she* loved me so much, and sharing this family lore with me was a way for her to express that. I didn't, at the time, know what I'd do next, but her love and support, and that of many others, helped make that unknown less daunting.

A TRANS PANIC, SO TO SPEAK

"This is a picture of stark realism," reads the sepia-toned title card projected on the screen in front of me, "taking no sides—but giving you the facts—All the facts—as they are today. . . . _You are society_—JUDGE YE NOT. . . . ."

With its random capitalizations, italicized dramatics, copious em dashes, and experimental take on ellipses, the disclaimer alone probably would've given me a pretty good idea of what I could expect from _Glen or Glenda,_ were I not already familiar with it before I took my seat. But I did know a few things about the late Ed Wood's infamous 1953 train wreck: It had a reputation as one of the worst films of all time; it had something to do with cross-dressing and was at least vaguely autobiographical; and, much like Wood's later _Plan 9 from Outer Space,_ it was supposed to be as idiosyncratically terrible as it was terribly idiosyncratic. Above all, I knew that I really wanted to see it. So when I learned that it was playing at a small independent movie theater here in Brooklyn,* I made plans to go. I even made a date of it, inviting along a guy I'd met through an app who wanted to meet up again, because why not, I figured: two birds, one stone.

Watching *Glen or Glenda* with this new guy was, perhaps, an ostentatious choice for a second date with a cis man, especially one who I definitely hoped would still want to fuck me afterward. While often billed as a deranged exploitation film about cross-dressing and sex changes—and it certainly is all that—*Glen or Glenda* is, at its core, an unexpectedly earnest plea for acceptance, one that begs its viewers to open their hearts and minds to all the poor transvestites suffering silently in their midst. In other words, it might be one of the least sexy things you could ever make a straight man watch. "Men don't like being told what to do," as Hari Nef once wrote in a tweet that for some reason got burned into my brain immediately upon reading it. But a part of me enjoyed the confrontation of it all. You know, like, if you wanna be my lover, you gotta get with this unhinged movie that's not about me but is also not not about me, as the Spice Girls famously never once said.

Glen or Glenda's portrayal of marginalized individuals and the mental anguish that such marginalization causes was almost certainly drawn from Wood's own experiences, given the filmmaker's well-documented history of cross-dressing in his own life. It's not like the director was trying to hide any of the parallels. I mean, he cast himself as Glen, and he cast his actual girlfriend, the actress Dolores Fuller, as his onscreen paramour, Barbara. In the movie, Glen likes to wear women's

---

* Spectacle Theater, you will always be famous.

clothing, especially Barbara's angora sweaters, and in an interview published years after the film's release, Fuller joked that she got the part because she "came [into the audition] with an angora sweater, and [Wood] loved angora." Still, I wonder how much Wood and Fuller's actual offscreen relationship paralleled that of Glen and Barbara's. Like at the end of the movie, when Barbara decides to accept Glen's transvestism as well as his feminine alter ego, Glenda. "Although I do not fully understand this, maybe together we can work it out," she tells Glen/da. "I love Glen. I'll do everything I can to make him happy." Was this autobiographical on Wood's part, or creative wish fulfillment? An indirect communiqué from the filmmaker to his girlfriend? Historical revisionism after a coming-out gone wrong?

There's also a fleeting B plot about a character named Alan, who only shows up briefly and not until the end of the film. Alan doesn't just want to wear women's clothes—he wants to *be* a woman. And with a suite of full-body surgical procedures and "hundreds of hormone shots . . . injected into various parts of his body," she does exactly that, becoming Anne.

While Glen/da appears to have been inspired by Wood's own lived experience, the transsexual character of Anne, an army vet before she transitioned, was inspired by news coverage of Christine Jorgensen, the postwar trans media personality whose widely publicized medical transition had made international headlines the year before *Glen or Glenda* was released. A now-iconic New York *Daily News* headline from the time declared, "Ex-GI Becomes Blonde Beauty." Unfortunately, and please imagine me saying this in the most Debbie Downer voice possible, that sensationalistic press coverage, however camp in hindsight, was entirely nonconsensual on

Jorgensen's part. She wasn't a public figure prior to her transition, nor had she alerted the media about her decision to undergo surgery in Denmark, a major destination for transsexual medical tourism in the postwar era. When Jorgensen arrived back home in New York after her extended stay in Europe, she was greeted by journalists eager to know all about what she had done. She made use of the platform foisted on her, acting as a transsexual ambassador to the non-transsexual public. She was happy to give "as much good publicity as possible for the sake of all those to whom I am a representation of themselves," as she once said, giving countless televised interviews, speaking on college campuses, and, in 1967, publishing a memoir. But her newly visible life was also one that was born of necessity, as she would never be able to hold down a normal job again, nor ever try to live a life away from the public eye.

It's curious that Wood would include the Anne narrative at the end of his film, slotted in out of nowhere just before its conclusion, since he takes such great pains to emphasize that she and Glen/da are not one and the same. But maybe that's the point: Glen/da is not a transsexual, and neither, by proxy, is Wood. The intended dissonance might not be fully legible to the modern viewer, who might mistakenly read them both as plainly transgender. But Glen/da is a transvestite: "Not half man, half woman," the narrator explains, "but man and woman in the same body, even though by all outward appearances Glen is fully and completely a man." Anne, on the other hand, is a transsexual, one whose medical transition was only permitted because doctors had determined that she was actually intersex.

The film pathologizes Glen/da and Anne for their respective non-normative genders, as well as for their failure to integrate into society. It presents a diagnosis and suggests a cure for both, tailored to each of their needs. Anne's problem is biological, and so her cure is medical, whereas Glen/da's is psychiatric in nature, stemming from her troubled relationship with her parents as a child, and so her cure is social. To become whole, all that Glen/da needs is for Barbara to accept her. Also, Barbara has to let Glen/da try on all her clothes. It's medicine. It's science. Ask the *DSM*!

Anyway, back to why Wood might've wanted to weave Anne into Glen/da's story, since the two apparently have nothing in common, as Wood repeatedly tells us. I would argue that Anne serves as a counterpoint to Glen/da, one who's meant to demonstrate just how normal the latter is by comparison. Earlier in the film, Wood similarly deploys a cruisey homosexual, who tries and fails to pick up a straight man. The straight man then turns around and tries to pick up Glen/da, dressed *en femme*, but this, too, proves unsuccessful. "The homosexual, it is true at times, does adopt the clothing or the makeup of a woman to lure members of his own sex, but this is not so for the transvestite," the narrator explains. "The transvestite is not interested in those of their own sex. The clothing is not worn to attract the attention of their own sex but to eliminate themselves from being a member of that sex." This was a common talking point in transvestite circles at the time, a way of normalizing themselves by drawing some distance between themselves and other sexual deviants. Rather than trying to find common ground with all the homosexuals, transsexuals, and drag queens who lived outside of the pristine bubbles of their redlined suburbs and idyllic retreats in upstate New York, they rejected those others wholesale. (And that rejection, to be sure, cut both ways. "[Transsexualism] is as distinct from transvestism as it is from homosexuality," writes Jan Morris in her 1974 memoir, *Conundrum*. "It is not a sexual mode or preference. It is not an act of sex at all. It is a passionate, lifelong, ineradicable conviction, and no true transsexual has ever been disabused of it.") As self-identified transvestites like Louise Lawrence and Virginia Prince noted in the pages of *Transvestia*, their penchant for cross-dressing did not mean that they wanted to be women, and it certainly didn't mark them as deviant, like those urban homosexuals and their seedier, filthier drag. Transvestites like Glen/da were good men. Family men. Respectable men. Heterosexual men! I wonder if women like Barbara agreed.

In the final minutes of *Glen or Glenda*, a therapist tells Glen/da and Barbara that in order for Glen to permanently excise Glenda from his psyche, he must first heal his childhood trauma. (If you guessed "he didn't receive enough love from his mother," surprise! You would be right.) To do that, he must transfer the love he feels from Glenda, a motherly stand-in he created to cope, onto Barbara, a task that will require her complete acceptance and unconditional love. "It's up to you, Barbara," the doctor tells her. "Love is the only answer. Glenda must be transferred to you." Barbara turns to Glen/da and smiles as she places her hand on his. "I'll do everything I can to make him happy," she tells him, without a thought in her head nor a want in her heart.

After the movie ended, my date and I wandered westward as we got to know each other better, stopping at an unoccupied stoop to make out before we reached the waterfront boardwalk. If you haven't been over to that side of Williamsburg, which when I first moved to Brooklyn looked nothing like its current state, the boardwalk that has since been built looks like, well, a boardwalk, only there's no life to it, no sense of identity like you'd find at Coney Island's or the one at Venice Beach. Walking around the Williamsburg boardwalk feels like walking through a photoshopped rendering of a boardwalk as dreamed up by developers to upcharge their new tenants. I mean, sure, it would probably look amazing in *The Sims,* but in real life the vibes are a bit too uncanny. Still, I can make out with anyone, any place, and this certainly was a place. So we parked ourselves at a picnic table on a patch of grass that lined the boardwalk, at the base of one of the waterfront highrises, with no one around but a group of teens who were smoking by the water. I perched on top of the table, and he leaned in between my legs, wedging himself between my thighs, and started to kiss me again. We'd stop to talk for a bit, and then make out some more, then stop and talk again for a bit, and then make out some more.

During one of those talking breaks, he explained to me the specifics of his particular practice of "ethical non-monogamy," a term that I'd frankly never heard before I started dating straight men. For those of you who might be unfamiliar with the term, it basically means that you're a gay guy over thirty but you're straight and you also could be twenty-six. This particular straight man was married and lived with his wife, but theirs was a marriage of mutual convenience, so their relationship was more like two friends who also happened to be roommates. His actual primary partner was his long-term girlfriend, and everyone involved would date people on the side.

At the time, I was two months out from a devastating breakup and wasn't looking for anything serious. So I set out on what I called my summer of fucking, hoping to find something consistent and intimate where no one got possessive or felt way too committed. What my date was looking for and what I was looking for seemed to be compatible, or at least compatible enough for us to go on a few more dates, so great. Fantastic. My summer of fucking went on.

We kept going back and forth like that, kissing and talking and groping and talking. And then during another one of our talking spells, he asked me about my hormones. What did I take? How long had I been taking them? How did I get them? How did they make me feel? He then started telling me about his relationship to his own gender, adding that he'd been questioning it for a while now and had even started contemplating possibly changing his pronouns. "I haven't told anyone this," he said.

My body tensed up as he spoke—not like in a horror movie, more like in an erotic psychological thriller—as I realized that the cis man who was currently wedged between my thighs probably wasn't actually cis after all. And although he didn't quite know it yet, he probably wouldn't be a man for much longer either.

In the back of my mind, I connected the dots as I pretended to give his confession the attention it deserved. This man didn't want me. He wanted to *be* me. Or, worse: He was looking for a mother, one who could shepherd him into womanhood, under the false pretense of a date. Why else would he be sharing all this with me, a literal stranger, just some random trans bitch that he'd met on an app, before talking about it with his wife or his girlfriend or anyone else in his life? I mean, surely he had friends? Had he specifically sought me out, convinced that I was his key, unwittingly jamming me into his innards in the hope that I'd unlock something buried deep within? This wasn't the first time that some guy I was dating had begun to question his gender after we'd met, and, as I probably could've guessed at the time, it would not be the last. I don't begrudge any of them for transitioning, something that I'd quite literally done myself, but if we're on a date, especially the first or second one, leave me out of your journey! I've journeyed enough! I'm good!

Whatever my date was going through, I had no wish to ferry him through it. All I'd wanted was to go see this deranged movie with some guy I was kind of into and then maybe go back to my place and probably have sex and—

Wait, I realized, as he droned on about his gender trouble. All that could still happen.

Sure, the guy probably wasn't a guy, or at least wouldn't be one for long, but was that really a problem? Did that totally throw off my night? His "journey," as they say, might be taking him somewhere else, somewhere I absolutely didn't want to tag along to, but he hadn't started down that road yet. Besides, I figured, if he was going to use me for my knowledge about hormones and stuff, then I was more than permitted to use him right back, if only for the night. I was Myra Breckinridge, whom no man will ever possess! And whom no man will ever dissuade from still trying to have sex with him just because he's an obvious closet case! So I listened a bit longer, peppered in a "yeah" or "hmm" whenever it felt appropriate to prove I was paying attention, told him what Callen-Lorde was, and then asked him to get us a cab. Was this Glen about to Glenda? It honestly didn't matter. He could find some other woman to take care of that for him—possibly even the one that he might very well turn into.

HUMOR ME

n the wake of the U.S. military's invasion of Afghanistan, the first strike in a twenty-year war that felt distant by design, American tabloid media cooked up something special in a seeming attempt to stave off cravings for class warfare at home.

"Stars—they're just like us!" declared *Us Weekly* in April 2002.

The brainchild of Bonnie Fuller, the magazine's then editor in chief, this new regular feature would take previously unusable paparazzi photos of celebrities doing mundane things and spin them into gold, or at least an additional page or two of printed content, with the goal of showing readers that stars? They're just like them. Marcia Cross eating salad on the set of *Desperate Housewives,* her flaming red hair all pinned up in rollers? "They really love lettuce!" the caption reads. Russell

Crowe getting caught with his finger up his nose? "They pick major boogs!" says another.

Though initially providing a refreshing change of pace from glamorous red-carpet photos and photoshopped magazine covers, this new breed of unmediated celebrity imagery began to look less authentic as its subjects developed a keen awareness for how to use the paparazzi to their advantage. Perhaps the apex of staged celeb candids, or at least my personal favorite, is a series of shots of *Hills* star Heidi Montag in 2008, sitting on what's clearly an indoor dining chair in the middle of a sidewalk, scrunching up her face in a visibly pained expression. She was deftly trying to use the negative reviews that the music video for her debut single had recently received in order to garner sympathy, or at the very least, further notice, a message that the composition of the pictures communicates quite clearly. In one of those pictures, she raises her left hand to her temple as if to cradle her head. In her right hand, she's clutching her own CD, or at least *a* CD standing in for her own. She's like a surged-up Saint Sebastian, wounded but alive.*

These days, the average American is a little wiser to the mechanics of paparazzi trickery. If a celebrity wants us to think they're authentic, they're going to have to give us their blood, sweat, and tears—literally. Their blood. Their sweat. And their tears. Take Bella Hadid, a supermodel who's graced the covers of *Vogue, Elle, W,* and so many others. In November 2021, she shared a carousel of tearstained selfies in an effort to show her Instagram followers that nobody's life is ever as perfect as their

---

* Totally unrelated, but Heidi Montag's 2010 *People* cover story about her "10 Procedures in a Day" plastic surgery experience and its accompanying before-and-after photo spread is one of the greatest, if underdiscussed, moments in ftf (i.e., female-to-female) history.

posts would have you believe. "Social media is not real," she explains in the caption. "Sometimes, all you've gotta hear is that you're not alone. So from me to you, you're not alone. I love you, I see you, and I hear you. Self help and mental illness/chemical imbalance is not linear, and it is almost like a flowing rollercoaster of obstacles . . . it has its ups and downs, and side to sides. But I want you to know, there is always light at the end of the tunnel, and the rollercoaster always comes to a complete stop at some point."

Her words resonated widely, as evidenced by the more than two million likes that the post has since accrued. But I would argue that it was her pictures, rather than her words alone, that really struck a chord with people. Looking at them, her pain is palpable. As she explained in later interviews, she'd started taking pictures of herself in that state in order to show her mom and her doctor, when she couldn't find words to tell them, exactly how much her depression and Lyme disease were affecting her. There's no doubt that her feelings were genuine. Her tears just look too real to fake, unlike those found—or rather, not found—in the myriad YouTube apology videos uploaded over the last decade. Beauty guru Laura Lee posted one such mea culpa in 2018 after fans of a rival content creator resurfaced racist tweets of hers from many years earlier. Lee, who is white, truly looks like she's struggling to conjure up tears in the clip. Her eyes get watery, occasionally a droplet drips past her bottom lash, but if you were to listen to only the audio, you'd think she was gushing waterfalls. Her voice is weak, barely crackling out of her mouth, and she keeps gasping and breathing irregularly as if she's close to breaking down. Through all that, however, her cheeks remain dry. So does her upper lip, which, despite her constant sniffling, is very clearly not pooling with mucus.

There's a certain weight that we ascribe to bodily fluids. To see them leaking out of someone tells us something visceral, something undeniably true, something that the person's words alone could never say half as convincingly. In the age of smartphones and visually driven social media, every piece of content that you scroll past can feel like a lie. Everyone, it seems, is trying to make themselves known through heavily curated images and tightly crafted narratives, even when their audience is just their friends and family. I'll occasionally stumble on a video where the creator says something like "Get ready with me while I do my makeup," only to realize that they've only got about two dozen likes and maybe a hundred followers. They have the influencer lilt down, but who are they even doing it for? And how would they deal if their nose started bleeding in the middle of that unbeheld Live? What if they suddenly projectile vomited, pissed or shit themselves, or spontaneously came?

Bodily fluids are humbling because they can betray us without warning. Their presence, like sweating when you're nervous or pissing yourself in fear, can expose our most shameful truths to others. They can also, in their absence, reveal things about us we'd rather hide, like a total lack of remorse by way of failing to shed actual tears. We know this as viewers, so we look for these telltale signs, whether or not we know it. Anyone can say that they're sorry, that they're in pain, but how can you be sure, if words are all you have to go by? If you don't see the tears or the blood for yourself? Are they really all that sick if they're not doubled over and vomiting? Is she really having an orgasm if you never see her squirt? There's a reason that straight women have gotten into asking for a "nut video with sound on," a popular shitpost from the early 2020s that reflects a broader desire. A nut video says more than a mere dick pic ever could. It speaks volumes, in fact, even with the sound off.

There's something nostalgically humoral about this worship of bodily fluids. Humorism, also known as humoral theory, was a system of medicine attributed to ancient Greek philosophers like Hippocrates and Galen that flourished in the Middle Ages. Doctors throughout much of the medieval world—from Western Asia to North Africa and Europe—viewed a healthy body as one that had balanced humors: blood, phlegm, yellow bile, and black bile. Each of these humors, in turn, corresponded to a different element—fire, water, earth, and air—and a different combination of properties—hot and wet, cold and wet, cold and dry, and hot and dry. Humoral theory also gave rise to the practice of phlebotomy, also known as bloodletting, which involved making small incisions at various parts of the body in order to relieve a diseased individual of whichever humoral surplus was said to be causing their ailment. Further signs of physical imbalance were even said to be evident in excretions like vomit, saliva, sweat, and feces.

Humorism was appealing at least in part for its ability to provide comforting, teleological answers for its devotees and practitioners, appearing to explain both the roots of otherwise unknowable diseases as well as give reason for one's bigotry and bias. On that latter point, for example, men's bodies were thought to be naturally hotter than women's, which explained why men were bigger and hairier: Heat makes hair grow. Their logic, not mine. Men were also said to be better at self-regulating the inevitable humoral buildup because they sweat and ejaculate so much. Women were therefore smaller, smoother, and weaker on average on account of their naturally frigid natures, and because of their inferior capacity for self-regulation, they had to menstruate every month to purge their excess humors.

My apologies to all the giant, hairy, cum-happy women and tender, fragile, menstruating men reading this, not to mention all the humorally ambiguous genderfuckers in between. Again, to all this I repeat: It's their logic, not mine.

Anyway, Middle Eastern doctors thought that northwestern Europeans were pale on account of their various humoral failings. "The warm humour is lacking among them," reasoned Abu al-Hasan al-Masudi, a tenth-century geographer and historian born in Baghdad. "Their bodies are large, their natures gross, their manners harsh, their understanding dull, and their tongues heavy," al-Masudi continued. "Their color is so excessively white that it passes from white to blue." Later, this supposed humoral dearth served to explain the Christian Crusaders' purported cowardice on the battlefield, as they were thought to be colder and therefore more feminine and fragile under their armor. Europeans in turn agreed that their Muslim enemies during the Crusades were undeniably hotter than them, humorally speaking, though they put their own self-serving, proto-eugenicist spin on it. They blamed this humoral difference on their belief that Arabs had too much blood in their veins, which resulted in not only their darker skin tones but also their allegedly violent disposition. Europeans using racism to excuse their global terrorism? Shocking, I know.

This was obviously all bullshit—well, obvious to us in the present—but that didn't stop doctors from practicing humoral theory well into the Enlightenment, with bloodletting carrying on for another few hundred years. Jack Hartnell, the author of *Medieval Bodies: Life and Death in the Middle Ages,* attributes the field's decline to two key factors: the broadening of medical and pharmaceutical knowledge, plundered through colonization, and advances in experimental chemistry made by the sixteenth-century Swiss physician Paracelsus and others. But echoes of humorist logic can still be heard today. Take Hadid's line about "chemical imbalance" when talking about mental health. Despite the widespread belief that depression is caused by deficits of serotonin and other neural transmitters, most scientists and doctors, and that includes psychiatrists, now view this as a discredited theory, or an oversimplification at best; brain structure and function, disturbances in neural circuitry, day-to-day stressors, and other psychological factors are all believed to affect one's propensity for depression just as much as, if not more than, neurotransmitter abnormalities. According to P. E. Moskowitz, a journalist who often writes about mental healthcare in the United States, the main proponents of the chemical imbalance model aren't medical providers but the American public, whose entire understanding of psychiatric issues is most immediately informed by advertising, not medical research. "While the cause [of depression] is unknown, depression may be related to an imbalance of natural chemicals between nerve cells in the brain," says one TV commercial. "Prescription Zoloft works to correct this imbalance."

In my view, this idea of the chemical balance has caught on because it works quite well as a metaphor, one that's helpful in describing whatever intangible psychological problems that one might be grappling with. When most people use this language, I don't think they literally mean that they're missing some kind of brain fluid. Nor do I think that they're stupid for doing so. (In the words of Lisa Simpson, it's apt. Apt!) Still, I find it interesting to note the similarities between contemporary discourses around mental health and the concept of treating imbalances that once undergirded humoral theory, as well as other lingering traces buried deep within our psyches.

In the fourth episode of *Love & Death*—HBO's dramatized true-crime miniseries about Candy Montgomery, the Texan housewife who, in 1981, was accused of murdering the wife of the man she'd been sleeping with—Candy, played by Elizabeth Olsen, is driving to church, trying to summon a façade of suburban normalcy mere hours after killing her neighbor. That façade shatters when she glances in her rearview mirror and sees a spot of blood dripping from a wound just behind her hairline, which she sustained in the struggle. "No, no, no," she mutters anxiously as she wipes it away with her fingers, knowing that the sight of it will give her away to her fellow churchgoers. Not as a murderer, per se, but as someone worth talking about, a ready-made topic of neighborhood gossip. "Please, please, please, please, please." She adjusts her bangs and covers up the evidence that something about her ain't right, and when she greets the other moms at church, no one suspects a thing.

The idea that our fluids might reveal something about us that we'd rather keep hidden from view, that a truth we've kept secret might literally leak out of us, is another vestige of humorism that has lived on, into the present. Looking beyond ourselves, we often tend to hold subconscious expectations of others' bodily fluids and their ability, or inability, to properly retain them. Think back to that viral video first uploaded to YouTube as early as 2021 that appears to depict a British police officer caught upside down on a wrought iron fence. His pants are down, or rather up, bunched around his ankles, and in the center of his exposed tighty-whities lies a big brown stain—an unmistakable skid mark. Though the video was actually staged as a prank on unsuspecting passersby, many of us might jump to believe it as real, as it confirms what we already think about cops: that they're rotted to their core and disgusting inside and out. Ergo, it's unsurprising. Look, a pig caught playing in shit.

A more sinister example can be found in legislation that would criminalize people living with HIV for the simple fact of their status. To this day, twenty-five states still have laws on the books that threaten seropositive individuals with fines and even jail time for allegedly exposing others to their bodily fluids. Some of those laws even explicitly name saliva as one of those dangerous fluids, despite the fact that it's literally impossible to transmit the virus that way, per the Centers for Disease Control and Prevention. The actual facts of HIV transmission matter less to the criminal justice system than does the widespread stigma attached to those who have HIV, whose perceived immorality and criminality is believed to be so intrinsic that it's found in their blood, spit, and semen, waiting to seep out and infect the rest of us too.

We hold certain humoral expectations of others just as they hold them about us. We can prove that we're fit by snapping a sweaty selfie in the mirror at the gym. We can prove that we're hurt, perhaps even that we were attacked, by capturing our wounds before the blood dries. We can prove that we're aroused or that we've just climaxed by photographing our fluids. In recent years, men, or at least those men who like women, have become obsessed with female ejaculation of all kinds. They've always lusted after trans women's ejaculate, of course; I've heard many an anecdote over the years about sex workers tweaking their hormone regimens in order to give clients and videographers the exact kind of high-flying, milky-white cum shot that they know will be expected of them. But as online video-streaming technology and cellphone cameras have advanced, so too have straight men increasingly wanted cis women to throw them into the splash zone, at least if Pornhub's data on search trends are to be believed. According to the X-rated video-streaming platform's report on 2021 trends, the UK saw a nearly 200 percent increase in searches for squirting videos, while an even bigger jump was observed among French users, and the term "squirt" was one of the platform's top twenty most-searched words among American users. Is this some modern-day expression of the age-old misogynist anxiety that women are deceptive, in this case, faking our orgasms? Or are they drawn to the supposed humiliation of watching us lose control? Maybe I'm overthinking it. Maybe they just like looking at cum. Or maybe they want a show, and now the technology's there to give it to them.

The technology has also unfortunately advanced to the point that this show can be stolen from us, with certain corners of the internet brimming with hacked nudes and revenge porn. Even our celebrities are not immune from such violent acts, as photographic proof is leaked to the public that they, too, drip and ooze and spill. In some sick way, it's like their seeping fluids humanize them for us. They evince a shared humanity and theoretical equality of being, and we're willing to dehumanize those same celebs in order to make that known. As the tabloids would say, they get digitally victimized! Stars—they're just like us.

LOST IN SPACE

As construction began on Palazzo Chupi in the fall of 2005, some of its soon-to-be neighbors picketed on the sidewalk outside, bearing signs that decried its owner and called for an end to such "monuments to greed." Julian Schnabel, the famed artist and filmmaker, had scooped up the Manhattan property for more than $2 million in 1997 with plans to build skyward, high above the many townhouses that lined the surrounding blocks. Eight years later, he set his plans in motion, transforming the old factory building that he'd bought, itself a former stable, into the bottom four floors of the rosy-pink villa that towers over the West Village today.

The hostile reception from some local residents hurt Schnabel's feelings. "In principle the protesters are right," he said at the time, "but they are wrong about me and this building." Not everyone hated Palazzo Chupi, of course. Paul Rudnick, a novelist and playwright who lived in the neighborhood, was one such vocal fan. "Personally, I adore it," he told *The New York Times* in 2008, by which time two of the property's five palatial units had sold for more than $12 million apiece— a staggering number, though far below the $24 million asking price on another of the remaining duplexes. "It's much more in the tradition of the West Village, which is supposed to be outrageous and theatrical, than all those glass towers," Rudnick continued, in reference to other new buildings in the neighborhood. "When the transsexuals left it seems they were reincarnated as real estate. At least the Palazzo does them proud."

But the transsexuals he spoke of had not simply left. They were, more accurately, forced out. "We were pushed out of the neighborhood years ago, and now you don't see us here anymore," says filmmaker Kristen Lovell in *The Stroll*, her 2023 documentary, in collaboration with Zackary Drucker, about the displacement of trans sex workers from the area. "I just can't believe how many times I had to go to jail for this Highline Park to be built," she adds later, in reference to a popular tourist attraction built atop an old railway.

In the film, Lovell describes how awed she was the first time that she visited the titular Stroll, then found in the Meatpacking District, a short walk north from Schnabel's palazzo. "It felt like [there were] hundreds of trans women out there," she says in the film. "It was just amazing to see strong Black trans women," people like her, whom the rest of society would've rather kept hidden. Sex work was one of the only ways that trans women could make money at the time—as opposed to now, when it's simply one of our most reliable sources of income; one option among many, at least for some of us, though regardless of our options, it usually pays the most. "Unless you had your ID changed, your social security card, you could not just walk into a place and get a job," says Egyptt LaBeija, the Overall Godmother of ballroom's legendary House of LaBeija, in an interview from the film. "Some people choose sex work because they want to. Some people choose it because they have no choice. A lot of us back then did not have that choice, because jobs were not accessible to us."

Some of those other transsexuals, the ones allegedly "reincarnated as real estate," had been living on the dilapidated piers jutting out into the Hudson River, a longtime refuge where queer New Yorkers could cruise, gather, and trick in relative seclusion—relative being the key word. "It's dangerous everywhere," concedes author and activist Leslie Feinberg in filmmaker Alisa Lebow's 1994 documentary, *Outlaw*. "But we've got to go somewhere. I don't think the piers are dangerous because we go there. I think where we go becomes dangerous, you know? Where people know they can go to find us is dangerous because that's where we go to find each other." By the 1990s, encampments had formed on the piers, even some multiroom shelters. Some residents lived there long-term, while others only came when they had nowhere else to sleep. There are "social penalties" for being trans, Feinberg explains at a later point in Lebow's documentary. Zie is standing on the New Jersey side of the Hudson beside hir spouse, the poet Minnie Bruce Pratt, as they face the New York skyline. "And some of those social penalties have been carried out right across this river on the Hudson piers."

Police had always been a fixture of the area, sometimes as arresting officers and other times as johns. But after former mayor Rudy Giuliani took office in 1994, the New York City

Police Department, under its newly appointed commissioner William Bratton, cracked down on the Stroll, ramping up arrests in the name of law and order. Prior to his appointment to the NYPD, Bratton had served as chief of the city's Transit Police, where, fueled by the now-discredited "broken windows" theory—which frames minor infractions like graffiti and litter as laying the foundation for far more serious urban crime—he increased the number of arrests for fare beating and other misdemeanors fivefold. With Giuliani's blessing, Bratton took that approach aboveground. Being "the window-dressing of social decay," as the poet Kay Gabriel once wrote, "a metonym for public space seductively in crisis," transsexuals were deemed a threat to public safety—but whose safety? And which public? The displacement of trans sex workers could not have occurred without the tacit support of the wealthier new property owners moving into the area. Some homeowners banded together to engage in a campaign of organized harassment, even picketing the sex workers on at least one occasion—the one thing the transsexuals do have in common with Palazzo Chupi, I guess. Some of those newcomers were the real-world counterparts to *Sex and the City*'s Samantha Jones, who once complained to her friends over brunch that she was "paying a fortune to live in a neighborhood that's trendy by day and tranny by night." As seen in Lovell's documentary, *The Stroll*, the residents of one block even hanged an effigy of a trans sex worker by the neck with HOOKER scrawled across its stomach. The message was clear: Transsexuals? Out.

In 1998, the city privatized the West Side waterfront, and the area became even more hostile to the trans people who'd been coming there for years, as well as and especially to those who lived on the streets. The city ceded control to an organization funded by neighboring property owners, which demolished some of the piers while preserving others for renovation. The group shut down some of the existing public bathrooms, put up new gates, and imposed stricter curfews, which destroyed the encampments once and for all.

One individual who called the piers home for many years was Sylvia Rivera, the liberationist movement leader who spent her life fighting for the unhoused and incarcerated. Another was Egyptt LaBeija, who shares a bit of that experience in *Atlantic Is a Sea of Bones,* a 2017 short film by the artist and activist Tourmaline. "I literally lived on that pier that's no longer there," she says in the opening scene. She's standing by the window of a nearby building as she looks out on the Hudson. "See that last one that's no longer [there]?" She points down to the empty waters where Pier 54 once stood. "I lived on there."

Pier 54 was demolished after Hurricane Sandy left it irreparably damaged in 2012. The waters in which it stood remained empty for many years, save for the crumbling wooden columns that had once held it aloft. Little Island, a floating island park, has since emerged in its place, replete with an amphitheater, vendor stalls, a playground for kids, and a gender-neutral bathroom. It closes to visitors at night, a rule that, like many of the city's urban planning decisions in recent years, seems designed at least in part to prevent unhoused New Yorkers from finding refuge there, just as those people later "reincarnated as real estate" once did on the piers. One borough over, on Brooklyn's remodeled northern waterfront, stands Marsha P. Johnson State Park, named for the artist and organizer who, along with Rivera, co-founded the Street Transvestite Action Revolutionaries, a collective that housed and provided for many of the city's unwanted trans youth in the early 1970s. Much like

Little Island, Marsha P. Johnson State Park also closes at night. Violating that rule risks a $50 fine, which jumps to $250 if one also erects a shelter.

The "Pier History" tab on Little Island's website describes how Pier 54 had once been "a safe haven" for queer and trans New Yorkers, one where "they could openly socialize without fear of harassment and discrimination." It's a touching story, but as a history, it's thoroughly revisionist, ironically celebrating the idea that trans women once gathered on that pier after every effort was made—by the city, by police, by neighboring property owners—to force them out of the area. The site similarly notes how the Lenape once used this land as a seasonal encampment for hunting and fishing "during the early colonization of America," without quite spelling out why that came to an end.

The idea of a trans woman is always easier to stomach than the actual transsexual herself, what with all her wants and needs, however inconvenient they might be. The idea of her, however, can be anything you want it to be: a legacy to celebrate; a walking broken window. She's got more faces than Janus and more forms than Meredith Brooks. She's somehow every woman yet often not a woman at all.

• • •

Panic and unrest gripped the Michigan Womyn's Music Festival as claims of a penis sighting swept through the camps.

The year was 1999, and the festival, held every August since 1976, had once again brought thousands of women to camp out together in a remote wooded corner of the Upper Midwest. Having grown out of the lesbian separatist womyn's land movement of a bygone era—which, at its height two decades prior, had amounted to about 150 or so intentional communities scattered throughout rural pockets of the United States—MichFest, as it was called, aimed to allow its female attendees to escape the patriarchy for one week out of the year, communing with one another without men or boys present. While lesbian-centered, the festival was not oriented toward lesbians exclusively, but founder Lisa Vogel did intend for it to be a women-only space, though not one that welcomed all women. After years of pushback over the festival's quieter exclusion of trans women, explosively culminating in the eviction of Nancy Jean Burkholder from the grounds in 1991, Vogel clarified that by "womyn," she meant "womyn-born-womyn," by which she meant cis women—not that any of the cis women who went to MichFest in those earlier decades would have called themselves "cis," even by the time of the great penis sighting of 1999. It would take another decade for the term to even gain traction among trans people, who had previously described their cisgender sisters as being "non-trans," "GGs" ("genetic girls" or "genuine girls"), and "bio girls" (and its variant, "bio women").

Despite the so-called "intention" for the space, trans women had been going to MichFest since its inception.* They weren't

---

* And trans women continued to go to MichFest every year, even after the 1991 ban. Bryn Kelly, the late writer and onetime Camp Trans organizer, once wrote that she felt both welcome and unwelcome when she went to MichFest in 2008. With respect to that latter experience, she explained that it could've been due to her transness or to the fact that she was there with her butch partner, and "many Fest-goers don't approve of butch-femme relationships." The couple received the occasional "stank-eye," but "for every nasty look we got (and really, there weren't that many) we got just as many 'Hey sisters! Welcome home!' enthusiastic greetings. There are a lot of women who love that land and are effusively welcoming, especially of newcomers." Still, she said she wouldn't go back. "There are just other ways I'd rather spend my time and energy," she wrote. "Take a look at newsletters in the Lesbian Herstory Archives in Park Slope, and you will see that we have been having these exact same arguments about [trans women's inclusion at the festival] for the last thirty years."

alone in their transgression. "Intersexuals, FTMs, [and] lezzie boyz" could also be spotted, as activist and author Riki Wilchins once explained in a 1999 interview with the radical trans newsletter *In Your Face*. The problem, she continued, was that "no one felt safe to do so openly," likening the unspoken dynamics of their exclusion from the Land, as the festival grounds were called, to the U.S. military's since-repealed "don't ask, don't tell" policy, which forced gay and lesbian service members to remain closeted or else be dishonorably discharged.

Knowledge of this de facto ban was enough to discourage many trans women from going to MichFest, Wilchins went on to say, just as similarly exclusionary politics had discouraged them from finding lesbian community in the world beyond the Land. Given all that, I was both surprised and heartened to learn that MichFest's attendees, if not its founder, were far more welcoming of trans women's inclusion than I would have assumed: A survey conducted during the 1992 festival found that out of 633 respondents, 463 of them (73.1 percent) believed that "male-to-female transsexuals should be welcome at Michigan," while only 143 (22.6 percent) did not; some voted no because, in their words, trans women "have been socialized as males" and "have male energy"; others voted no on the grounds that "they have penises," while still others objected to trans women's presence because "they are too feminine." (And they say that a woman *can't* have it all.)*

---

* This survey was actually organized by Janis Walworth, a friend of a friend of Nancy Jean Burkholder, the trans woman expelled the year prior. "Janis organized a bunch of people to go back in 1992," Burkholder says in Michelle Tea's "Transmissions From Camp Trans," which appears in the poet and writer's 2018 anthology, *Against Memoir: Complaints, Confessions & Criticisms*. "She brought her sister, a male-to-female postoperative transsexual, and also an intersex person and a butch female. They distributed buttons and leaflets and did a survey. The survey indicated that seventy-two percent approved of transsexuals being at the festival. Twenty-three percent did not, for a variety of reasons."

That on-the-ground support unfortunately never prompted a change in policy, however, so every transsexual who went to MichFest remained at risk of expulsion, just as Burkholder had once been forced to leave simply for being a trans woman—or "a known transsexual man," as Vogel described her in a public statement released at the time. The MichFest founder's choice of words recall those found in a bluntly transmisogynistic open letter that she signed in 1977, which sought to pressure the women's music collective Olivia Records into dropping Sandy Stone, a recording engineer better known today for her contributions to the academic field of transgender studies.

Those who disagreed with MichFest's exclusionary practices were split on how to proceed. Should all trans women be allowed on the Land, or only those who've had bottom surgery? What about trans men, especially those who'd participated in lesbian community for years, even decades, before they transitioned? Could those men who wished to do so be admitted as "womyn" too?

Discussions gave way to action, and in 1994, Camp Trans, a smaller festival of nearly thirty people, including Feinberg, Wilchins, and others, was held right across the road from MichFest, in protest of the latter's exclusion of trans women. It returned five years later, in 1999, campily redubbed as Son of Camp Trans. As part of its protest against MichFest's trans-exclusionary practices, a dozen Camp Trans activists wearing shirts that said TRANSEXUAL MENACE, the name of a then-active coalition of trans rights organizers, purchased festival tickets and entered the campgrounds, escorted by more than two dozen supporters, per Wilchins's account: a mix of "lezzie boyz, [Lesbian] Avengers, and leatherwomen." Some experienced immediate hostility. Wilchins, for example, has said that two women followed their crew for over a mile yelling, "Man on the Land!" every couple of minutes. Others didn't personally encounter much conflict over the mere fact of their presence. One trans woman, known only as "Michelle," said that her TRANSEXUAL MENACE T-shirt actually helped spur many constructive conversations with other festival attendees, who were themselves open to if not fully supportive of trans women's inclusion at MichFest.

Within hours, however, chaos erupted. Word spread that a group of "men" had invaded the outdoor showers, waving their exposed, erect penises at the women in their vicinity. I use quotation marks around the word "men" because, again, in Vogelspeak, "men" could have meant actual men as much as it could have meant trans women. It's all very squares and rectangles. Like, yes, squares are understood to be a type of rectangle, but that's only because of transphobia. Anyway, by noon, rumors that a group of men had been seen terrorizing women in the shower stalls had reached the main dining area, where Wilchins and others were "verbally assaulted" with cries of "Men, get out!" and "Penises off the land!"

There had, in fact, been at least one transsexual man showering at the same time as female attendees, but that transsexual man was just that: a literal transsexual man, one who happened to have undergone phalloplasty. By his own account, he had asked every woman present for permission to shower before he did so, including the nearby MichFest staff members, who had all given him their blessing. Furthermore, he was hidden behind a shower curtain for most of the time that he was nude, only briefly walking naked from one shower stall to another, after a neighboring woman had noticed that his hot water wasn't working and invited him to use hers.

So, how did the transmisogynistic fearmongering begin? It's simple: A transphobic individual saw a trans man and mistook him for a trans woman, and a violent one at that. It's a familiar narrative, one that exploits both our hypervisibility and the utter erasure of trans men from the broader cultural grammar in order to frame trans women as uniquely threatening to every cis woman and girl. For a more recent example, take the infamous photo of Mack Beggs, the one that shows the former high school wrestler pinning a teenage girl to the mat. The picture, taken in 2018, frequently goes viral in reactionary circles eager to believe the lie that "transgender males"—that is, trans girl athletes—are "just boys beating up on girls" in order to steal their scholarships. Now in his twenties, Beggs was indeed a boy wrestling against girls. (And beating them too; he won the Texas girls' class 6A 110-pound division state title in both 2017 and 2018.) But he was a *trans* boy, specifically—a literal transgender boy who'd transitioned from female to male—wrestling against female athletes solely because they shared the same sex assigned at birth, and only because the state had forced him to, having barred him from wrestling against other boys. But what good is a trans boy or a trans man when he could be a violent trans woman instead. And by a trans woman, I just mean a man—and by man, I mean violence incarnate. A penis. A rapist. A threat to womankind. How do we always cast a shadow even when we're not in the room? And why, even when they box with our shadows, are we still the ones getting bruised?

• • •

The first time that I met Cecilia Gentili was in the backyard of a house where some mutual friends lived. I, of course, already

knew who she was; you really would've had to go out of your
way as a trans woman in New York City in the mid-to-late
2010s to not know who Cecilia Gentili was. She was the activist I'd often see speaking at rallies, the charismatic storyteller
I'd sometimes catch at readings, the lady from Apicha's trans
health clinic who'd given half my friends hormones—she even
had a recurring role on the FX ballroom drama *Pose,* playing a
shady black-market silicone injector who helps the girls get rid
of a dead body.

When I realized that she was standing beside me, both of us
shielding our eyes as we stared up at the abandoned church
looming over us in the neighboring lot, I racked my brain for
something to say. She was really that magnetic, that through
her very presence you felt compelled to speak with her, as if
not letting the opportunity pass you by were a matter of life or
death. I told her that some of the other people who'd come to
this all-trans potluck at our friends' house had climbed over
the fence to explore the inside of the church. She continued to
gaze at the church, too lost in thought to respond. "It's so
sad," she said in breaking her silence. "People could live
there." And with a crick of the monkey's paw, now people
do—in a brand-new condo building built over where the
church once stood. Not quite what she meant, I don't think.

That was Cecilia, always thinking of others, often to a fault,
even on that Sunday when she didn't have to be working,
when she could've just been kicking back in the sun with a
bunch of her friends, a watermelon cocktail in one hand and a
tofu scramble in the other. Her tenacity and selflessness are
unmissable in the legacy she left behind. She led the fight to
repeal the infamous "walking while trans" law, which had
greatly contributed to police harassment against trans women
of color in the city. She also grew the Apicha Community

Health Center's fledgling trans health program from a handful of patients to more than five hundred by the time she took a new job as the policy director at GMHC, where she played a key role in the passage of New York's Gender Expression Non-Discrimination Act. She created the COIN Clinic, a free healthcare program for sex workers run out of the Callen-Lorde Community Health Center, sued the Trump administration for attempting to dismantle trans healthcare protections and won, and achieved countless other wins for all her communities: trans people, Latinas, sex workers, immigrants, people of color, artists, and so many more.

At her memorial in 2024, following her sudden death at the age of fifty-two,* I remember one of her close friends talking about how giving Cecilia was, that she literally gave this friend one of her chairs after hearing the friend say that she liked it. So many others shared similar stories about her endless generosity that night, as well as at her wake and her funeral over the course of the week that followed. She gave people money, clothing, food, a place to sleep—anything she could, even back when she didn't have much. It made me think about the time when she'd invited me over to her place in South Brooklyn, where she lived with her kind and devoted partner of many years, Peter. She made dinner for us, a delicious hearty pasta paired with a few rounds of pint-size cocktails, and then insisted on calling me a cab home, despite my repeated protestations that I lived too far north. She was more than what she did for me and what she did for others, but still it must be said: She truly did so much.

Every time I spoke with her, she made me feel so special. I don't know that I'll ever again feel as beautiful as I felt the

---

* Did you gasp? Cecilia would be furious if you didn't gasp. I mean, google her and tell me she looked anywhere near fifty-two!

times she greeted me with "Bitch! You look so *fucking* hot!" When she called you bitch or she called you a whore, "it meant she loved you," as the poet Kay Gabriel shared at Cecilia's memorial. She was a mother to Kay, as she was to many others—artists and organizers like Río Sofia and Gia Love, the fashion designer Gogo Graham, and the drag performer Chiquitita among them—but to me, she was my friend, one I only really got to know over the last couple of years of her life. I'm still bitter that we didn't have more time together, that our friendship ended when it did, just as I'm angry at how she was cheated out of the next few decades of her life, just when she really seemed to be entering her prime. She'd published her first book, the unthinkably hilarious survivor memoir *Faltas: Letters to Everyone in My Hometown Who Isn't My Rapist,* in 2021, and had planned to write at least two follow-ups: one about her years as a transsexual sex worker after moving to Rosario, in her native Argentina, and another about her life after moving to the United States in the early 2000s. *Faltas* won a Stonewall Book Award and earned plenty of deserved acclaim, though Cecilia told me that a lot of readers didn't get the humor, probably because it had the word "rapist" in the title, so she reworked some of those stories, as well as many others, into her next one-woman show, *Red Ink,* which ran off-Broadway in 2023. Her social life was thriving, her professional life even more so, though she was really making an effort to say yes to fewer work commitments, to stop spreading herself as thin as she had been over the past decade and a half. She was insecure about feeling behind in life, she told me, and was anxious to catch up now that she had the chance. "Some of my friends built their own legal practices or bought homes or had families and kids. I just kind of, like, survived. That's productive, right? But how we measure things like productivity or risk as trans people is different than it is for cis people," she told me once. "That's where that idea came from, that I'm making up for those twenty years where I just survived. It's why I have this extremely chaotic life where I can't say no to anything. Every opportunity is an opportunity I'm grateful to have because I didn't have any for a long time."

In writing about Cecilia, I feel pulled in three directions. I want to emphasize how exceptional she was by highlighting all that she accomplished for herself and for her communities. At the same time, I don't want to exceptionalize her, as doing so carries with it the implication that any of us should aim to do less, simply because we'll never be her. I also don't want to urge us all to model our lives after hers exactly, given how little time and care she often reserved for herself and how little she would have wanted us to do that to ourselves. There's no universal lesson to draw from Cecilia because she wasn't a lesson—she was Cecilia. Politicians like Kathy Hochul and Alexandria Ocasio-Cortez found it easy to cherry-pick those parts of her legacy that served their respective agendas in drafting public statements issued shortly after her death—that she was a trans icon, that she was an artist and activist—while omitting those seemingly unsavory bits that they'd rather not call out by name, like the fact that she'd been arrested only a few months before while protesting Israel's siege on Gaza. They also both failed to mention that Cecilia was a sex worker, or that for years she'd been a leader in the fight to decriminalize that labor—omissions that exemplify the central thesis of Jules Gill-Peterson's *A Short History of Trans Misogyny,* that transness is only made palatable by rejecting transsexual sex workers. We don't have to, though. We can hold on to that complexity, Cecilia's as well as our own and each other's. We can refuse any effort to box her in, this woman who never wanted to be anything less than everything she possibly could be.

It was a limitlessness that most others in her hometown of Gálvez denied her when she was growing up. Her grandmother, thankfully, wasn't among them. As Cecilia recounted in one of her stories that she used to perform live, which she adapted in part for one of the chapters in *Faltas*, she became convinced when she was younger that she must be an alien from another planet, stranded on Earth, as a way of trying to understand why she thought she was a girl. "Hmm, that makes sense. I am pretty sure you are from another planet," her grandmother told her. "For the time being, just stay with us and try to make the best out of it . . . I am sure that one day, you will find a planet where everybody is like you and where you feel totally at home." That happened for her, Cecilia explained, once she moved to New York in 2004. "I met such an amazing group of people—of trans people, immigrants, sex workers. All of those people became my community, and my community became that planet where I feel at home, where I feel understood, where I feel like I'm OK, where I feel like I'm taken care of."

VALIDITY

What are childless women to do in a society that expects them to become mothers? "Just One of the Guys," the lead single off of Jenny Lewis's second solo album, *The Voyager*, explores this anxiety, one that is all too familiar for so many women.

Released in June 2014, the song tends to the ache of alienation that one might feel upon becoming, as per the bridge, just another lady without a baby. It's not necessarily about how Lewis herself wants to have kids or that she regrets not having them; despite also being middle-aged and childless, Lewis's in-song narrator is not a direct stand-in for the singer-songwriter herself, as she once clarified in an interview conducted some years later: "My songs aren't the paper of record. There's a lot of wiggle room in there." It's more that she, and her narrator, must reckon with who they are after having withstood the immense societal pressure to become mothers, as do all women who don't have children, regardless of whether they wanted to become mothers or even had much of a say in the matter.

But that is only one of the ways to understand Jenny Lewis's "Just One of the Guys." Another read, and my own personal favorite, would unnecessarily and pedantically reframe the track as an entirely self-contained text of gender theory, one that almost perfectly maps onto our reality, if not quite our reality as we understand it. For just as there are "at least three" genders in the world, as President Joe Biden explained that one time someone asked him, for some reason, how many genders there were,* there are at least three distinct gendered categories that Lewis explicitly names in the lyrics to "Just One of the Guys." They are, in order of appearance: the girls, the guys, and the ladies without babies.

My deepest apologies to the nonbinary community, but as far as Lewis's song is concerned, those are your options— you've got to pick one.

What do we know about these three genders? Further reading of the lyrics certainly elucidates that which the ladies without babies are not. They're not girls, for one, because the girls, like the so-called child bride on a summer vacation who is dating one of the guys, stay forever young. So if the girls stay young, and the ladies without babies are decidedly not the girls, then the ladies without babies must, by definition, get older. They must age. They must decay. They must die and disappear. They yearn for the guys, who then spurn them for the girls, as well as for another as-yet-undiscussed group. For

---

* Honestly, the only time I'd ever willingly "hand it to Biden." I mean, he's right! There are literally at least three!

while Lewis explicitly names three distinct gendered categories over the course of the song, one could argue that there is a fourth gender that she implies, though leaves unnamed. For if there exist ladies *without* babies, then that would suggest the existence of ladies *with* babies. Why else would This Song's Narrator, hereafter referred to as T. S. Narrator, feel compelled to specify that which the ladies without babies lack, if not to distinguish the ladies *without* babies from some unspecified other? Why wouldn't she just say ladies? It takes more time to say "ladies without babies," and time is famously money—though, maybe it isn't in the world of Lewis's song? But back to the point: the ladies.

As you can see, Lewis's insistence on saying "ladies *without babies*" raises more questions than it answers—for example, these ones: What if, perhaps, the ladies *without* babies and the ladies *with* babies are not discrete genders unto themselves? What if they are actually two different subgroups of the *same* gender, that gender being ladies, full stop? By that logic, babies would therefore be more of an accessory to gender, a means of differentiating one kind of lady from another, like implants and Airwraps and ejaculating strap-ons. Having made that clarification, however, our gender count would still clock in at three: the girls, the guys, and the ladies, full stop.

Again, dear reader, you must choose from only the aforementioned genders. If you do not do so in a timely manner, one will be assigned to you by the person to your right. In the case that there is no person to your right who can decide your gender for you, just ask the little cop inside you, the very same one that T. S. Narrator sings about in the last chorus of "Just One of the Guys." He should be able to clear that up.

Returning to the thread, now that we have identified the probable existence of ladies, full stop, as well as the ladies with babies, even more questions remain. Who are these ladies? And what do they want? And where did their babies come from?

No, really. I'm asking. The song doesn't say how.

My research into the subject has led me to conclude that such neonatal acquisitions are somehow facilitated by the partnerships formed between the ladies with babies and the guys. Which, speaking of the guys, who are the guys? We know that the guys are not the girls, and we know that they're not ladies of any kind, and we know this because T. S. Narrator is, by her own telling, just another lady without a baby—which, as we've already established, is a kind of lady, full stop. Furthermore, it is precisely because she is just another lady without a baby that she cannot be just one of the guys, no matter how hard she tries—again, by her own telling. As a woman of academe, I do have to wonder, how hard is she actually trying? Because being just one of the guys doesn't sound all that hard, at least not according to Lewis's lyrics. One simply inserts oneself into a group of guys, then cycles through girls in rapid succession until one finds a girl with whom one could build a life—which is to say, have a baby—thereby remolding that girl into a lady, and a lady with a baby, specifically. How does a girl become a lady, trading eternal youth for a guy, a baby, and death's sweet release? In order for this to be possible, the three distinct gendered categories—the girls, the guys, and the ladies, full stop—would need to share mutable borders, thus allowing the girls to become ladies, the ladies to become guys, and the guys to become girls. Unthinkable, I know.

So, then, if T. S. Narrator is trying very hard to be just one of the guys, and the line between their genders is at least somewhat permeable, why does she not simply become just one of the guys? My theory is that this is because she does not want to be just one of the guys. Even if she were trying as hard as she claims to be trying—to be just one of the guys, that is—we, dear reader, should not mistake effort for genuine desire. As I see it, her attempts at acting like just one of the guys are a maladaptive concession to her own perceived failure—an expression of the cognitive dissonance that plagues her every waking moment. Her stated desire to be just one of the guys is but a cover for her true desire, which, at the risk of conjecture, is to become a different kind of lady. Being a lady without a baby is a life she lives by default. T. S. Narrator would rather have a baby instead. Since she is not a lady with a baby and cannot conceive of a way in which she might, well, conceive one, she lives out her days in a state of denial, confronting her lack in brief spurts of lucidity that leave her questioning whether she's even a lady, full stop, at all.

STERILITY

Most of the trees had stopped bearing fruit or were otherwise already stripped bare. They say that September is the best time of the year to go apple picking, but time had not been on our side when we set out to plan our big Sunday outing upstate. If we'd had other options, Hugo and I would not have chosen to give our tumultuous, passionate, on-again, off-again relationship yet another go in the middle of October, well after the plumpest, reddest apples had all been plucked by wiser apple pickers. But the middle of October was when our latest reconciliation had taken place. We needed to do something fast to prove to ourselves, and also to Instagram, that not only were we back on and that our love was for real, but that ours was a love for the ages.

Scanning the trees as we walked farther into the orchard, we finally found signs of life: gouached red-and-yellow apples tethered high up on the branches that most apple pickers apparently could not reach. I was not most apple pickers, though. I am six foot one. So, into the crosshatch of branches I reached, twisting down every apple I could, while he, at five foot two, began climbing the tree trunks to grab those fruits that were buried deep in the leaves. *My hero,* I thought, or some embarrassing variation of that same swoony sentiment, as he handed his spoils down to me. I paused my own apple picking to take some pictures and videos of him, already writing the Instagram Story arc in my head.

Looking over at a neighboring tree, I watched as a father lifted his daughter up to pluck one of the last remaining apples from its branches. In doing so, he accidentally smacked her head on one of its many fruitless boughs, and she promptly started wailing.

Behind us, I heard a little boy berate his mother in the "Shut up, Mom!" tone that a certain type of little white child is prone to. "Why would you take us apple picking when there aren't any apples?" he scolded her, seemingly indignant.

Hugo and I looked over at each other.

"Don't you just love being sterile?" he asked, and we both broke into laughter.

The fact of our shared infertility was something that I loved about our relationship. I would never be able to give him children, yet he still loved me despite my lack; perhaps he even loved me because of it. He couldn't have children either, nor did he want them. "It would be cruel to bring kids into a world on the brink of an all-out climate apocalypse," he would tell me whenever the subject came up. I would agree and then echo something similar as I quietly relished how compatible my body was with what he wanted for his own.

Looking back on one such discussion, I grow sad as I reflect on how willingly I would take my cues from him, as if I couldn't know myself or my desires unless they were first refracted through him and his. I remember that once while we were fucking, I asked him, "Do you want to go down on me?" He looked at me and asked, cocking one of his eyebrows, "Do *you* want me to go down on you?" It was a habit of mine he'd observed and would call out whenever he noticed it—that is, asking him if he wanted something that I wanted, instead of just outright asking for it.

The conversation we had about whether we wanted kids followed a similar track. I posed a question, he gave an honest answer, and then I mirrored his answer in giving him mine.

Besides, I knew that I couldn't have kids, thanks to a sterilizing surgery that I'd previously undergone, so the question of whether I wanted them, even in the abstract, felt unworthy of interrogation.

What I did know was that I wanted a boyfriend, one who would later become my husband. I knew that none of the "ethically non-monogamous" men I'd gone out with in the past, the ones who'd taken me out on countless hookups masquerading as first dates, had ever seen me as anything more than, at best, a disposable secondary partner. I knew that none of the faceless Grindr torsos I'd had over to my place had ever wanted anything to do with me after they'd shot their load. I believed, however incorrectly, that their lack of further interest had something to do with my inability to ever give them children. I believed, however incorrectly, that men my age—at the time, my late twenties—wanted a woman they could settle down with, and that settling down with a woman would probably mean having children with her. I knew that I could never provide that for them, so why, I believed, however incorrectly, would any of those burgeoning patriarchs ever choose to settle for me? Doing so would limit their options. I would narrow the future before them. So my procreative ineptitude thereby rendered me a clandestine fetish. An accessory to infidelity. An optional add-on. A terminal third. That was my fate. I imagined that in a decade or two, some of those men would find a nice trans girl half their age to spoil rotten, after their coveted, sought-after marriage eventually went down in flames. Older men, especially those who'd been divorced at least once before, always struck me as so much more comfortable with themselves, and more comfortable with their desire for me. I'd privately speculate that the failure of their marriage had forced them to "give up on the illusions that led to failure," as author Torrey Peters once wrote about the potential commonalities between trans women and cis divorcées. But I'd also lament the timing of their hero's journey and how it would, by design, never sync up with my life. Why, I would wonder, weren't there any men like that my own age? Men with whom I could stand on equal footing, functioning more so as peers? And while that may have been true, I also, in hindsight, can't help but wonder, why was I so intent on trying to build a future with men who never seemed to want to build one with me?

Hugo, however, did. Even after only a few weeks of dating, I knew that he was different, that maybe he was the one. He bought me gifts, like that fancy, rose-scented moisturizer to ease my irritation after an electrolysis appointment. And in the two years since I had transitioned, he was the first man to sleep beside me in my own bed. The men who'd come before him had been cis. Hugo, unlike them, was trans. I took those facts and ran with them, idealizing love between trans people, even as our relationship began to stray from that imagined ideal.

We'd break up and get back together, break up and get back together. Every time we rekindled our relationship, there would always be a grace period of a few weeks, in which the man I loved was the man I was once again dating, and our relationship felt like the one that I willed it to be in my head. But always, like clockwork, he'd grow cold and mean and distant, holding grudges over an endless list of wrongs that I never could seem to make right. He once told me that he'd heard through the grapevine that Lyle, an ex of mine whom I remained on good terms with, had told a mutual friend that he was glad we weren't dating anymore since I wasn't "marriage material." I was stunned. Though we had only dated briefly, Lyle had definitely gotten to know me well enough to know how much a comment like that would hurt. I immediately texted the mutual friend and asked her if Lyle had said that. She reassured me that he hadn't, that what he'd actually said was "Harron and I didn't work out, so I guess my search for a wife continues."

I was relieved for a moment and then upset all over again. Someone *had* said something deliberately hurtful about me, something that needled at one of my tenderest points. Someone had said I wasn't "marriage material," and that someone was my boyfriend.

"You texted her?" Hugo exclaimed when I confronted him. Evidently, as I should have guessed, he was the wronged party in all this. Once again, he had hurt me, but it was somehow my fault. "I can't believe you didn't trust me!"

After some resistance, I relented to his feelings, as I often did when we argued. He would get upset, and I'd respond in turn with submission—that is, until I couldn't submit anymore. In fleeting bouts of lucidity, I'd break up with him, though I'd always come crawling back in tears, begging him to take me back, horrified at what I'd given up, or maybe just scared of my own conviction.

I knew—or at least I *felt* I knew—that if I lost him, I'd plunge back into that Sisyphean dating hell that he'd mercifully plucked me out of. I knew—or, again, I *felt* I knew—that this was the best I could ever expect from a man, that I was only getting older and my options more limited. So I continued coming back, searching for signs of life in a nearly barren orchard, hoping to scrounge up enough apples to make a pie for someone else.

After our day trip to the orchard upstate, I quite literally did just that when we got back to his apartment. The resulting pie was watery—I hardly knew what I was doing—but after draining some of the liquid, he told me it was good. My nerves eased, I took a bite. "Yeah, it's pretty good."

FERTILITY

"So much of my decision to try to have a baby is accepting that I don't have it all figured out right now," Río told me.

We were sitting under the canopy of her queen-sized bed facing each other. Río had a bowl of Thai takeout nestled in her lap.

"But you know what?" she continued. "That's OK. I know that when Cyd gets pregnant—*if* Cyd gets pregnant—I'm gonna be fucking ready to go."

I have known Río—full name Río Sofia, a thirty-two-year-old Mexican-born artist and organizer from Miami who now lives in Brooklyn—for nearly a decade. We first met at one of the many big house parties that she and her roommates used to throw all the time before the pandemic. I remember how, at one such Halloween rager on the eve of Trump's election, I sat on the floor of her bedroom with at least a dozen others in the later hours of the night as she held court from her bed, topless with sparkly red devil horns poking out from beneath her long, chestnut hair. Envious of her mane, I, still obliviously pre-transition at the time, would later ask a mutual friend what Río did to get her hair so thick and healthy, to which he said, "Biotin? I think?" So I started popping those vitamins every day. (I know, I know, so embarrassingly "I saw Cady Heron wearing army pants and flip-flops, so I bought army pants and flip-flops.") And then a few months later, I realized something pretty major about myself—take a guess at what it was—and I promptly swapped out those vitamins for estradiol, the pills I didn't realize were the ones I wanted all along.

Acquaintances for years, we grew much closer after I interviewed her for a 2019 feature for *Out* magazine about trans women artists creating self-portraiture in opposition to the cis gaze. She became the kind of friend who would tell me over and over to dump some horrible boyfriend way before I finally did. The kind who, when we realized that I'd have to walk past some dreaded ex at the club in order to get to the bathroom, would loop her arm in mine and escort me all the way, cackling her head off as if I'd just said something perfect. One of the original organizers of the Body Hack fundraiser parties held every month out in Queens, she's the kind of friend who's somehow always got the time to put together something massive and major, like an end-of-the-election-cycle phone-banking campaign for a swing-district candidate eight states away, or the 2020 million-dollar fundraiser for GLITS, a trans-led organization here in New York that helps community members with all sorts of pressing needs, from finding stable housing to securing asylum. And she's so passionate about it, whatever it is, that you can't help but say yes when she asks for your help.

She'll never make you feel like you have to diminish yourself or pitch up your voice to avoid getting clocked. Whenever someone calls you both "faggots!" on the street, she'll yell back, "Suck my dick!" For as long as I've known her, Río has been an enemy of dread and nihilism, reminding me through her words and actions that there's always another way forward, beyond the one that I might feel resigned to.

This was no less true as we sat on her bed, discussing her hopes of becoming a mother.

"Right now, I'm in baby-making mode, so all of my focus is going towards that," she said, her chestnut hair now shorn down to a buzz cut. Her silver chain necklace had fallen into one of the rips around the collar of her faded pink tee, which read CANCEL ME HARDER DADDY in a blocky black font down the front. "If Cyd gets pregnant, *that* is what I'll be available for. I'll learn everything I have to learn if and when that time comes. I have to just give myself permission for that to be OK and not think twenty steps ahead of where we're at right now. Like, obviously, I know that there are some things you do have to be thinking about ahead of time and preparing for and stuff, but creating this expectation that you're going to be a perfect parent when you've never been a parent at all—it's just not realistic."

I agreed. "If that was enough to stop people, then, like, nobody would be a parent."

"Right?" she said. "I also try to remember that I'm such a compulsive caretaker, you know? With my roommates—really, with anyone who tells me they have some sort of minor inconvenience going on in their life, I'm always nonconsensually jumping in and trying to fix the problem."

That made me laugh. "That sounds just like a mother to me."

"Exactly," she said and grinned.

• • •

"Trans motherhood" as a concept can mean different things to different people. For some, like a pair of cis women who used to edit my work at a well-known news site, and, in fact, once killed a story I'd been working on concerning this very subject, "trans motherhood" meant trans men getting pregnant and giving birth to biological children. In other words, trans fatherhood.

That's not what I mean here.

When I talk about trans motherhood, and by extension trans mothers, I'm referring to, in the broadest sense possible, trans women who raise other people, whether they're biologically related to each other or not.

I prefer a simple yet broadly applicable definition like this, as it's big and flexible enough to contain so many different forms of trans motherhood, ones that might theoretically rule one another out, without imposing a rank or hierarchy or a sense that some are more "real" than others. It includes trans moms, life mothers, house mothers, and every other kind of intracommunal matriarch who takes it upon herself to shepherd less experienced transfemmes through a world that would rather destroy them. This particular chosen-family dynamic is often equal parts kinship and mentoring between trans women, with the elder teaching the newly out girl how to dress or do her makeup, how to navigate insurance and access hormones and surgery, how to date safely, how to make money, how to deal with transphobia—how to deal, in general—and other vital things that she might not learn otherwise. Avery Everhart, a professor at the University of British Columbia, has described this passage of life-saving knowledge as a kind of "reproductive labor" specific to trans women. I have also heard it called "folk wisdom," as a trans woman I met through Twitter many years ago once told me: "Folk wisdom is a really sacred, beautiful community resource. We also have to rely on it because we're not supposed to exist, and there aren't any other reliable sources of information."

Along with the trans women who mother other trans women, my definition of trans motherhood includes those trans women who literally mother literal children, the ones who raise kids in more normative family structures. I'm less intimately familiar with this type of trans mom, since I haven't met that many in my day-to-day life. Most of my exposure to this type of mom has been through her many mass-media counterparts, both fictional and not, like Felicity Huffman's Oscar-nominated turn in *Transamerica* or Laverne Cox's Emmy-nominated breakthrough role on *Orange Is the New Black*. There is also, regrettably, Caitlyn Jenner, the Olympian–turned–reality star–turned–wreaker of irreversible psychic damage on us all. Many in the community despise how big a platform she has and regret how self-destructively she wields it. I, personally, find it beautiful that she's out there, every day, proving to the world that the worst person alive might just be a trans woman—and that trans woman? Might just be a mother.

Anyway, like I said, I've met few trans moms of this type in real life. The few that I have met all started having kids before they transitioned. I've met even fewer trans women who had biological children after they chose to transition, and I can think of only one trans woman I've personally met who's having and raising kids with another trans partner, a type of coupling that I am, admittedly, most interested in because it mirrors my own relationship, and almost all the serious relationships I've been in over the past few years.

Now, I do want to make it clear that just because I don't personally know those couples, that obviously doesn't mean they don't exist. I'm wary of projecting unwarranted novelty onto trans people purely on the basis of my own limited experience. I'm nobody's elder, but even I've been around long enough to know that, at the risk of hyperbole, most of us have never done anything meaningfully new; we're not the first trans person to do anything, nor will we ever be—and that's OK. Trust me. We'll live. The obsession with claiming "trans firsts," both real and imagined, continues because "trans people are in a constant state of being discovered," as the historian and filmmaker Morgan M. Page once wrote. Due to our ongoing erasure from culture and history, "people—trans and cis alike—rush to plant the flag of the *very first*, to mark the significance of the moment as being unlike anything that has ever occurred before. After all, it feels good to be part of history, to be able to say 'I remember where I was when . . . ' " But such "historical narcissism," as she terms it, whether the cynical work of publicists or stemming from nobler intentions, serves to further that same cycle of erasure, thereby ensuring more false firsts to come. This cycle not only breeds ignorance and promotes incuriosity but encourages us to see one another as rivals rather than peers—and as the *first* trans woman to ever write a book, I really don't want to feed into it.

Still, although my observations here are obviously anecdotal, I don't think it's all that myopic to suggest that my firsthand experiences with trans women and motherhood might reflect the lack of reproductive options available to trans women, or that this lack compounds itself exponentially for those whose partners are also trans. I could point to a whole swath of evidence to back up this hypothesis, like how eight states still require that trans people undergo a necessarily sterilizing surgery in order to change the gender marker on certain identity documents, down from ten states as recently as 2019. (For those who wish to legally transition but would not otherwise pursue bottom surgery, this is tantamount to forced sterilization and has been condemned by the United Nations as a form of state-sanctioned torture.) I could also cite how less than a fifth of the nearly twenty-eight thousand people who responded to the 2015 U.S. Transgender Survey said that they were parents, or how that stat continued to hover below 20 percent in the survey's 2022 follow-up, whereas if you compare those numbers to the broader population, 69 percent of American adults are reported to have had kids.

I could also refer to Lola Pellegrino, a close friend of mine who works at a queer healthcare clinic in New York City. Before that she ran a local reproductive care center's gender-affirming hormone therapy services—or, in her own words, "I was the trans healthcare person at the women's clinic, and now I'm the women's healthcare person at the trans clinic."

In the spring of 2022, I called her up to discuss the state of trans women's reproductive healthcare.

"How would you describe the state of trans women's reproductive healthcare?" I asked her, not that I couldn't have guessed.

"Hmm," she humored me for a second. "I think it's pretty bad," she finally said and laughed.

But do I really need to turn to all these outside sources to confirm what I already know to be true? Journalistically speaking, sure, but personally speaking, no. I, at the age of thirty-six, could simply look around and notice with very little effort that more and more cis people I know are having kids, and that the trans women I know are almost entirely not.

Perhaps that could change in the years to come. It's not like there are no trans couples out there raising kids, even if they're not in my personal purview. One such pair, Myles and Precious Brady-Davis, even appeared in a one-off TLC docudrama special called *My Pregnant Husband,* which aired in 2020—though I, like many other trans people, first learned about them the year prior, when they shared a truly breathtaking set of paternity photos on Instagram. Styled in the vein of Black Romantic portraiture,* one of the images features the Brady-Davises, named a "Chicago Trans Power Couple" in 2019, standing together in intricately embroidered, regal all-white ensembles. A tiara rests atop Precious's head, while a halo encircles Myles's kufi. Holding a golden staff in one hand, she locks eyes with the viewer, while Myles gazes down at his exposed torso, unmistakably with child. In another portrait, Precious embraces Myles from behind, covering his chest, as he holds her arm in his. They're staring upward beyond the horizon at something out of frame, both of them looking content and at peace as they rest their other hands around Myles's belly. Behind them in both photos shines a blinding burst of light, as if what we're looking at is something akin to a prophetic vision shining down from the heavens.

---

* As the critic and organizer Jasmine Sanders once defined it, Black Romantic artwork of the late twentieth century is "representational, mixed media, superlative in its sentimentalism and in an unambiguous race pride owed to a glamorized, monarchical African past."

When those pictures hit Instagram, it felt like such a hyper-niche, intracommunal "break the internet" moment, to borrow the tagline that *Paper* magazine coined to promote its 2014 Kim Kardashian cover shot by Jean-Paul Goude. Literally every trans person I knew, it seemed, had shared one of the portraits to their Story, while all the cis people I followed carried on with their usual posting, totally unaware of the freak-out in their midst.

"We beamed black trans excellence, our owning and celebrating gender nonconformity, our defining what family meant to us, at the camera," Precious wrote about the photo shoot, which Myles directed and styled, in her 2021 memoir, *I Have Always Been Me*. "We would be part of the mantle of our ancestors both known and unknown, staring into the face of our own lineage as we declared generations-old curses null and void."

The road leading up to the birth of their daughter, Zayn YeMaya Echelle Brady-Davis, in December of that year wasn't always so heavenly. In the TLC special, Myles shares that he's "terrified navigating the world as a pregnant man." He was already so vulnerable to surveillance, harassment, and violence as a Black trans man, as he says in a confessional. Having a visible baby bump on top of that only calls further attention, thereby compounding those preexisting vulnerabilities. He recounts one particularly harrowing instance, in which half a dozen undercover Chicago police officers arrested him as he was leaving a store, accusing him of stealing something and hiding it under his shirt. He says that he yelled over and over, "Please be gentle, I'm pregnant!" but it was no use. It wasn't until one of the cops lifted his shirt and saw his baby bump for herself that they believed him. "That could've gone so many different ways," he says. "I feel like every father wants to protect their child, and I get to protect my child even before they're in the world." Out of fear for his safety and that of his future daughter, he ended up staying home more than he would've otherwise. "I'm looking forward to giving birth," he says. "I'm ready for this process to be over."

Elsewhere in *My Pregnant Husband*, both Myles and Precious describe instances in which mundane aspects of the birthing process caused them both to feel dysphoric. He describes feeling out of his body while not taking testosterone, which he wasn't able to resume until after he gave birth. Still, the couple found a lot of joy in these moments of degendering pregnancy and parenthood—or perhaps *re*gendering them, on their own terms—to make room for themselves.

"In some sense, it upsets me that I can't physically carry a child, but my husband can," says Precious. At the same time, "I think my husband's handsome in this state. He's glowing, and—"

"It's a very masculine glow, though," Myles cuts in. They both laugh.

Trans couples having children, like the Brady-Davis family, are uncommon but not an anomaly. Hopping from Chicago to Little Rock, Miss Major, the legendary activist and veteran of the Stonewall Riots who runs the House of GG, a trans community space in Arkansas, had a child with her partner, Beck Witt, in January 2021. "We had a baby!" she announced via Instagram and Twitter, prompting a similar, micro-niche, break-the-trans-internet moment in my corners of social media. "Beck and I are just beaming over this little guy." Gigi Gorgeous, a popular YouTuber and influencer, has also been very candid over the years about her efforts to have children with clothing designer and socialite Nats Getty. "We worked very hard on our baby journey," she told *Out* in 2024. "It's taken a lot of lifestyle changes. I wasn't able to create any of my own DNA, so then I changed everything around lifestyle over the years, and now we are here with six embryos. There's no baby announcement yet, but we are on the path to that, which is exciting."

"I actually have a bunch of t4t couples who are trying to have babies," Lola Pellegrino, my nurse-practitioner friend, told me. "I have yet to see a baby from start to finish," she added, stopping to laugh at her own needlessly clinical phrasing. "What I mean is that I have yet to see a couple where both parties have hormonally transitioned and they decide to have a baby, go at it, get pregnant, and then have a baby. I've seen many trans women who had babies before they were out and went from somebody's father to somebody's mother. I've seen plenty of people enter relationships with people who had kids already. I've seen people adopt. I have yet to see any trans couples have their own biologically related kids, though."

"As a provider, have you ever had a transfeminine patient report getting a transmasculine partner pregnant?" I asked.

"Yes," she said.

"Have you ever seen that happen when both partners were hormonally transitioning?"

"Yes," she said again. It's less likely to happen than if one or both partners were not on hormone replacement therapy, but it's not impossible. "There's a shit ton of misinformation about fertility and sterility and HRT. Talk to anyone you know, and each one will have been told a different thing. Patients on HRT will say they've been told they'll never be able to have kids, or that if they do try, their kids will have fucking birth defects because of the hormones," neither of which are true.

Part of this widespread ignorance among trans and cis people alike can be blamed on the utter dearth of available research into trans reproductive healthcare—or really trans healthcare, period. "We have to do our own research," said Josie Caballero, the U.S. Transgender Survey and Special Projects Director at the National Center for Transgender Equality, in a phone interview. "It's the wild, wild West out there for trans people."

That body of research has been growing in recent years, with one 2021 study finding a high occurrence of seminal abnormalities in trans women's sperm when compared to that of cis men, especially among those of us who'd previously undergone hormone replacement therapy, and another from 2023 suggesting that most trans women are still able to produce viable sperm samples should they stop HRT. But the pool of data remains small. Thankfully, providers like Lola are able to fill in some of those gaps by examining studies that concern "hypogonadal males"—that is, cis men who produce low levels of testosterone—then explore what fertility treatment options are recommended for such patients and extrapolate them to trans women. She can similarly cross-reference studies that involve "PCOS females," cis women with polycystic ovary syndrome who naturally produce higher levels of testosterone, to gain insight into potential fertility treatment options for transgender men.

"We can stimulate sperm production and clean sperm," she said. "Infertility treatment in this country is wild—almost completely unregulated, massively expensive. But there's all sorts of things we can do for trans women interested in fertility treatments."

If they can afford it, that is. Banking sperm can easily cost as much as $1,000, and storing that material can drain anywhere between $350 and $1,000 per year. For trans men who wish to retrieve and freeze their eggs, that initial figure skyrockets, sometimes costing more than $10,000. Given that trans Americans face disproportionate poverty rates and are twice as likely to be unemployed as the broader American public, it's no wonder that, when asked in the abstract, more than three-quarters of all trans people surveyed in one study said that they'd considered preserving their genetic material prior to starting HRT, but only 9.6 percent of trans women and 3.1 percent of trans men had actually gone through with it.

A handful of startups have jumped in to fill the gaps left by our profit-driven healthcare system, as startups are wont to do these days, what with them also being driven by profits. Dadi, launched in 2019, used to offer a mail-in sperm analysis kit, freezing, and a year of storage for just under $200, charging $9.99 a month for storage after that, or about $120 per year. Though not created with trans women in mind, in case you couldn't tell by the name, Dadi was otherwise "tailor-made" for that demo, as founder and CEO Tom Smith told the website *them* in 2020, two years before his company was acquired by Ro, a direct-to-consumer healthcare company that offers sperm storage and semen analysis at comparable prices.

Legacy, another fertility-focused startup, similarly views trans women as a profitable enough demographic to target with their marketing—at least, that's the conclusion I came to when I saw an ad with a trans woman's face on it whooshing past me on the side of a city bus a few years ago. The banner ad inquired, "Starting HRT? Preserve your fertility for free." The company, founded by Khaled Kteily in 2018, charges as little as $295 for analysis, freezing, and the first year of storage, and $145 a year after that. That's cheaper than standard sperm-banking costs, but it's still not free. Other startups, like Kind-body and Extend Fertility, provide egg-freezing services that trans men and other transmascs could make use of for as little as $6,500—less than the industry standard of $10,000 but still costly enough to render that difference inconsequential to many.

The ways in which cost-prohibitive fertility treatments render otherwise fertile individuals unable to have children is an example of what's called social infertility, Lola told me. Social infertility is different from biological infertility, she explained— that is, what we're usually talking about when we talk about infertility. Someone who's biologically infertile is unable to produce the genetic material needed to have a child, either because they were born that way or because they became sterile as a result of some later circumstance, like surgery. A socially infertile person, by contrast, is capable of producing the necessary material to conceive but can't actually do so because of some missing link in our country's medical infrastructure. Like, let's take a hypothetical lesbian couple. One of those women is cis, and the other woman is trans and on HRT. They're both covered through that first partner's health insurance, which she gets through work, but her plan doesn't cover the treatments and services that might be necessary for them to have a kid who's biologically related to them both, like sperm banking and in vitro fertilization. That gap in their insurance coverage has effectively made them infertile.

"If someone wants to have a genetic child, it should be covered by the government or insurance as a qualified medical benefit," Lola said. But it's not, which "results in so much social programming. Patients have told me, 'Because I'm a trans woman, I'm not fit to have a baby,' or 'I'm not supposed to have them.'"

"Were they actually saying those things in earnest?" I asked her, hoping that wasn't the case. "Or were they just ironically repeating things they'd heard from other people all their life?"

"No, no, no—these were people who felt shitty about being trans and wanting to become mothers," she clarified. "The vibe I got was that they felt like they were damaged or less than or deviant, and that deviant people do not and should not have babies."

• • •

"I remember when I was a teenager, I would get really sad when I imagined my future and how I wouldn't be a parent," Río told me, shifting in her frosty-pink crushed-velvet leggings so that she was now lying, stomach down, on the shaggy white throw on her bed.

Though she didn't come into her transness until she reached her early twenties, Río had been out as gay in high school. It was around this time that she internalized the idea that not only would she never have children but that queer people and children had no place in one another's lives. She began to wonder why she was the way she was and, after Catholicism proved no help, turned to science for answers, soon developing an ontological autotheory about serving as a buffer against overpopulation. "Basically, I thought that the whole point of my life was to not procreate," she said, which, needless to say, given her desire to do just that, depressed her.

Later, upon encountering radical queer politics and queer theory for the first time, she replaced that nihilistic raison d'être, one she didn't want but felt she was resigned to, with something that felt more empowering. "I started hearing things like 'breeder' and 'heteronormativity,'" she said. "That really gave me further ammunition to be like, 'Having a child is *so* not the thing.'"

It wasn't until Río met Cyd in 2016 that she began to rethink this mindset. "Having a baby had felt so out of the question for me that it was never something I ever fully considered." Cyd, an artist, herbalist, and political organizer, had made it known from very early on in their relationship that he wanted to be a father someday. Having long since convinced herself that she would never be a mom, Río continually deferred whenever the subject came up. "I was always pushing it into the future, like 'Let's talk about that in a few years,'" she said. "Just pushing it and pushing it and pushing it. I succeeded in doing that for a few years until one time when we were walking around Prospect Park. He had brought up parenting again, and I was like 'Let's talk about it when I'm thirty,' you know, just doing that same line again. This time, he got really sad. He told me, 'I want to talk about it now.' It was something he really wanted. I couldn't push it off anymore."

So she confronted the possibility, really sat with the idea, and spent a lot of time talking through it all with Cyd. In doing so, she realized that part of her hesitation at even imagining herself raising kids was because of how deeply she'd internalized various bigoted cultural messages that told her that she, as a trans woman, shouldn't be around children—and worse, that she was a danger or a threat simply because of who she was.

The roots of her anxiety, while totally unfounded, are more than understandable. Just look at the ongoing "groomer" panic sweeping the United States, which echoes a similar brand of homophobia peddled by Anita Bryant and other right-wing figures in the 1970s as part of their national campaign to push gay people out of public life. Kindred to this current wave of transphobic fearmongering is an intense legislative assault at every level of government, one that would criminalize doctors for giving trans kids healthcare and punish those kids' parents for not throwing them into conversion therapy.

"I had really internalized the idea that I was someone who is totally unfit to be around children," said Río. Dredging up that subconscious shame "brought its own set of obstacles that I then had to work through and get over before I could even begin to think about the possibility that I could even be a parent at all."

She and Cyd considered adoption at first, reasoning that there were already so many kids in the world who needed parents, why shouldn't they try to raise them? But after learning more about what the process would entail and realizing how difficult it is for anyone to adopt, even cis straight couples, they decided that adoption was not right for them, since they, as a queer trans couple, weren't right for most adoption agencies.

"We're two transsexuals," she explained. On top of that, "I'm an artist who has posed naked in her work, which is all on the internet."

They'd known cis gay men who'd found it nearly impossible to adopt, so what hope did they have? It wasn't like she knew any trans women who'd managed to become mothers through adoption, much less trans couples who'd become parents that way. But she did know of one couple, a trans couple who mirrored her own relationship, who had successfully managed to conceive. Maybe she and Cyd could do that. They decided, then, to try.

...

In "No Comment," a short story by the author Ayşe Devrim, first published in 2017's *Meanwhile, Elsewhere: Science Fiction and Fantasy from Transgender Writers,* a trans woman named Maryam unexpectedly becomes pregnant after receiving a trial uterine transplant. Nobody, not even her doctors, had known that the womb she was given, which previously belonged to a cis woman who died tragically young in a car accident, was gestating life, its minuscule fetus having not only survived but evaded detection.

As news of her immaculate conception spreads, Maryam is hounded by invasive reporters, violent protesters, fanatical worshippers, and soulless corporate advertisers hoping to spon a little con amid the chaos. To keep her safe from harm—or, really, to protect their research and keep everything on track—her doctors place her under strict surveillance, severely curtailing her autonomy, until she finally gives birth.

Maryam does not relish her newfound notoriety. She has no intention of capitalizing on her unsought fame like some trans Demi Moore, posing for the cover of *Vanity Fair* while clutching her naked belly. (Or like the Brooklyn musician Macy Rodman, in her video for "Greased Up Freak Pt. 1.") What she wants is for her body to be *her* body again. In a gambit to wrest control of her life away from the fetus inside her, she does the only thing she can think to do: She gets an abortion. "Why would you pass up the chance to be the first trans woman to have an abortion?" Maryam's friend asks her, as she's coaching Maryam through the decision. "You'll be taking the biggest step forward for trannykind since we stopped using the asterisk."

While Devrim's story might've been a work of science fiction, the possibility of a trans woman getting pregnant by way of a transplanted womb, or even giving birth following such a procedure, might not be all that far off. Though hardly common, surgeons worldwide have been performing successful uterus transplants for over a decade, with at least thirty of the nearly one hundred transplants done in the United States. Some of those recipients have even gone on to conceive and have children thanks to the procedure, with the first such birth recorded in Sweden in 2014.

Still, all those recipients have been cis women with uterine factor infertility, either because they were born without a uterus or because they have a womb that no longer functions as needed. There is, however, at least one surgeon out there who has publicly declared that he wants to perform a uterus transplant on a trans woman, though so far all he's managed to do is secure some nice press for himself.

"Every transgender woman wants to be as female as possible," said Dr. Narendra Kaushik of New Delhi in a 2022 interview with the UK's *Mirror*, to which I have approximately one million follow-ups, like, what does "female" even mean in this context? Does "female" mean having a functioning uterus? Does "every transgender woman" really want this? Is "every transgender woman" in the room with us right now? Thankfully, he went on to answer at least two of those questions, albeit while raising about one million more. "[Being female] includes being a mother," he said. "The way towards this is with a uterine transplant, the same as a kidney or any other transplant."

My discursive qualms with his statement aside—and oh, are they innumerable—I have to note that there's actually a pretty long-standing historical precedent for trans women getting uterus transplants. It's not a very good precedent, but it's a precedent all the same. The Danish painter Lili Elbe, perhaps regrettably immortalized on the silver screen by Eddie Redmayne in 2015's *The Danish Girl,* received a transplanted uterus in 1931. Unfortunately, her body rejected the new organ, and she died from complications about three months later. Had she been able to access the proper anti-rejection medications, which wouldn't be developed until many decades later, she might have survived. But even with those treatments at the ready these days, every uterus transplant, whether successful or not, is performed with the intention of eventually removing that transplanted womb once it's served its purpose— that is, allowed the recipient to get pregnant through IVF and give birth, with the newborn delivered via cesarean section.

"Would that just be a red herring?" I asked Lola, my medical provider friend. "To figure out how a post-op trans woman might deliver a baby through her vagina, I mean."

"I mean, if that's what people wanted," she said, somewhat warily. "I'm thinking about how there are people who say they don't want a cesarean when they give birth but wouldn't care in the end, as long as their baby is alive and healthy. I don't know anyone who's like, 'I simply must give birth intravaginally.'"

"Do you think a neovagina could properly stretch to accommodate the birthing process?" I asked. As a journalist, I had to ask—though having undergone bottom surgery myself, I felt like I already knew the answer.

"No," Lola told me. "It probably couldn't."

"I simply would not want to find out."

"Yeah— Oh my god! Wait. I did read this case study abou— You know what? I'm not going to terrorize you."

I mulled it over. "It's OK. You can terrorize me."

"I was reading this case study about a woman who got her neovagina perforated by a dick, and—"

Got it. Moving on.

So, intravaginal birth for trans women who receive uterus transplants would definitely be off the table. But that's the case for cis women who receive transplanted wombs too, as are other risks inherent to any sort of organ transplant. "You'd have to take anti-rejection drugs, which are rough," Lola continued. "Like, *really* rough." Those medications, taken to suppress the patient's immune system so that their body accepts the transplanted organ rather than attacks it, can cause nausea and vomiting, diarrhea, diabetes, high blood pressure, arthritis, weakened bones, and a host of other side effects, even an increased risk for developing cancer or a serious infection.

Assuming, then, that a trans woman's hypothetical uterine transplant would mirror the dozens of other transplants that have been successfully performed on cis women—pregnancy and birth as the impetus for the procedure, the intention to eventually remove the transplanted uterus, the prospective mother taking immunosuppressing anti-rejection drugs in the meantime—what would necessarily be different? Well, one of the biggest concerns would be whether she would be able to generate the necessary levels of progesterone and estrogens—specifically estrone, estradiol, and estriol—as well as produce those hormones at the proper intervals needed to sustain fetal development over a period of nine months. Synthetic versions of those hormones all exist, of course, but the question remains as to whether the patient's medical providers could figure out how to supply her with them on a daily, perhaps even hourly, basis, without keeping her strapped to a hospital bed 24/7, mainlining hormones in a prison of her own making—to say nothing of the cost! Barring a much-needed communist revolution or even full-scale American healthcare reform, I doubt that her insurance provider would willingly cover any of this. So I guess that's another thing that this hypothetical trans woman would have in common with cis women: a uterine transplant and all subsequent IVF treatments are almost impossibly cost-prohibitive.

My thoughts started racing as Lola and I spoke. The more we discussed it, the more impossible it all felt. Like, imagine you just got bottom surgery, perhaps even paid out of pocket for it, and then you had to drop even more on an unproven uterine—

Wait.

I was struck by an epiphany the size of a city bus, one with a broadside banner ad trying to get me to freeze all that sperm I don't have.

"Lola," I asked her, "assuming that this hypothetical trans woman's doctors are able to ensure that her womb functions as needed, that it's viable, that it can create a placenta, and that all the necessary hormones are flowing through her as they need to—let's assume that they could do all that. Since she would be having a C-section anyway, wouldn't it be theoretically possible for a trans woman to give birth without having to have gotten bottom surgery first?"

". . . Yeah," she said, pausing, as momentarily stunned as I had been by the thought. "Absolutely."*

"And if she didn't get bottom surgery, then she wouldn't have to remove her gonads," I continued, "so could she ges-

---

* Sometime later, I would stumble on the Mexican visual artist Chris Cortez's 2021 painting *Immaculada Concepción*, which very much depicts this scenario by way of Catholic iconography.

tate a fetus made from her own sperm, which she'd be able to retrieve at any time after pausing HRT? Like, if her partner could provide the egg but had no desire to physically carry the fetus themselves?"

"I think we could absolutely do conception and birth, but the actual pregnancy . . ." She trailed off. "The middle part would be the difficult part."

Later, after we hung up, once my thoughts had finally settled, I began to wonder whether such medical innovations like the ones that we'd talked about would actually do anything meaningful for trans people writ large. By that, I mean that I can't easily imagine that anyone beyond the small cohort of hypothetical trans women selected to take part in trial uterine transplants, or a handful of multimillionaires, likely all of them white, could ever possibly stand to personally benefit from such reproductive advances, as cool as they might sound on paper. Would we be barreling down the road at two hundred kilometers per hour in the wrong lane, as those fake lesbians from t.A.T.u. might say? Especially when there are ways to improve and sustain trans people's reproductive capacity that already exist—like IVF and sperm banking—and for much cheaper than an organ transplant, at that, however underutilized and ignored those methods might be?

"Ignored" is a funny word to use when talking about trans people's fertility, given the ongoing legislative derangement that claims it as a concern. American politicians have become obsessed with the subject, their fixation only growing with each legislative session. Take, for example, the 2022 letter that Republican senator Marsha Blackburn of Tennessee wrote to Robert M. Califf, the commissioner of the U.S. Food and Drug Administration, in which she expresses concern over "reports of increased off-label use" of gonadotropin-releasing hormone agonists, commonly referred to as puberty blockers. Though developed as a means of halting a precocious puberty in children under the age of ten, GnRH agonists have also been used in gender-affirming medical care for decades as a means of pausing or preventing the onset of puberty in trans adolescents who don't wish to physically develop as the sex they were assigned at birth. This off-label use "concerned" Blackburn; at least that's what she said. She had previously described gender-affirming surgery as a form of physical mutilation, though, so I think we all know what really "concerned" her. And chief among those alleged concerns was the potential impact that medications like leuprorelin or triptorelin could have on a child's "future fertility."

Blackburn is not the only politician to suffer from this neurosis. American lawmakers have introduced a host of transphobic legislation over the past decade, some of which specifically targets trans kids' access to gender-affirming medical care precisely on the grounds—or I should say, alleged grounds—of preserving those trans kids' fertility. Of the 278 bills introduced at the state level in 2022 that targeted LGBTQ people, 35 of them sought to restrict trans people's access to healthcare, many specifically taking aim at kids and adolescents. And in 2023, lawmakers introduced 510 anti-LGBTQ bills—nearly double the previous year's number—more than 100 of which impose age restrictions on gender-affirming care.

These bills are often given titles that feed into the "transgender predator" myth. Arkansas, for example, proposed the Save Adolescents from Experimentation Act, aka the SAFE Act. There's also the Protect Children's Innocence Act, introduced at the federal level, and South Carolina and Oklahoma both introduced a Millstone Act, named for a biblical passage that calls on Christians to drown those who lead children into sin. But despite the obsessive focus on trans people under eighteen, these bills would appear to be the first step in a broader effort to prevent anyone from medically transitioning, regardless of age. Terry Schilling, the president of the American Principles Project—a key lobbying group behind this legislative onslaught, alongside the Alliance Defending Freedom, the Family Policy Alliance, and the Heritage Foundation—has even said as much, freely admitting in an interview with *The New York Times* that his organization's long-term goal was to eliminate gender-affirming healthcare for all. They were targeting trans kids for now because that's "where the consensus is," he said. "This is a political winner." We can already see the shift. In 2023, for example, those Millstone Acts proposed in South Carolina and Oklahoma would criminalize the provision of trans healthcare for people as old as twenty-five. Oklahoma's bill was even written in such a way that it could potentially be used to forcibly detransition people who had already transitioned. South Carolina's version, meanwhile, didn't move forward, but another proposal that banned care for anyone under eighteen did pass in 2024. That law, the Children Deserve Help Not Harm Act, includes a prohibition for Medicaid coverage for gender-affirming care for people of any age, highlighting one of the ways in which this hateful campaign has targeted lower-income trans adults more covertly than, say, trans children writ large. Such legislative sadism is nothing short of disgusting, to say nothing of the health risks that such a law would impose. For those of us who can no longer produce hormones of our own on account of a previous surgery, it would basically serve as a legal mandate to develop osteoporosis.

Blanketing over this genocidal campaign to mandate trans people out of existence, to paraphrase what the ethicist Janice Raymond recommended in 1979's *The Transsexual Empire,* is an alleged concern for preserving trans people's fertility. Yet, at the risk of mounting too credulous a counterargument to what is clearly a bad-faith defense of eugenicist legislation, gender-affirming medical care does not, in any form of it, guarantee infertility. Transness is not synonymous with infertility, regardless of that narrative's political utility for those who would seek to destroy us. Certain surgeries are necessarily sterilizing, of course, but what little research exists suggests that hormone replacement therapy does not always lead to sterility. Even the widespread panic over puberty blockers is unfounded, as there's no evidence to suggest that GnRH agonists in any way cause permanent infertility.

Transitioning has, in fact, made many of us effectively infertile, but not for the reasons that our enemies would claim. We're infertile as a result of various systemic barriers, the same barriers that render cis people socially infertile as well. Maybe we don't have the right insurance, or any insurance at all. Maybe we can't afford to pay for IVF treatments, sperm banking, or other cost-prohibitive services. We're not always barren because we chose to be. Sometimes, it's what they chose for us.

• • •

When Río told me that she was in full-time baby-making mode, she was not at all kidding. For the ten months leading up to our conversation, she and Cyd had been doing all that they could to conceive, which included many sacrifices. One of the biggest was halting their respective HRT regimens so that their bodies could begin producing endogenous hormones once again.

For Río, that switch has been both a blessing and a curse. Some of the downsides of swapping estrogen for testosterone have been incredibly discouraging for her. "All of my facial hair grew back," she said. "My chest hair started growing back. I had basically gotten to a point after years of laser hair removal and electrolysis that I was shaving maybe once or twice a week. Suddenly, I'm shaving every day again, so that sucked. I can't cry anymore either," or at least not as easily as she could before. "It feels like I don't have as much emotional depth as I could access when I was on estrogen."

On the plus side, she told me, her sex drive has risen. As sex has always been a way for her to feel present in her body, she's more than welcomed this increase in ease and pleasure. "My relationship with my gender identity and my body never feels complete, so there's a way in which feeling unstable like this can really help me feel a lot more present," she said. "I was really excited about having my sex drive return," and the added emphasis on intentional physical intimacy has also been a boon for her relationship.

For the two to three days when Cyd is ovulating every month, the couple drops everything to focus on getting pregnant. "We're basically like, 'Let's have sex as much as we can,'" Río said. "It's always really cute after we have sex. I put a pillow under Cyd's butt, and we hang out like that for twenty minutes. You want to have your pelvis higher up so the cum seeps down to the cervix. It's honestly wild that your little sperm has this impossible job of traversing through a cervix."

We both laughed. It is wild! "That little waiting period also gives us space to plan our future together. I was never someone who liked planning things out in advance. I was always struggling to be in my body and to be in the present. Cyd's a prepper—like, literally a doomsday prepper—and has a lot of beautiful ideas about how he wants to live his life. The idea of raising a baby was scary to me because I don't even know what I'm doing next week, girl! You want to lock me into a lifelong commitment? But I knew in my heart and knew in my bones that I had made a lifelong commitment to Cyd."

"What will your future together look like?" I asked her.

"I have no idea," she said. "I still don't know what it looks like, but I feel much more able to make brave choices and feel able to give myself permission to imagine an abundant life for myself."

"Abundant how?"

"I still feel a lot of that scarcity mindset in my head," she said. "Even giving myself permission to have a family and live somewhere you can afford a house feels crazy."

"How would you want to raise your child?"

"The way I was raised had a lot of things to it that were really great," she said, "but a lot of aspects were really insufficient. Having a baby feels like an opportunity to address that wounded inner child in me and also create a space of safety for a new human. Giving your child something you weren't given, I imagine, can be a cathartic exchange."

"How would you approach gender?"

"I would want to prepare my child for the world that they're living in, but I would also want the baby to have as expansive an outlook on themselves as possible and have as much capacity and permission to be creative in the ways that they see themselves," she said. "I can't really say whether I'm going to raise the baby in a decidedly nonbinary way, because that also feels very decisive, you know?"

"An attempted Get Out of the Gender Binary Free card, or something."

"I don't think we're going to raise our baby without gender, because the baby is still going to have confrontations with being gendered whether they like it or not," Río said. "What I would do is make sure I do everything I can to make my baby feel like they have as much choice as possible on the matter."

After six months of trying to conceive on their own, the couple decided to book a consultation with a fertility specialist, whose costly services would thankfully be covered by the insurance Río receives through her job. After reviewing options in the United States and Mexico, they opted for a provider in Manhattan that promoted itself as "LGBTQ+ competent" and featured lots of queer couples in its promotional materials. But as Río could have predicted, that broadly claimed "LGBTQ+ competence" didn't exactly translate to trans competence. "The first experience we had there was with someone who could not figure out which one of us had the uterus," she said. Even after they cleared that up, the specialist continued to exhibit a baseline ignorance around how to engage with trans patients, for example, misgendering them both by constantly referring to "male" and "female" organs.

The couple hasn't had any luck conceiving yet. Every month has brought the same emotional whiplash, where they start to believe that what they want might have happened, only to realize it hasn't. "There was one time when Cyd was a couple days late," said Río. "We were super excited and got all of our hopes up, but then his period started. Getting the news that you're not pregnant is so insulting after all that buildup. It really sucks. Every month, we have to strike this tricky balance of wanting to hold out hope but also hedging our bets to soften the blow in case that doesn't happen."

Now that they're seeing a fertility specialist, they will at least be able to resume HRT in the not-so-distant future.

"It will be nice to go back on hormones," she said. "IVF would allow us to do that."

IN/FERTILITY

On its face, Imogen Binnie's 2013 novel, *Nevada,* is a story about one trans woman's stunning ability to never actually deal with her shit. After blowing up her life in New York and hightailing it out west in a car that she stole from her ex, the protagonist Maria stumbles upon a Walmart clerk in small-town Nevada who she's convinced, for good reason, is a closeted trans woman himself. He needs her assistance, she tells herself, in cracking his egg wide open. So rather than deal with her own shit—which she really should do at some point—she projects that shit onto a total stranger and goes about trying to fix it, subconsciously hoping that she might fix her own shit by proxy, or something very Freudian like that. She fails, of course—no shit is fixed—and the narrative ends with Maria glued to a *Munsters*-themed slot machine, waiting for a jackpot that'll probably never pour out.

It's a fabulous rebuke of trans narratives as we typically expect them to unfold—the traditional three-act structure often found in trans-authored memoirs: A troubled beginning gives way to a painful but hard-won transition, ending with its post-op narrator at peace, having solved the only problem that apparently ever plagued them. We see none of that messy middle part in the pages of *Nevada*—a true literary blue-balling of the voyeuristic cis reader, who might've been expecting to witness something "brave" or "important." Nor does the work present transition as some kind of mystical panacea. Maria is still very much fucked-up by the time we meet her, despite having transitioned many years before the story begins. The clerk she encounters will probably continue to be fucked-up too, at least in the ways that he currently is, regardless of whether he ends up taking the plunge for him—or her—self.

Beyond the engaging narrative and its clever meta-critique, *Nevada,* which is set in the late 2000s, also reads like a time capsule to me, depicting what life was like in New York on the eve of the Great Recession, or at least what that era was like for one fictional bike punk, before the state was willing to pay for gender-affirming surgeries. The impossibility of bottom surgery pervades the text. (To borrow a turn of phrase from the way that we talk about *Sex and the City,* the impossibility of bottom surgery truly is the fifth lady of *Nevada.*) Maria wants it, but she can't afford it. Piranha, her friend and the only other trans woman (or at least the only other *transitioned* trans woman) to appear in the text, does as well. Piranha has saved up for ten years in order to get it, but every surgeon she consults rejects her on account of her chronic health issues. Maria can't even get that far. "Maybe one day, when my seven hundred dollars of savings become twenty thousand," she says.

"In all these years of transitioning I haven't even been able to save up for a decent pair of boots."

Were *Nevada* set only a few years later, Maria's problems, or at least this particular one, would have been solved. In 2015, two years after *Nevada* was published, New York became the seventh state to authorize Medicaid coverage for hormone replacement therapy and certain gender-affirming surgeries, including bottom surgery, thereby reversing a seventeen-year ban on using state funds for such care. New York's Department of Health later expanded that coverage to include facial feminization surgery and other procedures that aim to "change the patient's physical appearance to more closely conform [to] the patient's identified gender," so long as they are deemed to be "medically necessary" and not "purely cosmetic." Given Maria's status as a perpetually broke retail worker, I think it's safe to assume that she would have been able to get coverage through Medicaid. Or if she happened to have been insured through the bookstore that she worked for, she might have been able to access surgery by taking advantage of a 2014 change in state law that requires private insurance providers to offer coverage for trans health services.

The expansion to New York state Medicaid coverage in the mid-2010s coincided not only with the much-discussed "transgender tipping point," a moment in which trans people achieved unprecedented levels of visibility in mainstream American culture, but with a broader expansion to gender-affirming care nationwide as well. Following the lead of San Francisco, which, in 2001, became the first municipality to offer comprehensive trans healthcare benefits to city employees, public and private insurance providers alike began covering HRT and surgeries, reversing course on decades of explicitly trans-exclusionary policies, initially imposed due to that care's purportedly "experimental," "controversial," and not "medically necessary" nature.

From Maria's hipster heyday to this expansion of care, nothing fundamentally changed about the treatment itself. For the people seeking it out, trans healthcare didn't actually become any more "medically necessary" or any less "cosmetic." Those with the power to change that designation simply decided to do so one day—after years of urging from activist groups and pressure from organized labor, of course. Swapping a few words out for some others was all it took to alter the course of so many people's lives. In imagining *Nevada*'s unwritten postscript, I'd like to think that Maria got to benefit from these changes, at least before the pendulum swung back, as has happened before and is happening again.

•••

In the early months of 2019 as a reporter for *Out* magazine, I covered what felt like a seemingly endless wave of bills coming out of South Dakota that targeted trans kids—attempts to ban them from using the proper restrooms at school, bar them from participating in after-school sports, prevent them from discussing trans issues in the classroom, and block them from receiving gender-affirming care. All those bills failed, but I didn't sleep any easier. I just knew that we'd see more of these bills in the next year's legislative session, and unfortunately I was right. The following year, lawmakers filed a record number of anti-trans bills, only to break that record again in 2021, and then again every year after that. By the spring of 2024, five years after that initial wave of South Dakota bills had failed, twenty-three states had instituted restrictions on gender-affirming care for trans people under eighteen, while other states—Texas, Oklahoma, Kansas, and South Carolina among them—had considered banning that care for adults as well.

To borrow a framework from Susan Faludi, who in her 1991 book, *Backlash: The Undeclared War Against American Women,* proposed that the 1980s had resulted in "a powerful counterassault on women's rights . . . [that retracted] the handful of small and hard-won victories that the feminist movement did manage to win for women," we are living through an anti-trans backlash in the United States. This backlash is, of course, connected to other global fascist movements, from Poland to Brazil, which blame "gender ideology," among other culprits, for the ills of capitalism and climate destruction. But it is also distinctly American, responding in no small part to specific healthcare expansions made over the previous decade and the impact those gains have had on the lives of trans people in the United States, particularly those who rely on welfare programs to receive insurance coverage, whose political demonization is as American as apple pie.

What could we accomplish—individually, and as a collective—if so many of our lives, trans or cis, didn't revolve around trying to get healthcare? What would we be capable of if none of us had to worry about answering that perpetual question of access? Imagine what we could do with all that time and energy, not to mention incalculable resources, were we not funneling it all into our various attempts to solve that Sisyphean problem. I'm certain that we could do quite a lot, just as I'm certain that our enemies in power—the lawmakers, the think tanks, and their propagandists in arms—are desperate to ensure that we never find out. They want us exhausted, distracted, and confused, and they're dusting off old tactics to keep us that way.

•••

There has never been a "good" moment for trans healthcare in the United States. There's never been a "good" moment for healthcare in the United States, period. But the decades that followed World War II saw "the proliferation and early consolidation of transsexual medicine," in the words of historian Jules Gill-Peterson, with different models of care providing access to hormones and surgery—well, at least in theory. The university research clinics that emerged in the 1960s limited the number of patients they took on through stringent gatekeeping practices, Gill-Peterson points out, while the private clinics that came to the fore in the 1970s provided access only to those who could actually pay for their surgeries. All that said, more people were able to medically transition through institutional means by the late '70s than had been able to a few decades earlier—an obvious fact, considering most of those institutions did not exist a few decades earlier, but still. More people were able to.

The final decades of the twentieth century saw what Gill-Peterson describes in *Histories of the Transgender Child* as "a certain kind of retrenchment for access to transsexual medicine." Years of research at university clinics culminated with a one-size-fits-all "standards of care," according to historian Susan Stryker, along with diagnostic criteria, which were used as the basis for "gender identity disorder," or GID, which was added to the American Psychiatric Association's *Diagnostic and Statistical Manual of Mental Disorders* in 1980. The formalization of GID led to the closure of many university clinics ("the 'problem' of transsexuality now seemingly solved," per an obviously sarcastic Stryker), some of which then became privately run. Of course, DIY means of medical transition—black-market hormones, body and facial feminization via silicone injections, stealing your mother's estrogen when she's not looking—surely remained as popular as ever, perhaps even more so, once institutional medical care was made more inaccessible.

There were efforts to get gender-affirming care covered by private and public insurance providers since at least as far back as the 1960s, as Gill-Peterson has noted, and the addition of GID to the *DSM* provided a possible, if fraught, pathway to receiving that coverage. Some were able to travel that path: Kate Bornstein, the author and activist, details what it was like for her to get bottom surgery in the mid-1980s in her 1995 memoir, *Gender Outlaw,* and writes that her insurance provider covered the full $8,000 cost. But that navigable course was all but wiped from the map in 1989, when the Department of Health and Human Services published a formal national coverage determination against the use of public funds to cover gender-affirming care. As Cristan Williams, editor of the website the *TransAdvocate,* has argued, this set a precedent not just for Medicare and state-run Medicaid agencies but for private insurers as well. In drafting that determination, HHS drew on a 1981 report by the Office of Technology Assessment that argued that public insurance providers shouldn't cover transsexual care, claiming that such care is "expensive" and "controversial" and therefore "must be considered experimental."

In the years after the HHS determination, some states took steps to codify their public coverage, so that state-run Medicaid agencies would explicitly exclude gender-affirming surgeries and other kinds of trans healthcare. (New York was one of them, in 1998.) By the turn of the century, access to trans healthcare in the United States was split along class lines, according to Canadian academic Viviane K. Namaste. The American healthcare system at large is one in which care is "offered as a commodity to be bought," as she writes in 2000's *Invisible Lives: The Erasure of Transsexual and Transgendered People*. When it came to trans people specifically, "poor transsexuals obtain[ed] hormones through an underground market economy," while the aboveboard route to medical transition—diagnosis, prescriptions, and supervised care—was "a luxury available only to transsexuals with money." This in turn created "a two-tiered system of health care for transsexuals," similar to what she observed in her home country, where "employed individuals are eligible for SRS funding [from the state], while transsexuals without full-time jobs who are not in school"—like street-based sex workers and other lower-income trans women—"must pay for their surgeries themselves."

Reading through these old Medicaid policies, some now outdated and others still very much in place, I find it interesting how people, or at least cis politicians, used to talk about trans people's medical care, before the age of "affirming" and "confirming" one's gender. ("As if all the doctors did was to throw your inner woman a big thumbs-up," as the critic Andrea Long Chu once wrote in a roast of this linguistic shift.) According to a 1992 Medicaid handbook, Wyoming used to exclude "transsexual surgery" from state coverage. (The state no longer has an explicit policy—for adults, at least; a law banning all forms of gender-affirming care for minors went into effect in 2024.) Wisconsin once withheld public funding for such care as well, formally denying coverage for "hormone therapy" and all other drugs "associated with transsexual surgery." (A 2019 legal decision overruled that exclusion.) Arizona still blocks funding for "gender reassignment surgeries"; Kentucky, for "gender reassignment services"; and South Carolina, for "gender transition services or procedures." Nebraska state Medicaid explicitly refuses to cover "sex change procedures," though it may cover any "repair" needed should complications from such procedures arise. Tennessee refuses coverage as well. In fact, the authors of that state's policy took no chances, knocking out both "transsexual surgery" and "sex change or transformation surgery." I'm not exactly sure what a "sex transformation surgery" is or where they got that term. If I had to guess, I'd say it's something like that scene from the first season of *Ugly Betty,* when the transsexual character, Alexis Meade, played by the model-turned-actress Rebecca Romijn, emerges from the full-body bandages that had kept her identity a secret for the show's first twelve episodes. Maybe the policy's authors were big fans of Betty's antics. Maybe they caught Romijn's big reveal and decided they'd have *none* of that, whatever it was, in their state.*

Even if these exclusions were all struck from the record, Medicaid agencies would likely still deny coverage for most of the gender-affirming procedures that trans people tend to pursue, because Medicaid policies typically exclude those same procedures for cis people too. Arizona's policy explicitly re-

---

* In perusing various states' Medicaid policies, I also can't help but notice what other types of care often receive a bullet point under the bolded subheader "not covered": abortions, various fertility treatments, voluntary sterilization, non-life-saving hysterectomies, the "medically unnecessary alteration of sexual anatomy or characteristics," egg retrieval, sperm banking, in vitro fertilization, embryo storage, and transfer between gestational carriers. There is a palpable anxiety, eugenicist to its core, undergirding these exclusions—a need to oversee and control who can have children and who cannot; more than that: There is a palpable anxiety over the fact that some people who "should" have children are choosing not to and that some people who "shouldn't" are.

fuses coverage for hysterectomies, something that many trans men and transmascs have had done. Kentucky also excludes hysterectomies, but solely "if performed only to prevent pregnancy." Tennessee refuses to cover breast augmentation, unless it follows "a mastectomy that was done to treat a disease," like breast cancer, and the patient would like "to create [a] symmetrical appearance." Tennessee also excludes "penile implant devices," while Missouri withholds coverage for "penile prostheses," often the very same devices and prostheses used during the final stage of phalloplasty.

A common thread of discourse that I see on social media is that cis people love gender-affirming medical care: Even if they don't want trans people to get it, they can't stop getting it themselves. There are two ways to interpret that, both of which are true: Cis people not only use hormones and surgery to actively mold their bodies in accordance with their sex, even if sometimes subconsciously, in order to shore up their manhood or womanhood, both for themselves and others; they also use all the same medications and undergo the same surgical procedures that we do, albeit often for different reasons. The estradiol pills that I used to take? The estradiol valerate I inject into my thigh every week? Both are used by menopausal cis women, as well as others who don't produce estrogen. The spironolactone I used to take to block testosterone? A heart failure and blood pressure medication that's also prescribed to cis women to treat hirsutism, acne, and other unwanted effects of polycystic ovary syndrome. I've never gotten phalloplasty and don't have any plans to, but the surgeon who did Michael Dillon's, the first known trans man to successfully undergo the procedure in 1949, developed his technique by operating on soldiers who were wounded in World War I and II. Even just recently, I fell down a TikTok rabbit hole, landing randomly in bodybuilder TikTok. I couldn't stop watching videos of cis women talking about Anavar, an anabolic steroid that some of them use to bulk up. They were sharing tips about how to take it in low-enough doses so as not to deepen their voices or induce any clitoral growth, and all I could think about was how many transmascs have made the exact same content about "microdosing" testosterone to avoid its full effects. I also couldn't stop thinking about how many times some trans guy has jumped at the chance to tell me that the first two things that T did for him were deepen his voice and make his dick bigger.

But back to the dicks at hand: politicians drafting exclusionary Medicaid policies. Whether or not states' Medicaid programs specifically exclude phalloplasty and other gender-affirming surgeries, such procedures are often still effectively excluded for being "experimental" or "cosmetic." Missouri, for one, denies public funding for "experimental or investigational procedures [and] drugs," as well as for "cosmetic surgery," including but not limited to breast augmentation and rhinoplasty, both of which I've personally undergone and both of which were covered by insurance, as my provider in both cases determined these were "medically necessary," "gender-affirming" surgeries. The labels that insurance companies use to grant or deny coverage to patients might seem self-explanatory—experimental, cosmetic, investigational, elective, medically necessary, gender-affirming, and so on—but they're anything but. Not only are these terms arbitrarily applied, differing from state to state and between insurance providers, they're also totally meaningless, as the Canadian journalist Alex V. Green has explained. "What is necessary and lifesaving, or what is cosmetic and ephemeral?" they once wrote. "These labels are political and variable," shifted as desired by those with the power to shift them.

Further exemplifying the absolute void of meaning at the core of all these terms, Ohio's Medicaid program explicitly excludes, as of 2015, "gender transformation," yet as of 2019, the state was reportedly still not enforcing that exclusion. Inversely, Idaho has no explicit exclusions for gender-affirming care, but, as a 2022 court case confirmed, many trans people in the state have had their requests for coverage indefinitely delayed, if not outright denied, on the grounds that their desired procedures are "cosmetic" and, therefore, not "medically necessary." My own facial feminization surgery was delayed for months following the onset of the COVID-19 pandemic, after New York decided to halt all "elective" surgeries for the foreseeable future. Overnight, a surgery that my insurance provider had assured me was "medically necessary" suddenly very much wasn't, and I just had to sit there and wait until once again it was.

My point here is not that my FFS was undoubtedly medically necessary, but rather that "medically necessary" is not a description but a tool, one given only to those who are truly deserving of medical care, as agreed upon by insurance companies, medical providers, and politicians. It can mean anything but also means nothing, its definition shifting the moment you cross a state line.

• • •

I remember back in 2023, reading about how Missouri wanted to restrict access to gender-affirming care, on the grounds that it was, according to Attorney General Andrew Bailey, who is-

sued the proclamation, "experimental." Like many other people, I'm sure, I had a knee-jerk reaction to this word: It was
just a flat-out lie, a sensationalistic mislabeling deployed for its
unfortunate but very real political expediency. I mean, how
could these treatments be considered "experimental" when so
many of them predate me—predate my grandparents, even?

But what could I do with that trump card? Challenge Bailey to a debate? Hop in his Twitter mentions and tell him he
used the wrong word? Bailey might very well believe that trans
healthcare is experimental, but honestly it doesn't matter. That
word does mean something within the context of American
healthcare, given the way that it's used to deny coverage for all
kinds of medical treatments, whether that treatment will save
one's life or simply improve its quality. To be experimental
means to be controversial, means to be not medically necessary, means to be unfit for coverage. Why won't my insurance
cover this treatment? Because it's experimental. Why is it experimental? Because if it weren't, insurance would cover it.
Without further context, it means nothing. "Experimental" is
just a maddening, binary, self-justifying code that decides
whether you're able to get the care that you want. When Bailey or any other lawmaker invokes the "experimental" nature
of gender-affirming care in order to pass some ban or other,
it's not a verbal snafu born out of ignorance but a reflection of
precisely how well they understand the medical establishment
and the ways in which they can wield its power against their
chosen, medicalized targets. No matter how well we present
them with the right words, they aren't going to use them.
They want us gone, plain and simple, and this is one way they
can do that.

IM/POSSIBILITY

I can't remember the last time that someone asked me if I wanted to have kids. But when people do, I always say something like "So many things would have to fall into place." A nonanswer, but it's the truth. Whether I want to have kids is kind of beside the point. The real question to ask is *how* I'd have kids, and no matter how I answer that, for it to be real, so many things would first have to fall into place.

• • •

Early in our relationship, Mike and I were lying in my bed, tangled together in a postcoital sprawl as the sunlight peered through my gauzy pink curtains. Our eyes to the ceiling, we were lost in one of those endless get-to-know-you conversations where you're trying to discern if the two of you are compatible, but you don't say that's what you're doing, because that would be weird. At one point, I asked him what he thought about marriage and kids, careful to phrase my question in the least psychotic way possible. I wasn't trying to scare him away, like Glenn Close in *Fatal Attraction*. I was just curious. Relaxed and curious. Don't worry, Dan. I *can* be ignored.

Immediately queasy at asking such a loaded question, I jumped in to first answer the question myself. I told him I wasn't really sure about kids. "Not that I don't want them, I guess, but so many things would have to fall into place." I said I was into marriage—not politically, just, like, "It's fine." I didn't grow up dreaming of weddings and don't feel compelled to have one. The relationship itself would always mean more to me than having a big wedding, despite how much I love being a guest at big weddings, and I never want to be monogamous, even though I'm basically only ever seriously dating one person at a time. "I just want to feel like I can go to a party and get drunk and hook up with someone and not feel like I did something wrong," I told him. "I just feel better going about the world like that. Even if I don't do anything with it, I just like having the option."

He told me that made sense to him and that he didn't want monogamy either, even though he's very much a "wife guy," as my friend Morgan once described him. He said that he liked kids and would love to be a dad, but that he also didn't necessarily know how that would happen. Sometimes, he told me, he toyed with the idea of getting pregnant—men's business, truly, so I appreciated his candor. But he said that he would only do that if he could do so in total seclusion, hidden away in the woods for a year, somewhere off the grid, and then return to Brooklyn with his swaddled babe in tow. Even hidden away, though, safe from the threat of public scrutiny and whatever harassment he'd otherwise deal with, the prospect of being a pregnant man was too daunting to seriously consider, he said. Going off testosterone for such an extended period, the dysphoric body horror that delivery would entail—none of it felt possible for him. I told him that made sense.

The sunlight diminished as the questions wore on and our bodily tangle adjusted itself. We talked about surgeries, mine and his. He told me that when he transitioned more than a decade ago, when he was still in college, top surgery had seemed so out of reach. So, convinced he'd never be able to do it, he shunted the thought from his mind—because if you'll never be able to do something, why even bother considering it?

It wasn't until many years later, when more and more guys he knew started to get top surgery—and not only that, get it covered by insurance—that he realized that he might be able to get it too. "I thought I didn't want it when I thought I couldn't have it," he said, rolling his head toward me. "It was easier to not want it than it was to deal with wanting it when I thought I wouldn't get it." Again, I told him that made sense.

His desire to have the surgery, long dormant though never quite gone, reawakened and spurred him to figure out how to get it himself. He talked to some of those guys he knew who'd undergone the procedure, asked them who they'd gone to and how they'd gotten it covered, and figured that his best bet was getting a job with good insurance, which eventually, after a few more years, he was finally able to do. He always thought that top surgery would cost too much, that it would always be just out of reach. And then suddenly, years later, thanks to sweeping policy changes and the precedents set by others like himself, that was no longer the case. Sometimes, things don't fall into place, but also sometimes they do.

• • •

The terror that reactionaries have incited over the years over doctors creating "lifelong slaves to the medical system," to quote one fearmongering commentator, sacrificing our fertility to turn a quick buck—it's all just been so cynical, so obviously false. They don't actually care about our fertility except insofar as they can politicize its loss and weaponize it against us, and much like with other matters of bodily autonomy, they also do not care that we might sacrifice it willingly.

I barely remember being asked if I understood that starting HRT might permanently impact my fertility. I know that I was—I mean, it's standard for clinics that operate on the basis of informed consent; famously, you're informed, so famously, you consent. But my memories from that day and the weeks surrounding that appointment tend toward the impressionistic, with scattered moments of absolute clarity. Getting the callback to schedule my intake appointment. Staring at a tube of surgical lube as I sat on the lip of an exam table, waiting for my doctor to show up. Walking down Eighth Avenue two weeks later after my next appointment, cuing up Whitney's "I'm Every Woman" as I popped that first estradiol in my mouth, savoring the sweet nothing of that Tiffany-blue pill as it dissolved and frothed under my tongue. I'd made a whole playlist for that day, I remember, filled with other tracks that were equally on the nose. Deee-Lite's "Runaway." Black Box's "Everybody Everybody." I thought that Martha was singing "set me free" in the middle of the verses, but I've since learned that she's actually saying, "sad and free, sad and free." Either way, it was apt for the day. I'd set myself free. Sad and free.

I freely gave up my surest pathway to motherhood, if not with the hormones, then with surgery some years later. I remember that surgeon asking me if I'd frozen any sperm. I told him the same thing I'd told my doctor at that HRT intake appointment: that no, I had not; that I didn't care; that I knew what I was doing; that I was fine with that exchange. I sacrificed something in making that trade, but there would always be a sacrifice, no matter what I chose. The life I live. The woman I am. The communities I have. The politics I've sharpened. It's like my friend Jamie said the other night when we were out at a bar with a friend of ours. That friend was nervous about an upcoming surgery, her first such procedure, and wanted to talk through that anxiety with us, given our shared experience. Jamie reassured her by talking about how "every choice you make forecloses on a life where you didn't make that choice," like the body you once had and the way it looked or functioned, the relationships you're building and those you left behind. What she meant, or at least what I understood her to mean, was that the past may seem better than the present at times, its options more expansive in hindsight. But when you had the chance to choose a different future for yourself, you seized that opportunity, which then foreclosed and opened others. Sometimes, things don't fall into place because you chose that other things would. Sometimes, things won't fall into place, but it's fine. You chose something else.

ACKNOWLEDGMENTS

Thank you to the people who've encouraged me over the years, the women and gay guys and everyone in between. Whether you actually, explicitly said something like "Your writing is good and you should keep doing it" or were unwittingly someone I'd project onto while writing to wonder if "X would think this was funny" or "Y would think this was corny," you played a vital role in this process. It's a nonexhaustive list, to be sure, but: Mitra Kaboli, Rider Alsop, Nia Nottage, Emma Quail, Cyd Nova, Emily Scanlon, Rex Santus, Hannah May, Erin English, Venus Stevens, Julianne Escobedo Shepherd, Suzanne Goldenberg, Chiquitita, Lena Ruth Solow, John Sherman, Eric Torres, Jo Livingstone, Marlowe Granados, Thora Siemsen, Alex V. Green, Penny Parkin, Eric Shethar, Alex Bedder, Sam Corbett, Macy Rodman, Parker Sargent, Katia Perea, Zarina Crockett, Katie Liederman, Joss Barton, Jasmine Sanders, Ty Mitchell, Chrystin Ondersma, Zefyr Lisowski, Suzy Exposito, Reed Jackson, Vidal Wu, Charlene Incarnate, Emily Lim Rogers, Liv Bruce, Kyle Lukoff, Kate Friggle, Max Steele, Charlie Markbreiter, Shon Faye, Jules Gill-Peterson, McKenzie Wark, Denne Michele Norris, Lena Pervez Afridi, Gaines Blasdel, Meredith Talusan, Raquel Willis, Grace Byron, merritt k, Sloane Holzer, Brittany Spanos, Cherie Nesfield, DJ Wawa, Zackary Drucker, Lenny Schnier, Stephen Ira, Liam O'Brien, Rachel Millman, Sara David, Erik Escobar, Mikelle Street, Mardi Pieronek, Ashley Reese, Frida Garza, Amy Rose Spiegel, Crissy Bell, Nea Ching, Mimi Zima, Mattie Lubchansky, Jaya Saxena, Haley Mlotek, Tuck Woodstock, Marian Bull, Oscar Díaz, Aurora Mattia, Davey Davis, Alyza Enriquez, Librada González Fernández, and more. To say that I couldn't have written this book without you would be an accurate and true statement. Someone should say it!

Thank you to my agent, Connor Goldsmith, for seeing something special in me when I was just blogging and tweeting. Thank you to my editors, Katy Nishimoto and Ben Greenberg; my work could not have been molded by better hands. Thank you to Jia Tolentino for the vital role you played in this book's genesis, and thank you to JP Woodham, Zora O'Neill, Cara DuBois, and everyone at Random House who worked hard to make this book what it is.

Thank you to Sheri Ford, Corey Williams, Amy El-Shafei, Kiersten Clark, Jesse Hasko, Rob Orlowski, Erin Bailey, Haig Moses, Noah Van Court, and everyone else at the studio who supported me in this process; thank you to Mark McAndrews and Cara Griffin for encouraging me to take time off to write.

Thank you to Larissa Pham and Tommy Pico for talking to me about writing and treating me like a peer before I'd ever written anything that I would've thought deserved it. Torrey Peters, my mentor-turned-friend, I'd be someone else entirely, someone stupider and worse at writing, if you'd ignored that annoying DM I sent you eight years ago. Paris—I mean, "P. E." Moskowitz, it's so fun and annoying being psychically handcuffed to you. I hope that key never turns up. Morgan M. Page, the TikToks and VMs you send me comprise an alarming amount of my daily nourishment. Thank you for being my friend and for continuing to make such paradigm-shifting work.

Thank you, Ceyenne Doroshow, the People's Pope, for creating and sustaining life for so many others. Thank you for always being so encouraging of my writing and for making me feel from the first time we met like I was someone worth talking to.

Thank you, Cecilia Gentili, the Mother of All Whores. Thank you, Anthony Brian Smith, Jack Rohman, and Spencer Barnett. I love and miss you all so much.

Thank you, Mom, for always thinking of me and for always trying to meet me halfway, and thank you Dad, Ben, Jac, Siobhan, Ken, Paulo, and every other family member who's shown me kindness, love, and support while working on this book (and also in the decades before that).

Thank you, Río Sofia, for always believing in me. Thank you for believing that a better future is possible and for modeling every day how we can work together to build it. Thank you, Joan Summers. Your brilliance, your beauty, your hateful reminders that you're seven years younger than me—you can *All About Eve* me any time that you want. Kay Gabriel, I love you, I love you, I love you. Thank you for being real, for being realer than real. Lola Pellegrino, a doctor among women (????), please sit next to me every time. Lo Burnett, you always have my back. I hope I've given you even half as much in return as you've given me since we first met. Tyler Morse, my oldest friend, you always groan when I bring up that old poem of yours, "NO-FILTER," but "you can make any ol' sound you want girl, you can make any sound you want, any sound you want girl—THAT'S THE SOUND YOU CHOSE? YOU CHOSE THAT SOUND?" has never not been true, instructive, jolting, and perfect. I love you so much. To the next eighteen years!

Muna Mire, there's no one I'd rather cackle with as the horrors of the future unfold. Charlotte Shane, every day I think about what I would do if some apocalyptic event shuts off our cellphones and we couldn't trade VMs back and forth every day. I can't say what I *think* I'd do without bringing down the mood, but trust me: It wouldn't be fab. And Jamie Hood, my sister, your friendship has changed me in every conceivable way. I've loved you from the moment that we first met eight years ago—down in Orlando! We were only nineteen.

Michael Funk, thank you for changing my understanding of what love could feel like. Thank you for never doubting that I'd actually finish this book. It's an honor, a privilege, a pleasure, and a thrill to love and be loved by someone so kind and so funny, so compassionate, talented, affectionate, supportive, considerate, protective, and hot as you are. Thank you for being in my life. Thank you for bringing me into yours (and Ezra's). Thank you for everything. Thank you. Thank you.

NOTES

vii **"to the association of certain ideas"**   Marcel Proust. *In Search of Lost Time, vol. I: Swann's Way,* translated by C. K. Scott Moncrieff and Terence Kilmartin. Modern Library, 2003.

vii **"Where is the body?"**   *RuPaul's Drag Race.* Season 11, episode 12, "Queens Everywhere." World of Wonder Productions, May 16, 2019.

OBVIOUS COMMUNITY MEMBER

3 **which was about to screen *Monica***   Andrea Pallaoro, dir. *Monica.* IFC Films, 2022.

4 **a 2022 Venice Film Festival favorite**   Jenelle Riley. "Trace Lysette and Patricia Clarkson on the Joys and Challenges of Making *Monica:* 'The Work Has Already Changed People's Lives.' " *Variety,* Jan. 4, 2024.

4 **"OK, go get 'em"**   Pallaoro. *Monica.*

PICK ME

9 **"Satan's Circus"**   Lucy Sante. *Low Life: Lures and Snares of Old New York.* Farrar, Straus and Giroux, 1991.

10 **began to move in en masse**   Adam Sternbergh. "Soho. Nolita. Dumbo. NoMad?" *New York,* April 8, 2010.

12 **President Donald Trump the day prior**   Anemona Hartocollis and Yamiche Alcindor. "Women's March Highlights as Huge Crowds Protest Trump: 'We're Not Going Away.' " *The New York Times,* Jan. 21, 2017.

12 **appear to be doing just that**   Stephanie Maida. "The BEST Signs from the Women's March in NYC." Guest of a Guest, Jan. 23, 2017.

13 **as the year before**   Amanda Arnold. "How Many People Were at the Second Annual Women's March?" *New York,* Jan. 21, 2018.

17 **scarfing down McDonald's at the mall**   Suzanna Andrews. "There's Something About Gisele." *Vanity Fair,* Oct. 2004.

19 **"someone to change her life"** Sandra Cisneros. *The House on Mango Street*. Arte Público Press, 1984.

21 **"Voices of Trans Employees"** "Lush Cosmetics Kicks Off Human Rights Campaign by Elevating Voices of Trans Employees," emailed press release. Lush Fresh Handmade Cosmetics, Feb. 2018.

22 **"have attempted suicide"** Rachel Dowd. "More Than 40% of Transgender Adults in the U.S. Have Attempted Suicide," press release. Williams Institute at the UCLA School of Law, July 20, 2023.

24 **"children six and under"** Harron Walker. "The Lobster Emoji Is Apparently a Trans Icon?" *Out*, Jan. 11, 2019.

24 **that was a reach** Miley Cyrus. "The Best of Both Worlds." *Hannah Montana*. Walt Disney Records, 2006.

25 **half a billion every year** Sarah Butler. "Lush Paid Managers £5m in Bonuses After Taking £5m in State Support." *The Guardian*, July 30, 2023.

26 **"on behalf of LGBTQ causes"** Carlos A. Ball. *The Queering of Corporate America: How Big Business Went from LGBTQ Adversary to Ally*. Beacon Press, 2020.

27 **where do I exist?** Sophie feat. Cecile Believe. "Immaterial." *Oil of Every Pearl's Un-Insides*. MSMSMSM, Transgressive, & Future Classic, 2018.

DISCONTENT

30 **access to their insurance coverage** Lena Ruth Solow. "The Scourge of Worker Wellness Programs." *The New Republic*, Sept. 2, 2019.

30 **but for media labor organizing** Robert Luketic, dir. *Legally Blonde*. MGM, 2001.

37 **in that same time span** Angela Fu. "US Lost More Than Two Local Newspapers a Week This Year, New Medill Report Finds." *Poynter*, Nov. 16, 2023.

37 **"have ever worked under"** Joan Summers. "Dissociating at the Tranny Factory." Curran, Sept. 19, 2023.

38 **the industry over the past decade** Angela Fu. "Not Just a Wave, but a Movement: Journalists Unionize at Record Numbers." *Poynter*, July 16, 2021.

39 **was scheduled to happen** Isaac Scher. "New York City Hospitals Will 'Go Broke' from the Coronavirus Crisis Unless the Federal Government Steps In to Help, Says Mayor Bill de Blasio." *Business Insider*, March 24, 2020.

WHAT'S NEW AND DIFFERENT?

41 **"The Chanel boots? Yeah, I am."** David Frankel, dir. *The Devil Wears Prada*. 20th Century Fox, 2006.

44 **"at all times. Got it."** Ibid.

44 **"there's no denying that"** Carly Stern. *"The Devil Wears Prada* Author Reflects on 'Wild' Experience of Being *Vogue* Boss Anna Wintour's Assistant: 'It Was a Crazy Entrance into the Working World of New York City.'" *The Daily Mail,* June 11, 2021.

45 **in *A Room of One's Own?*** Virginia Woolf. *A Room of One's Own.* In *The Selected Works of Virginia Woolf.* Wordsworth Library Collection, 2007.

47 **"because I invented it"** Lady Gaga, dir. "Marry the Night," music video. Interscope Records, 2011.

49 **between 2008 and 2009** Sam Becker. "News and Media Layoffs Keep Piling Up After One of the Worst Years Since the Financial Crisis." *Fast Company,* Feb. 23, 2024.

54 **contemporaneous to the term's origins** Nancy Meyers, dir. *The Intern.* Warner Bros. Pictures, 2015.

55 **but not too seriously** Sophia Amoruso. *#GIRLBOSS.* Penguin Publishing Group, 2015.

55 **"I'm sure you aren't either"** Ibid.

55 **Mukhopadhyay once put it** Samhita Mukhopadhyay. "The Girlboss Is Dead. Long Live the Girlboss." *New York,* Aug. 31, 2021.

55 **per the critic Jamie Hood?** Jamie Hood. "The Girlboss and the Anti-Woke Cool Girl." *The Drift,* Jan. 31, 2022.

55 **like Miki Agrawal** Noreen Malone. "Sexual-Harassment Claims Against a 'She-E.O.'" *New York,* March 2017.

56 **exec Sheryl Sandberg?** Dawn Foster. "Sheryl Sandberg's Trickle-Down Feminism Stands Exposed." *Jacobin,* Dec. 2018.

56 **funds the slaughter of an occupied people?** "Biden Admin Quietly Approves 100+ Arms Sales to Israel While Claiming Concern for Civilians in Gaza." *Democracy Now!,* March 7, 2024.

56 **the better cinematic example** David Fincher, dir. *Gone Girl.* 20th Century Fox, 2014.

62 **exploiter of secretaries herself** Mike Nichols, dir. *Working Girl.* 20th Century Fox, 1988.

64 **because of their similar titles** Lizzie Borden, dir. *Working Girls.* Miramax, 1986.

65 **fails to improve their conditions** Lizzie Borden, dir. *Born in Flames.* First Run Features, 1983.

65 **told me in a phone interview** Lizzie Borden. Personal interview, Sept. 1, 2020.

66 **"pièce de résistance"** Borden. *Working Girls.*

67 **described this dynamic** Erika Stallings. "When Black Women Go from Office Pet to Office Threat." Zora, Jan. 16, 2020.

68 **in a territorial contralto** Borden. *Working Girls.*

74 **"What's new and different?"** Ibid.

MONKEY'S PAW GIRL EDITION

81 **"but they don't"** *RuPaul's Drag Race Untucked!* Season 5, episode 5, "Snatch Game." World of Wonder Productions, Feb. 25, 2013.

83 **"treat them, too"** "TEDxToronto Women: Nina Arsenault." *She Does the City,* Oct. 15, 2015.

86 **that didn't catch on** "A Guide to the Buzzy Micro-Neighborhood of Stuyshwick." *New York,* May 30, 2019.

89 **claim to womanhood** Lisa Allardice. "Chimamanda Ngozi Adichie: 'America Under Trump Felt Like a Personal Loss.' " *The Guardian,* Nov. 14, 2020.

89 **for the first time** Vondie Curtis-Hall, dir. *Glitter.* 20th Century Fox, 2001.

90 **the coronavirus pandemic** Harron Walker. "How Essential Is My Facial Feminization Surgery?" *Esquire,* June 9, 2020.

92 **didn't mean to turn you on?** Mariah Carey. "Didn't Mean to Turn You On." *Glitter.* Virgin, 2001.

93 **twenty-two states and counting** "Identity Document Laws and Policies." Movement Advancement Project website.

SHE WANTS, SHE TAKES, SHE PRETENDS

99 **"all of her friends"** Sinéad Bligh. Personal interview, March 16, 2022.

99 **ruled a suicide** Joyce Randall Senechal. Afterword to *Sketchbook, September 1977,* by Greer Lankton. Primary Information, 2023.

100 **as a book in 2023** Lankton. *Sketchbook.*

100 **mass-produced doll, as she once said** Bridgitte Engler. "Shocking Dolls." *Paper,* 1984. The Greer Lankton Collection, Mattress Factory Museum, Pittsburgh, Penn. (on future reference GLC, MFM).

101 **and transsexuals used to say** Charlene Incarnate. "RuPaul's Version of LGBT History Erases Decades of Trans Drag Queens." *BuzzFeed,* March 8, 2018.

101 **"ventricles of her heart"** Kay Gabriel. "Top Ten: Kay Gabriel." *Artforum,* Nov. 2022.

101 **"somebody's sins but not mine"** Patti Smith. "Gloria." *Horses.* Arista, 1975.

101 **to give birth to oneself** Juliana Huxtable. *Mucus in My Pineal Gland.* Capricious, Wonder, 2017.

102 **once said of her dolls** Interview found during in-person visit to the GLC, MFM, March 16, 2022.

102 **for us or anyone else** Kali Hays. "*Out* Magazine Dogged by Unpaid Contributors." *Women's Wear Daily,* Jan. 28, 2019.

102 **magazine of the same name** Harron Walker. "Making Work in Her Own Image." *Out,* April 25, 2019.

103 **"suffering on the streets"** Alex V. Green. "Trans Visibility Won't Save Us." *BuzzFeed News,* Dec. 4, 2019.

103 **presenting them for public view** Tourmaline, Eric A. Stanley, and Johanna Burton. Introduction to *Trap Door: Trans Cultural Production and the Politics of Invisibility.* MIT Press, 2017.

103 **"go beyond mere procreation"** McKenzie Wark. *Love and Money, Sex and Death.* Verso, 2023.

104 **"have to show up"** Cecilia Gentili. *Red Ink.* Rattlestick Theater, New York, Nov. 2023.

104 **"captivating, you know?"** Zackary Drucker. Personal interview, March 2019.

105 **limp three-quarter angle** Photo album, c. 1975–c. 1990 (GL.PA.00001). GLC, MFM.

107 **born in Flint, Michigan** Hilton Als. "Doll Parts: Hilton Als Recalls Some of His Most Poignant Memories of Artist Greer Lankton." *Document Journal,* Oct. 30, 2014.

107 **a nearby village** Nan Goldin. "A Rebel Whose Dolls Embodied Her Demons." *The New York Times,* Dec. 22, 1996.

107 **born in Chicago** Pat Butler. "Her Tortured Past Yields Bright Future." *Lincoln-Belmont Booster,* Aug. 5, 1992. GLC, MFM.

107 **that has since closed** Photo album, c. 1975–c. 1990 (GL.PA.00001).

107 **once told a reporter** Phyllis Feuerstein. "Young Sculptor: Stuffed Shirt a Specialty." *The Star,* Jan. 10, 1974. GLC, MFM.

108 ***One from the Vaults*** Morgan M. Page. *One from the Vaults.* Podcast episode 31, "It's About Me Not You," Aug. 6, 2019.

108 **liked to make puppets himself** Interview found during in-person visit to the GLC, MFM, March 16, 2022.

108 **she was still a student** Feuerstein. "Young Sculptor."

108 **pretend that it was her hair** Cathi Cunningham. "[Greer] Is a Super Sophomore." *The Torch,* 1974. GLC, MFM.

109 **"they didn't move right"** Interview found during in-person visit to the GLC, MFM, March 16, 2022.

109 **"talking about it all the time"** Sarah Hallett. Personal interview, March 16, 2022.

109 **excelling at everything he could** Lankton. *Sketchbook.*

109 **"so I got the sex change"** Grace Byron. "Trail-blazing Trans Artist Greer Lankton Gave the Girls the Dolls We Need." *Xtra,* Aug. 25, 2022.

109 **"straighten me out"** Butler. "Her Tortured Past."

110 **conversion therapy instead** Julia Serano. *Whipping Girl: A Transsexual Woman on Sexism and the Scapegoating of Femininity,* second edition. Seal Press, 2016. *See also:* Jules Gill-Peterson. *Histories of the Transgender Child.* University of Minnesota Press, 2018. Susan Stryker. *Transgender History.* Seal Press, 2008.

110 **sketchbook from 1977** Lankton. *Sketchbook.*

111 **"certainly delivers well"** Cunningham. "Super Sophomore."

111 *and the Bloodshed* Laura Poitras, dir. *All the Beauty and the Bloodshed.* Neon, 2022.

111 **"too tanned and too rich"** Dylan Jones. "Greer Lankton Talks to Dylan Jones." *i-D,* 1984. Press clipping packet, c. 1982–c. 1985 (GL.PL.00157). GLC, MFM.

111 **afterword to that 1977 sketchbook** Randall Senechal. Afterword to *Sketchbook.*

111 **while living in Park Forest** Photo album, c. 1975–c. 1990 (GL.PA.00001).

111 **Renée Richards, and Christine Jorgensen** Randall Senechal. Afterword to *Sketchbook.*

111 **"sex change was the only answer"** Greer Lankton. Unspecified correspondence, c. 1976–77 (GL.C.3161). GLC, MFM.

112 **"I swear to become my body"** Lankton. *Sketchbook.*

112 **orange and then black** Photo album, c. 1975–c. 1990 (GL.PA.00001).

112 **"I will become."** Lankton. *Sketchbook.*

112 **dullest person she'd ever met** Greer Lankton. Artist statement, *It's all about ME, Not You.* Mattress Factory Museum, Pittsburgh, Penn., 1996.

112 **next to it in shaky caps** Photo album, c. 1985–c. 1994 (GL.PA.00002). GLC, MFM.

113 **captioned another set of photos** Three sets of photos in this paragraph from photo album, c. 1975–c. 1990 (GL.PA.00001).

113 **"allow me to function"** Lankton. *Sketchbook.*

114 **"that wasn't the issue"** Phyllis Feuerstein. "Trapped in 'Wrong' Body, Transsexual Seeks New Life." *Suburban Trib,* July 31, 1978. GLC, MFM.

114 **masculine portraiture** This and images in next paragraph from photo album, c. 1975–c. 1990 (GL.PA.00001).

115 **"exciting about him"** Jones. "Greer Lankton Talks."

115 **Thirty-first Street in New York** Ibid.

116 **she once told *i-D*** Ibid.

116 *Eye* **in 1984** Carlo McCormick. "Greer Lankton." *East Village Eye,* Nov. 1984. GLC, MFM.

116 **"naïve, pious, or complaisant"** Eve Kosofsky Sedgwick. "Paranoid Reading and Reparative Reading; or, You're So Paranoid, You Probably Think This Essay Is About You." *Touching Feeling: Affect, Pedagogy, Performance.* Duke University Press, 2003.

117 **once said in an interview** Interview found during in-person visit to the GLC, MFM, March 16, 2022.

118 **"protect herself in public"** Byron. "Trail-blazing Trans Artist."

119 **"a night of classical musical theater numbers"** *La MaMa's Squirts,* Night 3, curated by Charlene Incarnate. La MaMa, New York, June 2, 2019.

120 **"the way I'd like to look"** McCormick. "Greer Lankton."

120 **documentary *Paris Is Burning*** Jennie Livingston, dir. *Paris Is Burning.* Off-White Productions and Prestige Pictures, 1990.

121 **"abortion," she told me** Mardi Pieronek. Personal interview, March 10, 2023.

121 **interview for *New York* magazine** Cecilia Gentili. Personal interview, Sept. 21, 2022.

122 **"I learned with them."** Ibid.

122 **" 'standards of care' brain," she said** Pieronek. Personal interview, March 10, 2023.

124 **"not really that bad"** Written statement, found during in-person visit to the GLC, MFM, March 16, 2022.

125 **"soft sculpture" in 1984** Ellen Lubell. "Eye of the Beholder." *The Village Voice,* 1984. GLC, MFM.

125 **"it was anatomically correct"** Beauregard Houston-Montgomery. *NY Talk,* Oct. 1984. GLC, MFM.

125 **"transsexual that makes dolls"** Jones. "Greer Lankton Talks."

125 **for the *East Village Eye*** Sylvia Falcon. "Greer Lankton." *East Village Eye,* Oct. 1983. GLC, MFM.

126 **"rather than celebration"** Als. "Doll Parts."

127 **a photograph of it** "*Charred Woman* Doll Standing Against a White Wall" (GL.S.270) and subsequent photos in series. GLC, MFM.

128 **with respect to her gender** Interview found during in-person visit to the GLC, MFM, March 16, 2022.

128 ***The Village Voice* in 1984** Lubell. "Eye of the Beholder."

129 ***The Gentrification of the Mind*** Sarah Schulman. *The Gentrification of the Mind.* University of California Press, 2013.

129 **"deep voice," she once said** Jones. "Greer Lankton Talks."

129 **between $75 and $500** Consignment agreement with Civilian Warfare Gallery, 1984 or 1985. GLC, MFM.

129 **Iggy Pop**   c. 1990 Research and Documentation Slides, Iggy Pop with *Princess Pamela* sub-series (GL.S.2432–44). GLC, MFM.

129 **restaurateur Pamela Strobel**   Mayukh Sen. "She Was a Soul Food Sensation. Then, 19 Years Ago, She Disappeared." Food52, Feb. 2, 2017.

129 **for many thousands**   Civilian Warfare Gallery price list for one-woman show by Greer Lankton, 1984 (GL.EA.84). GLC, MFM.

130 **one of her old CVs**   Greer Lankton. CV, 1984 (GL.EA.29). GLC, MFM.

130 **"just part of the anatomy"**   Interview found during in-person visit to the GLC, MFM, March 16, 2022.

130 **"what it means to be a person"**   Greer Lankton. Artist statement, n.d. GLC, MFM.

131 **"concentrate on the change"**   This and following photos and captions from photo album, c. 1975–c. 1990 (GL.PA.00001).

133 **commercial work here and there**   Photo album, c. 1981–c. 1986 (GL.PA.00003). GLC, MFM. *See also:* "Girls in Pearls." *Mademoiselle,* Sept. 1984. GLC, MFM.

133 **"still be doing what I'm doing"**   Lankton. *Sketchbook.*

133 **"in your apartment making things"**   Interview found during in-person visit to the GLC, MFM, March 16, 2022.

134 **"worried about Greer," he writes**   Paul Monroe. Letter to Bill and Lynn Lankton, n.d. (GL.C.1484). GLC, MFM.

135 **goth boutique that opened in 1976**   Butler. "Her Tortured Past."

135 **Mia Farrow in *Rosemary's Baby***   This and photo in next paragraph from photo album, c. 1985–c. 1994 (GL.PA.00002).

135 **"recovering dope addict"**   Butler. "Her Tortured Past."

136 **average trans-authored memoir**   Jonathan Ames. Introduction to *Sexual Metamorphosis: An Anthology of Transsexual Memoirs.* Vintage Books, 2005.

136 **"because I'm over it"**   Lankton. Artist statement, 1996.

TALES FROM THE HOSIERY COUNTER

137 **queer like herself**   Jia Qing Wilson-Yang. *Small Beauty.* Metonymy Press, 2016.

137 **might have also been trans**   Casey Plett. *Little Fish.* Arsenal Pulp Press, 2018.

139 **needed to buy a house**   Timothy Noah. "Let's Give Black World War II Vets What We Promised." *The New Republic,* Nov. 10, 2023.

140 **trans-oriented periodical of its kind**   Susan Stryker. *Transgender History.* Seal Press, 2008.

140 **many of them called home** Jules Gill-Peterson. "Feeling Like a Bad Trans Object." *Post45,* Dec. 9, 2019.

140 **pages of *Casa Susanna*** Michel Hurst and Robert Swope, eds. *Casa Susanna.* PowerHouse Books, 2004.

140 **Latin music stations** Sébastien Lifshitz, dir. *Casa Susanna.* PBS, 2022.

140 **even sometimes unmarried straight men** Stryker. *Transgender History.*

143n **"salesperson in the store"** "The Consultant Teaching Trans Women How to Be 'Feminine.'" *Broadly,* May 15, 2016.

146 **love you so much today** Author's aunt. Personal interview, May 15, 2023.

A TRANS PANIC, SO TO SPEAK

147 **"*JUDGE YE NOT*. . . . ."** Ed Wood, dir. *Glen or Glenda.* Screen Classics, 1953.

148 **immediately upon reading it** Hari Nef (@harinef). "when i got asked to get on the mic for @gq i thought about." Twitter (X) post, Feb. 24, 2021.

149 **"and [Wood] loved angora"** "Dolores Fuller on Ed Wood Jr., Being Dissed By Sarah Jessica Parker Interview." YouTube video, uploaded by Si Melzer, July 4, 2007.

149 **"to make him happy"** Wood. *Glen or Glenda.*

149 **becoming Anne** Ibid.

149 **coverage of Christine Jorgensen** Hal Hinson. "Ed Wood." *The Washington Post,* Oct. 7, 1994.

149 **"Becomes Blonde Beauty"** Ben White. "Ex-GI Becomes Blonde Beauty: Bronx Army Vet Undergoes First Widely Known Gender Reassignment Procedure in 1952." New York *Daily News,* Dec. 1952.

149 **nonconsensual on Jorgensen's part** Christine Jorgensen. *Christine Jorgensen: A Personal Autobiography.* Excerpted in *Sexual Metamorphosis: An Anthology of Transsexual Memoirs,* edited by Jonathan Ames. Vintage Books, 2005.

150 **about what she had done** Ibid.

150 **publishing a memoir** Andrew J. Zilavy, Richard A. Santucci, and Maxx A. Gallegos. "The History of Gender-Affirming Vaginoplasty Technique." *Urology,* April 21, 2022.

150 **"fully and completely a man"** Wood. *Glen or Glenda.*

151 **"member of that sex"** Ibid.

151 **and other sexual deviants** Susan Stryker. *Transgender History.* Seal Press, 2008.

152 **"disabused of it"** Jan Morris. *Conundrum.* Signet, 1974.

152 **"happy," she tells him** Wood. *Glen or Glenda.*

HUMOR ME

157 **"They pick major boogs!"** Ruth Graham. "One of *Us*." *Slate*, Sept. 22, 2016.

158 **"a complete stop at some point"** Carolyn Twersky. "Bella Hadid Opens Up About Mental Health in Tear-Filled Instagram Post: 'Social Media Is Not Real.'" *W*, Nov. 9, 2021.

158 **clearly not pooling with mucus** "Laura Lee apology video with original captions." YouTube video, uploaded by Melissa, Aug. 20, 2018.

160 **saliva, sweat, and feces** Jack Hartnell. *Medieval Bodies: Life and Death in the Middle Ages*. W. W. Norton & Company, 2019.

161 **purge their excess humors** Ibid.

161 **allegedly violent disposition** Ibid.

162 **Paracelsus and others** Ibid.

162 **neurotransmitter abnormalities** Hal Arkowitz and Scott O. Lilienfeld. "Is Depression Just Bad Chemistry?" *Scientific American*, March 1, 2014.

162 **by advertising, not medical research** P. E. Moskowitz. "Breaking Off My Chemical Romance." *The Nation*, March 23, 2022.

162 **it's apt. Apt!** *The Simpsons*. Season 13, episode 6, "She of Little Faith." Gracie Films & 20th Television, Dec. 16, 2001.

163 **no one suspects a thing** *Love & Death*. Season 1, episode 4, "Do No Evil." David E. Kelley Productions, Blossom Films, Whatever Lola Wants Productions, and Lionsgate Television, May 4, 2023.

164 **exposing others to their bodily fluids** "HIV Criminalization Laws." Movement Advancement Project website.

164 **Control and Prevention** "How HIV Spreads." Centers for Disease Control and Prevention website, Jan. 18, 2024.

165 **among American users** Rae Witte. "How Women Squirt on Camera, According to Porn Stars." Mashable, Aug. 30, 2023.

LOST IN SPACE

166 **"monuments to greed"** Penelope Green. "The Painter and the Pink Palazzo." *The New York Times*, Nov. 12, 2008.

166 **"me and this building"** Ingrid Sischy. "Artist in Residence." *Vanity Fair*, Feb. 27, 2008.

167 **the remaining duplexes** Green. "The Painter."

167 **sex workers from the area** Kristen Lovell and Zackary Drucker, dirs. *The Stroll*. HBO, 2023.

168 **"go to find each other"** Alisa Lebow, dir. *Outlaw*. Women Make Movies, 1994.

169 **other misdemeanors fivefold** Malcolm Gladwell. *The Tipping Point: How Little Things Can Make a Big Difference*. Back Bay Books, 2002.

169 **Gabriel once wrote** Kay Gabriel. *A Queen in Bucks County.* Nightboat Books, 2022.

169 **on at least one occasion** Lovell and Drucker. *The Stroll.*

169 **"tranny by night"** *Sex and the City.* Season 3, episode 18, "Cock-a-Doodle-Do." HBO, Oct. 15, 2000.

169 **across its stomach** Lovell and Drucker. *The Stroll.*

170 **funded by neighboring property owners** P. E. Moskowitz. "Back on Christopher Street: Charting the Change of West Village's Gay Haven." *Out,* April 3, 2017.

170 **says in the opening scene** Tourmaline, dir. *Atlantic Is a Sea of Bones.* Visual AIDS, 2017.

170 **damaged in 2012** Marley Marius. "An 'Invitation to Dream' at Little Island, New York's Newest Park." *Vogue,* May 20, 2021.

170 **in the early 1970s** Sessi Kuwabara Blanchard. "At STAR House, Marsha P. Johnson and Sylvia Rivera Created a Home for Trans People." *Vice,* June 8, 2020.

171 **erects a shelter** "Rules & Regulations: §1-07 Penalties." New York City Department of Parks & Recreation website.

171 **"harassment and discrimination"** "Pier History." Little Island website.

172 **pockets of the United States** Rina Raphael. "Why Doesn't Anyone Want to Live in This Perfect Place?" *The New York Times,* Aug. 24, 2019.

172n **"the last thirty years"** Bryn Kelly. "XOJane It Happened to Me: I Was a Trans Woman Who Went to MichFest." Tumblr post, Aug. 5, 2014.

173 **newsletter *In Your Face*** Interview with Riki Anne Wilchins. *In Your Face,* Aug. 18, 1999. Michigan/Trans Controversy Archive at eminism.org (on future reference M/TCA).

173 **"they are too feminine"** Nancy Burkholder. "Results of 1992 Gender Survey at Michigan Womyn's Music Festival," April 28, 1993. M/TCA.

173n **"for a variety of reasons"** Michelle Tea. *Against Memoir: Complaints, Confessions & Criticisms.* Feminist Press, 2018.

174 **statement released at the time** Lisa Vogel and Barbara Price. "Festival Womyn Speak Out," Nov. 19, 1993. M/TCA.

174 **signed in 1977** Lisa Vogel et al. "Letter to Olivia Records," June 1977. M/TCA.

174 **"Avengers, and leatherwomen"** Wilchins interview. *In Your Face.*

175 **women's inclusion at MichFest** "Michelle [last name redacted]'s Account of Camp Trans '99," Aug. 1999. M/TCA.

175 **given him their blessing** Tony Barreto-Neto. "The Showering Penis S-P-E-A-K-S!!!" Aug. 1999. M/TCA.

176 **steal their scholarships** Michael Majchrowicz. "Fact-Checking Viral Image of Transgender High School Wrestler." WRAL News, June 14, 2021.

176 **both 2017 and 2018**   Associated Press. "Transgender Texas Wrestler Wins Second High School Girls Title." NBC News, Feb. 25, 2018.

180 **"cis people," she told me once**   Cecilia Gentili. Personal interview, Sept. 21, 2022.

180 **Israel's siege on Gaza**   Nicole Acevedo. "Late Trans Activist and Actress Cecilia Gentili Honored from New York City to Congress." NBC News, Feb. 15, 2024. *See also:* Brody Levesque. "Cecilia Gentili, Trans Latina Activist and Actress, Dies at 52." *Washington Blade,* Feb. 7, 2024.

180 **rejecting transsexual sex workers**   Jules Gill-Peterson. *A Short History of Trans Misogyny.* Verso, 2024.

181 **her grandmother told her**   Queer|Art (@queerart). "Reposting this beautiful, beautiful video of our treasured Cecilia Gentili." Instagram post, Feb. 9, 2024.

VALIDITY

182 **familiar for so many women**   Jenny Lewis. "Just One of the Guys." *The Voyager.* Warner Bros. Records, 2014.

182 **"wiggle room in there"**   Allison Stewart. "Rebound, Rediscovery, Rebirth: How Jenny Lewis Made Her Best Album in More Than a Decade." *The Washington Post,* March 15, 2019.

183 **how many genders there were**   Daniel Avery. "Joe Biden Says 'There Are at Least Three' Genders in Iowa Campaign Stop." *Newsweek,* Aug. 11, 2019.

FERTILITY

193 **"right now," Río told me**   Río Sofia. This and all following quotes in chapter from personal interview, Nov. 17, 2021.

194 **"army pants and flip-flops"**   Mark Waters, dir. *Mean Girls.* Paramount Pictures, 2004.

194 **to the cis gaze**   Harron Walker. "Making Work in Her Own Image." *Out,* April 25, 2019.

197 **specific to trans women**   Harron Walker. "My Trans Mother, Myself." *W,* April 6, 2021.

197 **"sources of information"**   Harron Walker. "Where Are All the Ads for HRT?" *Into,* Sept. 15, 2017.

198 **Page once wrote**   Morgan M. Page. "Never Be New Again." *Valley of the D,* Jan. 19, 2021.

199 **as recently as 2019**   "Identity Document Laws and Policies." Movement Advancement Project website.

199 **of state-sanctioned torture**   Kristen Gelineau. "Dubbed Torture, ID Policies Leave Transgender People Sterile." Associated Press, Nov. 11, 2022.

199 **that they were parents** Sandy E. James, Jody L. Herman, Susan Rankin, Mare Kiesling, Lisa Mottet, and Ma'ayan Anafi. *The Report of the 2015 U.S. Transgender Survey.* National Center for Transgender Equality, 2016.

199 **survey's 2022 follow-up** Sandy E. James, Jody L. Herman, Laura E. Durso, and Rodrigo Heng-Lehtinen. *Early Insights: A Report of the 2022 U.S. Transgender Survey.* National Center for Transgender Equality, 2024.

199 **reported to have had kids** Megan Brenan. "Americans' Preference for Larger Families Highest Since 1971." Gallup, Sept. 25, 2023.

199 **"person at the trans clinic"** Lola Pellegrino. Personal interview, Feb. 3, 2022.

200n **"monarchical African past"** Jasmine Sanders. "Image Conscious." *Artforum,* Jan./Feb. 2021.

200 **"Chicago Trans Power Couple" in 2019** Ashton Blatz. "Chicago Trans Power Couple Announce Pregnancy." *The Advocate,* July 2, 2019.

200 **shining down from the heavens** Precious Brady-Davis (@preciousbradydavis). "May our ancestors who labored before us be pleased" and following untitled post. Instagram, Dec. 15, 2019.

201 **shot by Jean-Paul Goude** Amanda Fortini. "Break the Internet: Kim Kardashian." *Paper,* Nov. 12, 2014.

201 **memoir,** *I Have Always Been Me* Precious Brady-Davis. *I Have Always Been Me.* Topple Books & Little A, 2021.

201 **"as a pregnant man"** *My Pregnant Husband.* Crazy Legs Productions and TLC, July 24, 2020.

202 **Witt, in January 2021** Matt Baume. "Miss Major Griffin-Gracy and Partner Announce Birth of First Child." *them,* Jan. 20, 2021.

202 **corners of social media** Miss Major (@missmajor1). "We had a baby!" Instagram post, Jan. 14, 2021.

203 **"which is exciting"** Bernardo Sim. "The Unstoppable Gigi Gorgeous on Motherhood, Red Carpets & Joining OF." *Out,* March 7, 2024.

204 **"out there for trans people"** Josie Caballero. Personal interview, Feb. 16, 2023.

204 **compared to that of cis men** Kenny A. Rodriguez-Wallberg, Jakob Häljestig, Stefan Arver, Anna L. V. Johansson, and Frida E. Lundberg. "Sperm Quality in Transgender Women Before or After Gender Affirming Hormone Therapy—A Prospective Cohort Study." *Andrology,* March 8, 2021.

204 **should they stop HRT** V. S. Wells. "Trans Women Who Stop Hormones Are Still Fertile, According to a New Study." *Xtra,* Jan. 19, 2023.

205 **$1,000 per year** "Sperm Banking." Alliance for Fertility Preservation.

205 **more than $10,000** "Egg Cryopreservation." Alliance for Fertility Preservation.

205 **disproportionate poverty rates** James et al. *Early Insights. Compare with:* "Income, Poverty, and Health Insurance Coverage in the United States: 2022." United States Census Bureau, Sept. 12, 2023.

205 **twice as likely to be unemployed** James Factora. "Trans Adults Are Twice as Likely to Be Unemployed as Cis Adults." *them,* Nov. 15, 2021.

205 **actually gone through with it** Matthias K. Auer, Johannes Fuss, Timo O. Nieder, Peer Briken, Sarah V. Biedermann, Günter K. Stalla, Matthias W. Beckmann, and Thomas Hildebrandt. "Desire to Have Children Among Transgender People in Germany: A Cross-Sectional Multi-Center Study." *The Journal of Sexual Medicine,* May 1, 2018.

205 **told the website *them* in 2020** Lauren McCarthy. "These Startups Are Opening a New World of Fertility Preservation for Trans Patients." *them,* Jan. 21, 2020.

209 **gay people out of public life** Natalie Wynn (ContraPoints). "The Witch Trials of J. K. Rowling." YouTube video, uploaded April 17, 2023.

210 **"stopped using the asterisk"** Ayşe Devrim. "No Comment." *Meanwhile, Elsewhere: Science Fiction and Fantasy from Transgender Writers.* Topside Press, 2017.

211 **transplants done in the United States** "Uterus Transplant." UAB Medicine website.

211 **birth recorded in Sweden in 2014** Mats Brännström, Anders Enskog, Niclas Kvarnström, Jean Marc Ayoubi, and Pernilla Dahm-Kähler. "Global Results of Human Uterus Transplantation and Strategies for Pre-transplantation Screening of Donors." *Fertility and Sterility,* July 2019.

211 **interview with the UK's *Mirror*** Adrian Addison and Rosaleen Fenton. "Doctor Planning Risky Womb Transplant to Allow Transgender Woman to Carry a Baby." *The Mirror,* May 5, 2022.

212 **complications about three months later** David Cox. "The Danish Girl and the Sexologist: a Story of Sexual Pioneers." *The Guardian,* Jan. 13, 2016.

216 **commonly referred to as puberty blockers** "Blackburn Calls for FDA Investigation into Use of Puberty Blockers on Minors," press release. Office of Sen. Marsha Blackburn, Sept. 22, 2022.

216 **restrict trans people's access to healthcare** "Tracking the Rise of Anti-Trans Bills in the U.S." Trans Legislation Tracker website.

216 **age restrictions on gender-affirming care** Annette Choi. "Record Number of Anti-LGBTQ Bills Were Introduced in 2023." CNN, Jan. 22, 2024.

217 **lead children into sin** Serene Jones. "Stop Using the Bible to Dehumanize Transgender People." *Newsweek,* Jan. 23, 2023.

217 **"This is a political winner"**   Maggie Astor. "GOP State Lawmakers Push a Growing Wave of Anti-Transgender Bills." *The New York Times,* Jan. 25, 2023.

217 **people as old as twenty-five**   Brooke Midgon. "Oklahoma 'Millstone Act' Seeks to Ban Gender-Affirming Care Under Age of 26." *The Hill,* Jan. 5, 2023. For South Carolina, see: South Carolina House Bill 3730, introduced Jan. 18, 2023.

217 **people who had already transitioned**   Erin Reed. "Oklahoma Could Force Trans People Under 26 Years Old to Detransition Medically." *Erin in the Morning,* Jan. 5, 2023.

217 **say, trans children writ large**   Savannah Moss. "South Carolina Gov. McMaster Signs Bill Outlawing Transgender Care for Trans Youth." *The Greenville News,* May 21, 2024.

218 **in 1979's *The Transsexual Empire***   Janice Raymond. *The Transsexual Empire: The Making of the She-Male.* Beacon Press, 1979.

IN/FERTILITY

223 **probably never pour out**   Imogen Binnie. *Nevada.* Topside Press, 2013.

224 **ever plagued them**   Jonathan Ames. Introduction to *Sexual Metamorphosis: An Anthology of Transsexual Memoirs.* Vintage Books, 2005.

225 **"a decent pair of boots"**   Binnie. *Nevada.*

225 **state funds for such care**   Gus Rosendale, Maggie Freleng, and A. B. Fox. "Top NYC Hospital Racing to Specialize in Transgender Healthcare." NBC 4 New York, May 8, 2015.

225 **not "purely cosmetic"**   "New York State Medicaid Update—January 2017 Volume 33—Number 1." New York State Department of Health, Jan. 31, 2017.

225 **coverage for trans health services**   "New York State Acts to Remove Medicaid Ban on Transgender Health Care." *Erie Gay News,* Dec. 16, 2014. *See also:* Anemona Hartocollis. "Insurers in New York Must Cover Gender Reassignment Surgery, Cuomo Says." *The New York Times,* Dec. 10, 2014.

225 **visibility in mainstream American culture**   Katy Steinmetz. "The Transgender Tipping Point." *Time,* May 29, 2014.

225 **benefits to city employees**   Associated Press. "San Francisco to Cover Sex Changes." *The Washington Post,* Feb. 16, 2001.

226 **from receiving gender-affirming care**   Harron Walker. "South Dakota Lawmakers Are Targeting Transgender Children." *Out,* Jan. 30, 2019.

226 **record number of anti-trans bills**   "Trans Rights Under Attack in 2020." American Civil Liberties Union website.

226 **again every year after that** "Tracking the Rise of Anti-Trans Bills in the U.S." Trans Legislation Tracker website.

227 **care for trans people under eighteen** "Equality Maps: Bans on Best Practice Medical Care for Transgender Youth." Movement Advancement Project website.

227 **care for adults as well** Oriana González. "GOP Lawmakers Expand Gender-affirming Care Restrictions to Adults." Axios, March 29, 2023.

227 **"to win for women"** Susan Faludi. *Backlash: The Undeclared War Against American Women*. Three Rivers Press, 1991.

227 **capitalism and climate destruction** Judith Butler. *Who's Afraid of Gender?* Macmillan, 2024.

228 **well, at least in theory** Jules Gill-Peterson. *Histories of the Transgender Child*. University of Minnesota Press, 2018.

228 **"access to transsexual medicine"** Ibid.

228 *Mental Disorders* **in 1980** Susan Stryker. *Transgender History*. Seal Press, 2008.

229 **as popular as ever** Nina Arsenault. *The Silicone Diaries*, anthologized in *TRANS(per)FORMING Nina Arsenault: An Unreasonable Body of Work*, ed. Judith Rudakoff. Intellect Ltd., 2012. *See also:* Joann G. Layne. *The Champagne Slipper*. iUniverse, 2005. Harron Walker. "Cecilia Gentili Opens Her Burn Book." *New York*, Nov. 3, 2022. Gill-Peterson. *Histories*.

229 **as Gill-Peterson has noted** Gill-Peterson. *Histories*.

229 **full $8,000 cost** Kate Bornstein. *Gender Outlaw: On Men, Women, and the Rest of Us*. Routledge, 1994.

229 **private insurers as well** Cristan Williams. "Fact Checking Janice Raymond: The NCHCT Report." *The TransAdvocate*.

230 **one of them, in 1998** "New York State Acts." *Erie Gay News*.

230 **"pay for their surgeries themselves"** Viviane K. Namaste. *Invisible Lives: The Erasure of Transsexual and Transgendered People*. The University of Chicago Press, 2000.

230 **this linguistic shift** Andrea Long Chu. "Extreme Pregnancy." *Boston Review*, Aug. 10, 2018.

230 **According to a 1992 Medicaid handbook** "Medicaid Handbook: Your Guide to Wyoming Medicaid." Wyoming Department of Health, Oct. 2016.

231 **overruled that exclusion** *Flack v. Wisconsin Dep't of Health Servs*, cited in Wis. Admin. Code Department of Health Services § DHS 107.03.

231 **"gender transition services or procedures"** Ariz. Admin. Code § R9-22-205. *Kentucky Medicaid Provider Manual*. WellCare of Kentucky, 2022. *Physicians Services Provider Manual*. South Carolina Department of Health and Human Services, April 1, 2024.

231 **should complications from such procedures arise** "Equality Maps: Medicaid Coverage of Transgender-Related Health Care." Movement Advancement Project website.

231 **"transformation surgery"** This and following Tennessee regulations are from Rules of the Tennessee Department of Finance and Administration, Division of Tenncare, Chapter 1200-13-13.

232 **transmascs have had done** Ariz. Admin. Code § R9-22-205.

232 **"to prevent pregnancy"** *Kentucky Medicaid Provider Manual.*

232 **"penile prostheses"** This and following Missouri regulations are from *Physicians Provider Manual.* MO HealthNet, Sept. 1, 2023.

232 **World War I and II** Morgan M. Page. *One from the Vaults.* Podcast episode 4, "Valentine's Day Special!" Feb. 14, 2016. Brandy Schillace. "The Surprisingly Old Science of Living as Transgender." *Scientific American,* March 18, 2020.

234 **the power to shift them** Alex V. Green. "The Case for Facial Feminization Surgery." *BuzzFeed News,* July 28, 2020.

234 **excludes, as of 2015, "gender transformation"** Ohio Admin. Code § 5160-2-03.

234 **not enforcing that exclusion** Michael Ollove. "States Are All Over the Map When It Comes to Transgender Healthcare." *The Washington Post,* July 22, 2019.

234 **therefore, not "medically necessary"** Kelcie Moseley-Morris. "Idaho Health Department Asks Court to Dismiss Trans Discrimination Lawsuit." *Idaho Capital Sun,* Nov. 29, 2022.

234 **who issued the proclamation, "experimental"** "Missouri Attorney General Andrew Bailey Promulgates Emergency Regulation Targeting Gender Transition Procedures for Minors," press release. Office of Missouri Attorney General Andrew Bailey, 2023.

IM/POSSIBILITY

239 **turn a quick buck** "Allie Beth Stuckey Says Doctors Who Treat Trans Patients Are 'Creating Lifelong Slaves to the Medical System.'" Media Matters for America, Sept. 12, 2022.